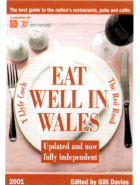

Welcome to the third e
truly independent. Excell
and the Welsh Developm

Independence means that every restaurant, hotel, cafe, pub, tea room, bistro, and bed and breakfast included in the guide has been inspected, anonymously. No free meals have been given, and there has been no negotiation between inspector and establishment. Of the 250 establishments that we have inspected, 213 were good enough to be included. On receiving a good report, we simply contacted the proprietors to ask for their details.

There were 20 inspectors eating hard throughout Wales last autumn and it is hard to quantify the total weight gain! Being paid to eat out seems like a dream ticket to most people, but, writing the reports is not as easy as it might appear. All the inspectors had impeccable credentials, usually having been restaurateurs themselves, or food journalists – sometimes both, so the reports they wrote have been edited as little as possible. We hope you like the mix of writing styles and critics. No doubt as a seasoned guide reader, you will be able to pick out the sweet-toothed inspector or the one who enjoyed his house wine!

Mixed with the surprising and delightful discoveries all over Wales of truly good cooking and excellent dining there have been some truly awful eating experiences – one report began 'No one should go here to eat!' However, compiling this guide has generally been a voyage of discovery and pleasure. Enthusiasm for producing the best cooking using the best ingredients always shines through, and for all inspectors working on the guide has been a very rewarding experience. If you are not asking when the next is to be published, they certainly are!

As you read through The Red Book no doubt you will find that we missed some out – please let us know on the form at the back of the book, and we will follow up your recommendations for edition No 4.

We hope you eat well in Wales this year.

Sainsbury's in Wales

We've been adding new ingredients to our stores in Wales, combining innovative new product ranges with the best of Welsh produce to 'Bring home the true taste of Wales'.

Sainsbury's has a long history in Wales. It opened its first store in 1976 in Cwmbran and now has nine stores, serving around 200,000 customers each week.

Seven of the Sainsbury's stores are in the south – Colchester Avenue and Thornhill in Cardiff and a new Sainsbury's Central in Cardiff, Newport, Swansea, Llewellyn Road (Cwmbran) and Bridgend (McArthur Glen Shopping Centre), and two are in the north – Rhyl and Wrexham.

Sainsbury's is committed to sourcing Welsh produce wherever possible. Sainsbury's promotes regional products such as Welsh lamb, Welsh cheeses and Welsh butter throughout the UK. The Welsh stores offer around 230 Welsh product lines sourced locally to reflect the wishes of our Welsh customers. We have introduced around 60 new lines this year.

Sainsbury's purchases £76 million per year of products from over 55 food and non-food suppliers processing products in Wales.

Take home the true taste of Wales

Some products are sourced specifically for sale in the eight Welsh stores, including Welsh favourite Joe's Ice Cream, and others are sold throughout the UK. The products include bread, biscuits, eggs, cheese, milk and dairy products, ice-cream, beer, fruit juices, processed chicken, ready meals, frozen foods, household cleaning materials, confectionery, and organic foods.

In conjunction with its meat, fruit and vegetable suppliers, and their suppliers - the farmers and growers - Sainsbury's has established Partnership schemes. In Wales, 26 suppliers have formed partnerships with Welsh farmers and growers through Sainsbury's Partnership in Livestock and Partnership in Produce schemes.

Sainsbury's relationship with lamb supplier Oriel Jones illustrates well the benefits of the Partnership schemes. Oriel Jones, with whom Sainsbury's started trading in 1989 and who are now Sainsbury's largest fresh lamb supplier, supply on average 75 tonnes of fresh lamb per week to Sainsbury's. For the last two to three years, through partnership schemes, Sainsbury's has promoted local products delivered directly from growers into stores.

In conjunction with the Welsh Development Agency, Sainsbury's is looking for new ways of extending its Welsh supplier base and its promotion of Welsh products. For example, in April 2000, Sainsbury's hosted a 'Meet the Buyer' event in Cardiff at which 23 potential new suppliers were identified.

Because of these initiatives, Sainsbury's stores in Wales are offering its customers to 'Take home the true taste of Wales'.

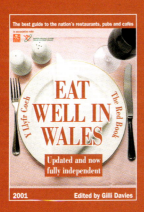

Published by Western Mail Books

Editorial
Gilli Davies
Martin Greeves

Design and Typesetting
Western Mail & Echo Ltd
© Western Mail Books
Thomson House,
Havelock Street, Cardiff CF10 1XR

Printed by
Colourprint Division,
Western Mail & Echo Ltd

All rights reserved.
No part of this publication may be reproduced, stored in a retrieval system, or transmitted in any form or by any means, electronic, mechanical or otherwise, without the prior permission of the copyright holder.

Entries in The Red Book represent the views of our inspectors at the time of their visit.

The details quoted in this guide are as supplied to The Red Book and to the best of the company's knowledge are correct on going to press.

ISBN: 1-900477-18-1

Contents

Introduction	1
Acknowledgments	2
How to use the Guide	4
The Red Book Awards	6
Shopping Lists	25
A Welsh Cheeseboard	32
Welsh Wine List	33
The Red Book Entries	
North Wales	34
Mid Wales	78
South West Wales	108
South East Wales	144
Youth Hostels	178
Award-winning Recipes	180
What are your comments?	188
Maps of the regions	
North & Mid Wales	189
South-east & South-west	190
Index of Establishments	191

With special thanks to Martin Greaves for his editing skills and to the research team of Ken Goody, Diana Richards, Peter Ball, Adam and Penny Rathenbury, Annette Yates, Frances Roughley, John Idris Jones, Manisha Harkins, David Richards, Richard Crowe, Nerys Lloyd Pierce, Alan and Anne Heason, David Hancock, Sue Wilshire and Jacky Palit.

How to use
The Red Book

Quality is the main priority of The Red Book, with great emphasis given to the sourcing of the ingredients, the standard of cooking, the service and the general ambience of the establishment.

Where there is accommodation, this is noted with a description of the type and number of rooms and their cost. Additional discounts often apply for stays of more than one night, while in many cases there may be a supplement for single occupancy.

Once you have decided where you wish to stay – or dine, book ahead if you can to avoid disappointment. Many of the smaller establishments are busy all year, and find it difficult to cater for those who turn up unannounced.

All establishments listed in The Red Book have passed a demanding inspection by one of our team. Those establishments who failed to gain entry this time have been offered advice and will be encouraged to re-apply.

The Red Book has divided Wales into North, Mid, South West and South East, and all entries are listed alphabetically under the nearest town or village which can be found easily on road maps. Places of local interest are also listed.

We are particularly interested in readers' comments, and would welcome recommendations on any other excellent establishments you think should be mentioned in our next edition. Or if you think an establishment fails to meet the standards we have set, please discuss the problem with the proprietors before contacting us. A form for your comments is at the back of the book.

Key to Symbols

	Chef proprietor (i.e. one of proprietors or their family personally cooks or supervises all of the cooking).	Cogydd berchennog (h.y. un o'r perchnogion, neu'r teulu, sydd naill ai'n paratoi'r bwyd neu yn cadw llygad ar yr holl goginio).
	Children's portions or menus, usually with facilities for children, e.g. high chairs.	Plateidiau bach a bwydlen arbennig i blant, ynghyd â chyfleusterau, fel rheol, megis cadair uchel.
	No smoking in the dining room.	Dim ysmygu yn yr ystafell fwyta.
	Circled cigarette symbol – No smoking at all, or in limited areas only.	Dwy sigaret – dim ysmygu o gwbl, neu, mewn llefydd cyfyngedig yn unig.
	Access to premises and accommodation suitable for wheelchairs.	Mynediad i'r adeilad a'r ystafelloedd yn addas ar gyfer cadair olwyn.
	Food is served and can be eaten outside.	Darperir bwyd ac mae modd bwyta y tu allan.
	Excellent seafood served here.	Darperir bwyd môr ardderchog yma.
V	Wide choice of vegetarian dishes available: usually also cater for special diets.	Dewis helaeth i lysfwytawyr ac, fel arfer, darpariaeth hefyd ar gyfer anghenion arbennig.
	Special dietary needs.	Anghenion arbennig deiet.
	Organic or free-range ingredients.	Defnyddiau rhydd neu organic.
CHS	Good selection of Welsh cheeses available.	Cynigir amrywiaeth dda o Gaws Cymru.
	Wine list which offers especially good choice, quality and value for money.	Rhestr winoedd yn cynnig dewis ardderchog, safon uchel a gwerth am arian.
	Full range of beers, including real ales.	Dewis helaeth o gwrw, gan gynnwys cwrw go iawn.

For Example

86   Penybont ar Ogwr

Ma's Davies' Coffee Shop

Cwmscwt Road
Aberllyn Goch
Wrexham
AB1 2CD
Tel: 01234 567890
Fax: 01234 098765

Housed in the former waiting room of Dinas Station on the old Llansantffraid line, Genni Davies' commendable café with rooms has been a regular whistle-stop for walkers and twitchers for over twenty years. Slate-topped tables for al-fresco eating occupy the platform, an ideal spot to enjoy the marvellous views across the Skewy Valley, spanned by its now disused railway bridge above the mediaeval stepping stones.

The splendid buttered cheese scones, bara brith and other fine home baking for which Genni is justly famous are as popular as ever, be it for a mid-morning snack or afternoon tea served with wafer-thin cucumber sandwiches and home-made conserves.

Her additional lunchtime offerings, too, would shame any trackside buffet: pizza topped with melted Pencarreg cheese, various savoury flans, ploughman's of cheese, ham or pâté (do try the smoked mackerel for a real treat), two daily soups which might be parsnip and apple or carrot and coriander, with light flaky apple turnover to follow or the deliciously decadent tipsy almond cake flavoured with just a hint of Red Dragon Whisky.

The picturesque postage-stamp of a garden has just enough room for a children's swing and slide and is safely enclosed: indoors, however, space considerations preclude entry to prams and pushchairs, while both dogs and smoking are similarly prohibited.

MEALS: L 12-.30 approx £1; Sunday L 12-2 approx £15;
D 7-9 approx £21.90;
Cards: All major
CHEF: Genni Davies. PROPRIETOR: Marion Greaves

WTB: 3 ★★★
Rooms: 4, £46.50 S, £41.50 D.

LOCAL INTEREST. Waterfalls, all outdoor pursuits.

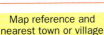

Map reference and nearest town or village	
Name and details of establishment	This appears beside entries where our inspectors found excellent use of local ingredients.
Inspector's report	
Meal times and prices where applicable - accommodation details and prices may also be given	This is awarded by the Taste of Wales scheme (see page 11), following an annual inspection to establish that set quality standards, involving use of local ingredients, have been achieved.
Classification - See Left	

Colour code

The background colours shown, above, are for coding purposes only, with exception for the symbol line.

5

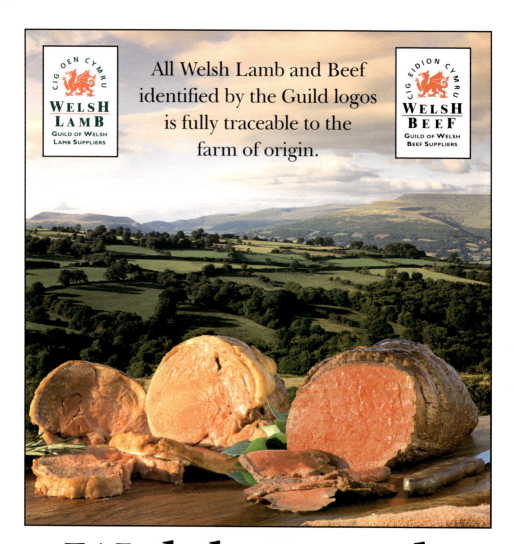

Welsh Lamb & Welsh Beef

For further information contact
Tel: (01970) 624011 Fax: (01970) 624049
Web: www.welshlambandbeef.co.uk

By day, FEAST YOUR EYES. By night, SIMPLY FEAST.

Rolling hills and valleys are draped in early morning sunshine. Sand shimmers as beaches stretch into the distance. The sun dips gently into a rippled mountain lake. Then, as evening draws in, you can settle down to fine food and drink in a cosy restaurant. Discover locally reared Black Beef, organically grown vegetables, fine Welsh cheeses and surprisingly extensive wine lists.

A feast awaits you in Wales, so send for our Wales brochure or visit our website for a real taste of escape.

For your free brochure
Freephone 080 80 1000 000
www.visitwales.com

WALES CYMRU

Two hours and a million miles away

Llangadog Creamery

... bringing high quality Welsh foods to the local customer

WELSH SALTED BUTTER
MENYN LLANGADOG

LUXURY RICE PUDDING
PWDIN REIS LLANGADOG

READY-TO-SERVE CUSTARD
CWSTARD LLANGADOG

Located in the beautiful Towy Valley, Llangadog Creamery has been producing dairy products since 1961.

As a major supplier of products such as rice pudding, custard, butter and evaporated milk to the multiple retailers, Llangadog's quality standards are second to none.

The Creamery has an enviable reputation within the dairy industry, regularly receiving awards for supreme quality butter at major dairy shows.

In order to build upon this success the decision was made in 1994 to launch a premium quality butter to match the old recipe with a traditional Welsh taste.

Menyn Llangadog provides the creamy taste and texture demanded by the local market. Launched in 250g, 9g and 7g portion packs, it has since carved a space for itself on the shelves of numerous retailers, wholesalers and cash and carrys throughout Wales.

Pwdin Reis Llangadog, a luxury rice pudding is the ultimate premium product in the canned rice pudding sector. Packed in a 425g can, this delicious, thick and creamy pudding offers a high quality alternative to the local consumer.

Custard Llangadog, a smooth, rich, pour over sauce for desserts, is the third produce within this premium quality range. Also available in a 425g can, this custard sauce is certain to complement any meal occasion.

All packaging within this range contains an eye-catching illustration of the beautiful Towy Valley, targeting the products directly to customers from the principality.

Contact: Ellis Davies, Llangadog Creamery, Carmarthenshire SA19 9LY. Tel: 01550 776300 Fax: 01550 777032

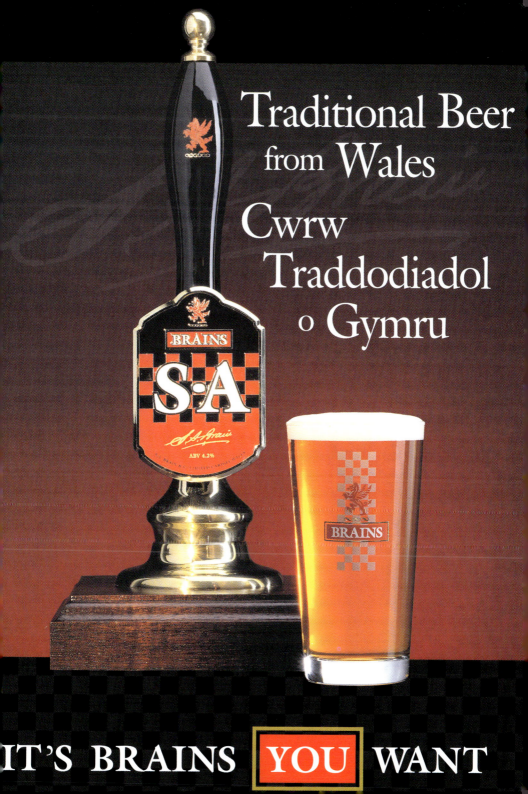

Chefs reputations depend on the quality of their source

Creating great tasting dishes depends on the quality of the food source. That's why Welsh produce is the chef's choice. A traditional approach to farming means Welsh produce tastes like it should. Our lamb tastes like...lamb, our cheeses are full and flavoursome and our seafood tastes exactly the way nature intended. As any chef will tell you, it's all the inspiration they need.

For more information contact Taste of Wales.
Tel: 08457 775577
or visit our website on www.tasteofwales.com

THE PRODUCE OF WALES   *A source of inspiration*

Experience Welsh Food ~ The True Taste

By Wynfford James, Welsh Development Agency Agri-food Director

So much of what we eat today is prepared and packaged to within an inch of its natural flavour. It can be difficult to tell the difference between chicken and pork, between real butter and margarine. We've almost forgotten what real food tastes like.

Welsh food and drink can refresh your memory, and your tastebuds.

Welsh Lamb, reared on rich pastures is deliciously sweet and succulent. Welsh dairy produce bursts with the freshness of the green pastures. Welsh seafood, harvested off the rocky coastline, tastes delicate and pure.

And when produce is this good, it is a natural inspiration for producers and chefs everywhere. French chefs are buying and using our lamb and seafood in growing quantities. Our cheeses are finding their way on to more and more of the best-dressed cheese boards.

Wales offers great quality foods that come from a rich and varied natural landscape and which inspire a rich and varied array of foods. And to support Wales' modern and exciting food and drink industry, the WDA runs a number of key programmes. These include:

The Taste of Wales Hospitality Scheme – wherever the sign is displayed you can expect the highest quality service, and the finest food made from the best Welsh produce. Dining out in Wales – a guide to Taste of Wales members makes choosing a good place to eat in Wales easy and straightforward. With over 370 members you'll find a great selection covering all price ranges – everything from friendly farmhouses to luxury country house hotels, historic inns to family cafes and teashops. For a free copy of Dining Out in Wales call us on Tel: 029 2082 8984.

The Welsh Culinary Team – sponsored by Taste of Wales, has brought together Wales' finest chefs to promote our food in competitions at home and abroad. Acting as ambassadors for Wales, the team has cooked for heads of state, royalty, senior politicians and celebrities.

Through our **Events Programme** – the WDA works to put Welsh food and drink on the map, promoting and marketing our produce throughout Wales and internationally. We support industry events, from regional food and agricultural fairs and shows, through to large international food fairs and exhibitions, providing financial and marketing support to producers.

The **Market Channels Programme** assists food and drink companies in promoting their produce via the supermarkets. Success to date has ensured that hundreds of excellent Welsh food items are appearing on the shelves of major supermarkets within Wales itself. We are confident that these quality products will be increasingly available in branches of these supermarkets across the UK.

A public/private sector **Agri-Food Partnership,** to which the Food Directorate provides the secretariat, was established in spring 1999 - to ensure co-ordination and co-operation across the industry. Action Plans have been produced for four key agri-food sectors – Lamb and Beef; Dairy; Organic, and Farm Development. There is determination and a joint effort within the industry to ensure Wales keeps on producing excellent food.

These are just some of the things the WDA is doing to ensure that Wales' thriving food culture goes from strength to strength. The rest is up to you – the consumer, and your commitment to buying, and asking for, Welsh produce, wherever possible.

CASTELL DEUDRAETH

Castell Deudraeth Bar & Grill in the grounds of Portmeirion.

Open from end May 2001
11.00 - 11.00 daily
(with free admission to Castle and Gardens)

Open for morning coffee, lunches, teas, bar meals and suppers.
Local Seafood a Speciality

Children Welcome

No pre-booking required

Castell Deudraeth Bar & Grill, Portmeirion
Gwynedd LL48 6ET
Tel: 01766-770280 Fax: 01766-771331
email: castell@portmeirion-village.com

Award Winning in Both Accommodation & Restaurant

Tre-Ysgawen Hall

Driving over the Britannia Bridge one enters the enchanted land of Anglesey. We cannot offer a royal palace but the unashamed luxury offered by this lovely hotel will surely suffice. An elegantly restored Victorian mansion in landscaped grounds, Tre-Ysgawen Hall was opened as an hotel as recently as 1990, and to the wide-eyed guest of today it offers stylish modern furnishings well in keeping with the opulence of former years. A magnificent oak staircase leads to classically designed guest rooms with tasteful drapes and practical contemporary appointments. The drawing room of regal decor, invites complete relaxation, while the chef's art is displayed to perfection in the impressive dining rooms.

Brasserie Restaurant
and for the more intimate occasion, candlelight dining in our
Capel Coch Restaurant
A La Carte & Table d'Hôte

Tre-Ysgawen Hall, Capel Coch, Llangefni, Isle of Anglesey LL77 7UR
Tel: 01248 750750 Fax: 01248 750035

exclusively vegetarian

46 Plassey Street, Penarth CF64 1EL
Tel: 029 2070 6644
www.tomlinsvegetarianrestaurant.co.uk

The
PRIORY HOTEL & RESTAURANT

Beautifully located hotel and restaurant stands in the historic village of Caerleon, only 5 minutes from the M4 motorway.

Our renowned dining room offers a vast selection of daily fresh fish, seafood, Welsh beef and game. This complemented by a superb choice of fine wines, champagnes, ports and brandies.

WTB ★★★

Each of the 22 bedrooms boasts en-suite bathrooms, satellite TV, mini bar, tea/coffee facilities.

Indeed a truly unique experience!!

High Street, Caerleon, Nr Newport NP18 1AG
Tel: 01633 421 241   Fax: 01633 421 271
Web site: www.traveluk.com.plc

Care
Comfort
Cuisine

Be warmly welcomed and well looked after. Experience the friendly atmosphere at this tastefully appointed and comfortable award-winning retreat.

Join Jacky and Miles and their team of chefs

Open evenings to Non-Residents

PENBONTBREN FARM HOTEL
Glynarthen, Ceredigion SA44 6PE
Tel: (01239) 810248 Fax: (01239) 811129

Allt Yr Ynys

Country House Hotel & Restaurant
Abergavenny

Tranquility, elegance, quality and beautiful surroundings are the hallmarks of Allt Yr Ynys, centred around a 16th Century manor house in stunning Black Mountains scenery, with its own landscaped and walled gardens.

Les Routiers Welsh Hotel of the Year - 1999

Fine dining for residents and non-residents in our restaurant or on walled garden terrace. Light meals and bar snacks available.

Other facilities include: 19 luxury en-suite bedrooms, Conference facilities for up to 100 delegates, Licensed for Civil Wedding Ceremonies with facilities for up to 200 wedding guests, Indoor heated swimming pool, sauna and spa bath, Private clay shooting and river fishing, 16 acres of grounds.

Stunning Black Mountains scenery
- ideal for walks, cycling and riding.

Weddings and Conferences, and other functions and events are our speciality.

Family bookings welcomed.

Visit our Website on www.allthotel.co.uk
Just north of Abergavenny, off the A465 at Pandy
Phone for details and bookings on 01873 890307
or Email: us on allthotel@compuserve.com

Paul & Martine welcome you to their newly refurbished restaurant 'The Armless Dragon', only five minutes from Cardiff City Centre.

Come and enjoy a unique mix of contemporary Welsh food made from fresh local ingredients and served in a warm and friendly environment. Prices are sensible and we welcome groups and individuals alike.

'Excellent innovative cookery' Harden's 2001

We're open for lunch between Tuesday and Friday 12noon-2pm and dinner between Monday and Saturday 7pm to 9pm.

Call the Armless Dragon Restaurant on:
Tel: 029 2038 2357
97-99 Wyeverne Road, Cathays, Cardiff, CF2 4BG.

The Wynnstay
Machynlleth

The Wynnstay Hotel, Machynlleth, Powys.
Tel: 01654 702941 Fax: 01654 703884.
www.wynnstay-hotel.com

After nine years at the Red Lion, Llanfihangel, Radnorshire, Gareth Johns, one of Wales' (and Britain's) most acclaimed chefs, moves to the Wynnstay.

Gareth is a leading member of the Welsh National Culinary Team (one of the most successful international teams in the world), he worked with Alistair Little and at The Ritz. At his previous establishment he won awards from Michelin, The Red Book, the AA, and was awarded "Restaurant of the Year" (Twice!) by The Good Food Guide. He won "Mid Wales Chef of the Year" and had glowing write ups from Jonathan Meades of The Times and Colin Pressdee of The Western Mail amongst others. Gareth, Welsh and proud of it, will bring his particular mix of traditional and modern Welsh cookery, using fresh, local produce to Wales' ancient capital. "I'm delighted to have such a stage to promote the glories of Welsh food, which I feel is second to none", says Gareth.

"We're very fortunate at The Wynnstay to have such a wealth of wonderful local produce. Welsh lamb, of course, but we also have wonderful beef and farms producing interesting hams & cheese. Salmon and Sea Trout fresh from the great Dovey River. Then there's the delicate crab and lobster from Cardigan Bay. In the autumn the wonderful wild mushrooms arrive, especially the ceps. Then there's all the game. It is our belief that we can satisfy both the arch traditionalist and the gourmet, with the same menu: after all they are both simply after great food, well prepared."

For the very best in Mediterranean/Turkish cuisine

Try the most exquisite Mediterranean & Turkish cuisine, lovingly and expertly prepared by Nerman - our award winning chef with over 18 years experience.

Relax and enjoy as you take in the fabulous views of the Waterfront.

EXTENSIVE WINE LIST

Examples from extensive menu:

Cold Starter: Avocado with raspberry viniagrette (this delicous viniagrette is a combination of avocado served with green salad leaves - £3.95

Hot Starter: Feta Cheese Pastrie (Golden triangles of cheese filled with a delectably mixture of feta cheese, fresh dill & spinich) - £3.25

Grilles & Entrees: Kleftico (knuckle of roast lamb served with roast potatoes)

Also Set 4-Course Menu for Lunch & Dinner at only £14.95 available

31 Mermaid Quay, Cardiff Bay. Tel: 029 2048 7477

PLAS BODEGROES

Restaurant with Rooms

A Georgian Manor House beautifully located on the spectacular Llyn Peninsula. Lovely gardens feature an avenue of 200-year-old beech trees, and wisterias and roses perfume the verandah.

Acclaimed as one of Britain's top restaurants, with awards in all food guides. Plas Bodegroes serves modern dishes making use of superb local ingredients. Specialities include lamb in puff pastry, seatrout with coconut leeks and chilli salsa and cinnamon biscuit of rhubarb and apple with elderflower custard.

The 11 bedrooms are fully equipped and decorated tastefully to retain the charming character of the house.

PLAS BODEGROES IS A WELSH RAREBIT HOTEL

Breaks only Tues-Fri • 5-Star Grading

Tel: 01758 612363
email: gunna@bodegroes.co.uk
www.bodegroes.co.uk

Ye Olde Bulls Head Inn

Beaumaris, Isle of Anglesey. LL58 8AP

A minor revolution has taken place at the Bull of recent. Five centuries of tradition are retained in the ancient beamed bar but elsewhere there is evidence of changing times. A stylish new brasserie offers imaginative food in an informal setting whereas the first floor restaurant, recently refurbished, continues to meet the highest standards. Accommodation of 15 comfortably appointed bedrooms makes a stay an absolute must.

For further details:
Tel: 01248 810329 Fax: 01248 811294
Email: info@bullsheadinn.co.uk

Members of Welsh Rarebits

---

38 Woodville Road
Cathays
Cardiff
Tel: 029 2023 5731

The Greenhouse Cafe

Licensed

International Vegetarian and Seafood from the finest local ingredients.

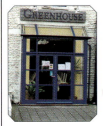

The small menu changes weekly with local organic produce and daily seafood specials brought in from a Swansea trawler. The vegetarian options are modern, fresh and exciting, hedonistic by design, wholesome by accident.

MIDWEEK SPECIALS EVERY TUES/WED EVENING
3 Courses (normally £13.50) Only £11.75
available March-Dec 2001

Open Tuesday to Saturday from 7pm.

Just 5 minutes from City Centre and only 2 minutes from Sherman Theatre.

Wales Tourism Award 2000
Winner of the hotel of the year

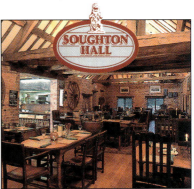

THE STABLES RESTAURANT

For a virtual Tour of our superb restaurant please access our web site
www.soughtonhall.co.uk

Soughton Hall, Northop, Nr. Mold,
Flintshire. CH7 6AB
Tel: 01352 840577 Fax: 01352 840382

QUAYSIDE Brasserie

The Quay, Carmarthen

Situated on the banks of the River Towy, within walking distance of the town centre, the restaurant specialises in using fresh local meat, fish and seafood produce.

It has a comprehensive wine list which includes new and old wines.

The two course special lunch menu is changed daily and children are catered for until early evening. Baby changing facilities and disabled toilets are provided.

Open 7 Days, Lunch & Dinner.
Children's Meals available until 7.30pm.

Two minutes walk from town centre

For further information & reservations -
Tel: 01267 223000
Fax: 01267 232444

Belle Vue Royal Hotel

A combination of Victorian architecture and modern sophistication makes The Belle Vue Royal Hotel a very elegant, spacious and comfortable place to stay.

Set in an enviable position on the Aberystwyth sea front, the hotel offers a magnificent view of Cardigan Bay with its spectacular sunsets.

The hotel serves a wide selection of wines and local produce from succulent steaks to fresh fish for lunch and dinner.

The Belle Vue is the ideal venue for your Conference or Wedding Reception and whether you require a professional or personal approach we will cater for the occasion.

The perfect base for sightseeing, golf with discount rates, walking - in fact, just about everything.

The Promenade, Aberystwyth, SY23 2BA.
Tel: 01970 617558 Fax: 01970 612190
www.bellevueroyalhotel.co.uk

AA ★★★ AA   RAC ★★★   WTB ★★★ Highly Commended

PEPPERCORN
COOKWARE SPECIALISTS
5 KING STREET, LLANDEILO, DYFED SA19 6BA.
Telephone: 01558 822410. Fax: 01558 824228

Cook Well - Eat Well

Top Quality Kitchen Equipment

Gadgets Galore

Catering for the Basic Cook or The Hotel Chef

CHRISTOPHER and GLORIA VAUGHAN-ROBERTS

For a taste of the exquisite east...

57/59 Lower Cathedral Road, Riverside, Cardiff.
(opposite Backpackers)

A vast array of whole and ground spices, unusual flours and pulses - boxes of Asian greens and herbs. Aubergines and gourds, Fenugreek and curry leaves. Shelves jam packed with the exotic items to in demand currently.

Why not try one of Mrs Madhau's delicious hot snacks, made on the premises? Choose from • Kachories • Samosas • Aluwadas • Onion Bhajis • Bhel and many more both sweet and savoury.

• New Cafe Bar Opening Soon •

Tel: 029 2037 2947

THREE COCKS HOTEL

situated just four miles from Hay on the A438 to Brecon and is a fine specimen of a spacious, rambling 15th Century Hostelry, richly furnished with antiques, oil paintings, oriental rugs, log fires and seven modernised ensuite bedrooms still retaining their original charm. To relax in we have an elegant oak panelled drawing room or you can enjoy the garden with a fine Belgian Beer.

The restaurant serves continental cuisine with the accent on Belgian Dishes.

AA ® ®
Rosette Award for cooking & Quality Rating 73%

Tel: (01497) 847215

Abersoch, Pwllheli,
Gwynedd LL53 7BU.
Tel: 01758 713333
Fax: 01758 713538

Porth Tocyn occupies a stunning position overlooking Cardigan Bay and the mountains of Snowdonia and provides an ideal base from which to tour the area. With easy access to the mountains and nearby attractions and the glorious beaches of the Lleyn Peninsula on its doorstep, the Hotel's situation combines the best of both worlds.

Beautiful gardens surround the Hotel and are criss-crossed by paths leading to secret nooks where guests can enjoy a tea or coffee in the open air. An outdoor swimming pool, which is heated from May to September, offers the chance to cool down on a hot summer's day and an all-weather surfaced tennis court provides the perfect venue in which to work up an appetite for dinner.

The Hotel's Restaurant has been continuously praised by good food guides for decades and dinner here provides the high point of a holiday for residents and diners from all over the Peninsula. A panoramic outlook from the Dining Room's huge pcture window and polished antique dining tables provide a wonderful setting in which to enjoy Porth Tocyn's famous cooking.

All the bedrooms have private bathrooms and showers, most have marvellous seaviews and all are thoughtfully furnished with antiques and knick-knacks. Three of the rooms are on the ground floor enabling disabled guests to stay.

Port Tocyn attracts a broad spectrum of people interested in watersports, golf, walking or just relaxing.

MUSEUM OF WELSH LIFE CATERING

*F*rom the moment you enter the tearooms, you will experience traditional atmospheric settings that will enhance your enjoyment of dishes cooked and served to the highest standards. Whatever the occasion you can relax and be confident that we will cater accordingly; whether it be a wedding reception, seminar, annual dinner, birthday or school party, corporate event, Sunday lunch or a tea dance. All our food is home made and we use traditional recipies with the freshest local produce.

- Vale Restaurant
- Gwalia Tea Rooms
- Castle Tea Rooms
- Iolo Morganwg Restaurant

For bookings and further information please contact:

Apple Catering Restaurant Services, The Museum of Welsh Life, St Fagans, Cardiff 029 2056 6985

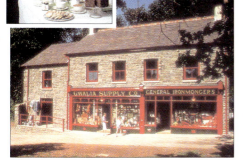

Basil's Brasserie

OPEN MONDAY - SATURDAY
LUNCH 12.00-2.30PM DINNER 7.00PM-10.00PM
(SATURDAY EVENING OPEN 6.30PM)
2 EASTGATE, COWBRIDGE
TELEPHONE: (01446) 773738

at Basil's you can taste the difference

Leonardos Delicatessen

○ Welsh Food ○ Organic Produce
○ Homemade Foods

Well Street, Ruthin, Denbighshire.
Tel: 01824 707161

With a menu as exciting as its eclectic, The Stable Door offers the best of Thai, Italian, British & Vegetarian Dishes to cater for all tastes.

Opening times: 7-10.30 Thurs-Sat & Sunday Lunch, Winter, Wed-Sat night 7-10.30pm, high season 6-10.30 Sun Lunch 12.30-2.30 from £10.20.

The Stable Door, Market Lane, Laugharne, Carmarthenshire, SA33 4SB.
Tel: 01994 427777 /
Fax: 01994 427819

Credit Cards: Visa / M/C (No American Express)

Do you expect delicious food, superb wine & excellent service when dining out? – GOOD!

because we know a place that delivers all this – and more...

Earl's of Llandaff

48 High Street, Llandaff, Cardiff

Examples from wide and varied menu:~

Starter: Chunky Fish Broth with lemongrass £4.90 (try this with our Gewürztraminer, Bin no 9)

Main Course: Crispy Bombay Duck roasted with honey glaze £12.90 (we recommend the Pirot Noir, Bin no 17 to accompany this)

~ Special Lunch Menus ~
£5.95 ~ 1 Course or £8.95 ~ 2 Courses

Sunday Roast £7.95

Daily Specials Available. All lovingly prepared by our renowned chef – Earl.

Tel: 029 2056 7711

Herbs Cookshop

162 High Street, Bangor
Tel: 01248 351249

For a quick coffee, tasty snack and a glass of wine or a meal in our informal friendly restaurant.

Herbs provides delicious home cooked fare with an emphasis on vegetarian eating, using only the best quality local Welsh produce.

Our wide range of freshly prepared foods includes soups, pastries, hot dishes, salads, breads & patisseries. Whist we also stock a high quality range of ground coffees, teas and cheeses.

In addition to this we also offer an outside catering service for any occasion.

Your pleasure is ours

The New House Restaurant

Situated on the fringes of Cardiff, nestling into Caerphilly Mountain, the Restaurant boasts unrivalled views over the city.

The award winning restaurant offers local Welsh produce mixed with an international style such as ham shank with a black bean sauce over root vegetables; or a matelot of local fish and seafood under a pastry case with saffron butter sauce.

A Member of Best Western
"The world's largest group of fine independent hotels"

Thornhill Road,
Thornhill
Cardiff CF14 9UA
Tel: (029) 2052 0280
Fax: (029) 2052 0324

AA ✦✦
email: newhousecountry@bestwestern.co.uk
www.newhousehotel.com

Carmarthen's newest and very exciting delicatessen

AARDELI

12A Mansel St, Carmarthen. Tel: 01267 236769

Call in and see our huge range of salamis, pastas, pickles and fresh pasties, also cheeses, wines, organic meats, chocolates, cakes and other gifts.

Cottage Delight and Carluccio's our specialities.

Small Shop - Big Choice!
Live a little - get the Aardeli habit

The Drovers Rest Restaurant & Tea Rooms With Rooms

The Square, Llanwrtyd Wells,
Powys LD5 4RA

Tel: 01591 610264
Website:
www.food-food-food.co.uk

Lunches ~ Welsh Teas ~ Dinners

Caldey Island

A range of delicious products from Caldey Island.

- Chocolate • Shortbread • Clotted Cream
- Yoghurt • Dairy Ice Cream • Cheese

Also available from Caldey Island Shop,
Quay Hill, Tenby. Tel 01834 842296

Visits to Caldey Island:
BOATS FROM TENBY HARBOUR
Easter to early October. Mon-Fri from 10am.
Also
Saturdays in June, July & August.
Phone: 01834 844453/842879/842296

Fine French Cuisine using the finest local produce cooked to perfection with a twist of originality

Also exhibitors of collectable contemporary art, specialising in ceramics, glass and sculpture.

63 Main Street,
Pembroke
Tel: (01646) 622333

THE CORS

Treat youself to the best in the most amazing setting

Proprietor, Nick Priestland welcomes you to his superbly original establishment, The Cors. Built in the 1830's, the house is set amidst $1^1/_2$ acres of glorious landscaped gardens. The restaurant offers an excellent á la carte menu which changes weekly. The food covers a variety of styles using the best fresh local produce. An extensive wine list complements the expertly prepared haute cuisine.

The Cors Country House Restaurant, Laugharne
Tel: 01994 427219

Brava

Brava is a delightful cafe/restaurant, located in the heart of Cardiff's Pontcanna district.

Our food is freshly made on the premises using local and organic ingredients whenever possible.

Superb breakfasts, baguettes, soups and daily specials.

• Afternoon Cakes • Voted 10/10 for our coffee!

Terrace & Garden in summer

Tel: 029 2037 1929
71 Pontcanna Street, Cardiff CF11 9HK

GORNO'S SPECIALITY FOODS LTD.

FRANCO GORNO MAITRE CHARCUTIER

The Authentic Italian Delicatessen

We Make with Care

Pepperoni Sausage
Traditional Italian Sausage
Mexican Chilli Sausage
Milano Sausage
Merguez Sausage
Toulouse Sausage
Natural Cooked Ham
French Garlic Sausage
Pastrami
Salt Beef
Chorizos
Cacciatori
Rillettes de Porc
Rillettes de Canard
Pancetta Affumicata
Dry Cured Bacon
Selection of Salamis
Prosciutto
Coppa

"A little taste of Italy, in Wales"

We produce, in our own factory, superior quality sausages manufactured from the finest ingredients, made to very old traditional Italian recipes. We have a delicatessen shop attached to the factory offering a wide range of scrumptious continental foods and delicacies - direct to you the public.

Unit 3, Fairfield Ind. Est., Pentyrch Rd, Taffs Well, Cardiff
(8 minute drive from City Centre)
Tel: 029 2081 1225
Fax: 029 2081 1299

Penally ABBEY

Country House Hotel & Restaurant,
Penally Nr Tenby, Pembrokeshire SA70 7PY, Wales, UK.
Tel (01834) 843033 Fax: (01834) 844714

Penally Abbey is a gem, commanding spectacular views across Carmarthen Bay. The hotel, a dignified Grade II listed mansion offers the rare experience of true country house accommodation by the sea. Genial hosts Steve and Elleen Warren and their welcoming staff are renowned for their hospitality and have awards to prove it.

The food - delicious but unpretentious, mirroring the style of the hotel - has also won praises. Dinner is an intimate candlelit affair with tempting seasonal delicacies, completing the picture of pure romance. Penally Abbey - The Perfect Place to unwind.

The Farmers Arms

Cwmdu, Nr Crickhowell, Powys NP8 1RU.
Tel: 01874 730464.
Web: www.thefarmersarms.com
Email: mail@thefarmersarms.com

The Farmers Arms is a traditional country inn, nestling in the foothills of the Black Mountains, 5 miles northeast of the quaint market town of Crickhowell.

We pride ourselves on providing all our customers with efficient, friendly service, good ales, inexpensive fine wines & consistently excellent food! How do we know? All the top independent pub/food guides are telling us so! Come and try for yourselves.

Contact Susan or Andrew to reserve your table
(Don't forget - we do accommodation as well!)

BLAS AR FWYD

Premier Welsh Delicatessen
Superior Selection of World Wide Wines

AMSER DA

Quality Restaurant in Llanrwst
For the Real & Fresh Taste of Wales
☎ 01492 640215 / 01492 641188

Windsor Lodge
HOTEL & RESTAURANT

Mount Pleasant, Swansea,
South Wales SA1 6EG.
Tel: 01792 642158 Fax: 01792 648996

The public restaurant grew from the hotel dining room which has long been appreciated by hotel guests. Its style is one of simplicity based on bought-fresh daily ingredients using British and French influences changing with the seasons. Vegetarians are especially welcome. The restaurant has received food awards from the AA and RAC and is open for dinner Monday to Saturday, booking by telephone, and for lunch by arrangement.

In 1992 Windsor Lodge was included in the AA's top twenty one-star hotels in the United Kingdom.

The Restaurant with the Difference

*E*njoy the warm ambience and informality of an authentic Spanish Bodega.

Now fully air-conditioned for your added comfort. Where fresh food is complemented by an extensive selection of wines and champagnes to cater for all palates.

In addition to our A La Carte menu, whether it's business or leisure, lunch should be a pleasure from our £6.95 for two courses menu.

28 Wind Street, Swansea.
Tel: 01792 469683
www.labrasseria.com

Good Food Good Wine.
Privately owned, professionally run.
Open Monday to Saturday 12 noon - 2.30pm and 7.00pm - 11.30pm

PENMAENUCHAF HALL

*E*xperience this elegant Country House Hotel overlooking the beautiful Mawddach Estuary where the emphasis is on comfort, cuisine and service.

*E*njoy our innovative and exciting menus, our varied and extensive wine list, our sumptuous oak panelled dining room and our professional and friendly staff.

*W*hether you are staying for afternoon tea, lunch or dinner we promise a warm welcome and a pleasurable experience.

Penmaenpool, Dolgellau, Gwynedd LL40 1YB
Tel: 01341 422129 Fax: 01341 422787
Email: relax@penhall.co.uk

George III Hotel
PENMAENPOOL, DOLGELLAU,
GWYNYDD LL40 1YD.
TEL: 01341 422525
FAX: 01341 423565

The George III is superbly situated on the banks of the beautiful Mawddach Estuary. The main hotel was built around 1650 as two separate buildings, pub and ship chandlers.

The adjacent lodge is a victorian building built as a waiting room, ticket office and station masters house for the railway, now closed.

AA RAC   WTB
★★ ★★   ★★★

The hotel is owned and personally run by John and Julia Cartwright and their family. Guests may choose between accommodation in the hotel or in the lodge. Each of the eleven rooms is full of character, comfortably furnished and has a wonderful view of the estuary.

Great emphasis is placed on the food with Welsh Lamb and seafood being the specialities in either the a la carte restaurant or bars.

The hotel is ideally located for exploring the surrounding area. Fishing permits are available free to guests to fish 12 miles of the estuary. Mountain bikes can be hired from the hotel to cycle the 7 mile old railway track along the estuary.

*A warm welcome awaits you
at The George*

EMAIL: reception@george-3rd.co.uk   Website: www.george-3rd.co.uk

16th C Manor House set in terraced gardens, surrounded by mountains and meadows in the spectacular scenery of south Snowdonia.

Resident owners offer a warm friendly welcome and superb food and wines in elegance, peace and tranquillity.

Ideal for touring or for the more energetic walking, fishing and mountain biking.

Recommended by Johansens, "Which?" Hotel Guide, The Good Food Guide and Ashley Courtenay.

A Non-Smoking Hotel

Plas Dolmelynllyn
Country Hotel

Ganllwyd, Dolgellau, Gwynedd LL40 2HP
Tel: 01341 440273
Fax: 01341 440640
Email: info@dolly-hotel.co.uk
Website: www.dolly-hotel.co.uk

★★★
*Wales Tourist
Board Country
Hotel*

★★★
*Rosette
for Food*

*P*icturesque National Park location central to Snowdonia's mountains and coast. Delightful en-suite bedrooms with bath and shower, satellite TV, telephone, tea/coffee, hairdryer, laundry. Spectacular views across the River Conwy. Our elegant AA Rosette awarded Queens Restaurant has an enviable reputation for its cuisine, enhanced by friendly attentive service.

*A*lternatively, dine in our less formal Kings Brasserie (pictured) - great atmosphere, great food, great fun. Open log fires, cosy residents lounge, we usually tempt you to stay longer than you expected!!

Trelriw (nr Betws-y-Coed),
North Wales LL27 0JP
Telephone: 01492 640592
Facsimile: 01492 640559

Shopping for Welsh Ingredients

Shopping for good food in Wales has not always been easy, and no one has complained more loudly than our chefs. In the past they have experienced great difficulties in finding sometimes the simplest of supplies like fresh fish or local vegetables. In compiling our shopping list we looked to them for advice, and were encouraged to discover a great improvement over the past couple of years.

Les Rennie, recently-arrived chef at Ynyshir Hall was delighted at what he found in Wales. "You can get any ingredients you want, as long as you plan well ahead." Les, who has cooked in some of the most prestigious restaurants in Britain says that the meat, lamb, beef and venison is first class in Wales. Fish arrives from two suppliers, sometimes by a phone call from the local harbour. Dairy produce is excellent with enough top quality Welsh cheeses to grace a first class board.

There are pockets of good food all over Wales, with well stocked delicatessens, top class butchers and farm shops to tempt the most hardened shopper. Since we found our best leads from the various restaurants, hotels and bed and breakfasts, we suggest that you ask your hosts, if you want to buy the best of local fish in each region.

Food producers/retail outlets may be seasonal or have special hours, please ring ahead for special conditions.

North Wales - Food List

ABERDOVEY
Butcher	David Roberts, Copper Hill St	01654 767223

ANGLESEY
Sea salt	Halen Mon, Anglesey Sea Zoo, Brynsiencyn	01248 430871
Butcher	Owen Roberts, Amlwch	01407 830277
Butcher	E T Jones, Bodedern, Holyhead	01407 740257
Traditional handmade cakes	Strawberry Farm, Pentraeth	01248 722564
Livestock, local produce stalls	Llangefni Market, County Counoil	01248 723332
Wholefoods	The Whole Thing, Llangefni	01248 724832
Welsh speciality products	Cegin Cymru, Llanfair PG	01248 717171
PYO fruit	Gwydryn Hir, Brynsiencyn	01248 430322
Herbs	Cae Gwyn, herb nursery	01248 470231

BANGOR
Oysters	Menai Oysters, Ger y Mynydd	01248 361313
Fishmongers	H&S Open Shores, High St	01248 351814

BARMOUTH
Delicatessen	Goodies, High St	01341 281162
Bakery	Kith'n Kin, King Edward St	01341 281071

CAERNARFON
Delicatessen	Just Natural, Pool St	01286 674748

COLWYN BAY
Delicatessen	Speronis Delicatessen, Conwy Rd	01492 533101
Wholefoods/organic produce	Country Kitchen, Seaview Rd	01492 533329

CONWY
Butcher (Welsh Black beef & saltmarsh lamb)		
	IG Edwards, High St	01492 592443
Free range/welfare assured pork	Oakwood Park Farm, Sychnant Pass Rd	01492 573573

DENBIGH
Organic produce	Ty Newydd Farmshop, A525	01745 812882
Bakery	Alwyn Thomas Bakery, Vale St and High St	01745 812068
Yogurt, dairy desserts	Llaeth y Llan Dairy, Llannefydd	01745 540256
PYO fruit	Maes y Wern Fruit Farm	01824 790762
Rainbow trout, fresh sea fish	Old Forge Trout Farm, Bodfari	01745 710305

DOLGELLAU AREA
Delicatessen/bakery	Popty'r Dref, Upper Smithfield St	01341 422507
Organic nursery, wholefoods	Panteidal Organics	01654 767322

HARLECH
Handmade preserves	Mountain Garden, Maes Y Neuad, Talsarnau	01766 780319
Delicatessen	Bwtri Bach Delicatessen, High St	01766 780373

LLANBERIS
Honey	Snowdon Honey Farm, High St	01286 870218

LLANDUDNO
Fishmongers	The Fish Shop, Builder St	01492 870430
Fresh local produce	Bodafon Farm Park	01492 545702

LLANGOLLEN
Herbs	Gill Thomas Herbs, WI Market, Friday	01978 860508
Bakery	Megan's Kitchen, Bishop Trevor	01978 860063

LLANWRST
Bakery	Sigwr a Sbeis (bakery)	01492 641775
Local foods, deli, preserves	Blas ar Fwyd, Heol yr Osaf	01492 640215

MOLD
Hand-made pates	Fat Cats Fine Food (handmade pates)	01352 731652
Delicatessen	Fresh & Fancy, Daniel Owen Precinct	01352 757386
Bakery	Roberts' Bakery, Wrexham St	01352 753119
Delicatessen	Roberts' Deli, Wrexham St	01352 755339

PORTHMADOG
Fish, organic veg	Joe Lewis, High St (fish, organic vegetables)	01766 512229
Ice cream	Cadwallader's Ice Cream, High St	01766 514235

PRESTATYN
Delicatessen	Cahill's Delicatessen, High St	01745 853199

PWLLHELI
Butcher	Tony Page, Jail St	01758 612136
Organic produce	Rhosfawr Nurseries, Rhosfawr	01766 810545
Rose beef & saltmarsh lamb	Cig Rose Llyn, Bwyd Llyn, Mynytho	01766 512288

RUTHIN
Natural Welsh honey to order	Ty Brith Honey (natural Welsh honey, to order)	01978 790279

TYWYN
Honey shop & reduced calorie choc bars		
	Halo Foods, Pendre	01654 711171

WREXHAM
Butcher; rose beer to order	Mike William, Caergwrle	01978 761078
Fruit and veg	Bellis Country Market, Holt	01829 270304

BORDERS
Organic produce	Discount Organics, Chester (farm shop)	01244 881209

Mid Wales - Food List

ABERAERON
Fishmongers	Fish on the Quay, the Old Wharf	01545 571294
Welsh speciality products	Cegin Cymru, Market St	01545 570460

ABERYSTWYTH & NEARBY
Brewery/pub - own brews	Harvest Moon, Oatmeal St, Flannery's, High St	01970 612334
Delicatessen	Cork n' Bottle, Pier St	01970 617332
Organic produce	The Tree House, Baker St	01970 615791
Organic dairy produce	Rachel's Dairy, Dolybont, Borth	01970 625805
Farmhouse cheese, goats	Merlin Cheeses, Ystrad Meurig	01974 282636

BRECON & CRICKHOWELL
Butcher	W.J. George, Talgarth	01874 711233
Organic fruit, veg, herbs	Primrose Organics	01497 847636
Deli, wholefoods	Top Drawer 2, Brecon	01874 622601
Natural venison/deer farm	Welsh Venison Centre, Bwlch, Brecon	01874 730929
Smoked produce	Black Mountain Smokery, Llangenney	01873 811566
Single estate apple juice, cider	Gellirhyd Farm, Llangenny	01873 810466
Organic veg, meat	Green Peas, Crickhowell Market - Saturday	01873 830554

BUILTH & LLANWRTYD WELLS

Delicatessen	Cheese and Chives, High St	01982 551171
Farmhouse cheese, goats	Pencerrig Home Farm, Llanelwedd	01982 553177
Bakery	Bernards Bakery, Irfon Crescent, Llanwrtyd Wells	
		01591 610391

HAY ON WYE

Wholefoods	Hay Wholefoods, Lion St	01497 820708

LAMPETER

Farmhouse cheese, Caerffili	Gorwydd Caerffili	01570 493516

LLANDRINDOD WELLS & NEARBY

Butcher/baker	Grosvenor Stores, Wellington Rd	01597 824369
Delicatessen, local foods	Van's Good Food Shop, Middleton St	01597 823074
Organic/additive free meat	Graig Farm, Dolau	01597 851655
Herbs	Whimble Nursery, Kinnerton	01547 560413
Cider	Ralph Owen, Kinnerton	01544 350304
Original Roman recipe sauces	Apicius Sauces Limited, Knucklas, Knighton	01547 528376

LLANIDLOES

Butcher	Edward Hamer, Plynlimon House	01686 412209
Bakery	Meredith Bakery, Great Oak St	01686 412628

MACHYNLLETH

Traditional flour	Felin Crewi Watermill	01654 703113
Organic gardens	Centre for Alternative Technology	01654 702400

MONTGOMERY & NEARBY

Wholefoods	Castle Kitchen, Broad St	01686 668795
Organic & traditional flour	Bacheldre Watermill, Montgomery	01588 620489
Montgomery Natural Spring Water		
	Harry Tuffin Ltd	01588 620226

NEWTOWN

Wholefoods	MacBeans, High St	01686 627002

WELSHPOOL & LLANFYLLIN

Butcher	John Langfords, Severn St, Welshpool	01691 648246
Delicatessen/wholefoods	Down To Earth, Narrow St, Llanfyllin	01691 648841

THE BORDERS

Wholefoods	Georges, Kington	01544 231400
Fish	The Grapevine, Kington	01544 231202
Food shop	Hussey's, Kington	01544 230381
Organic cider	Dunkerton's Organic Cider, Pembridge	01544 388653
Wine	Wroxeter Roman Vineyard, Shrewsbury	01743 761888
Bakery	Moray & Son, Bishops Castle	01588 638458

South West Wales - Food List

SWANSEA, THE GOWER & NEARBY
Cockles, laverbread, fish, cheese, baking

	Swansea Market	01792 654296
Butcher	H. Howell & Son, Caefolland, Penclawdd	01792 850371
Butcher	Colin Davies, Killay Shopping Precinct, Killay	01792 290114

LLANDEILO
| Cookware shop | Peppercorn, Llandeilo | 01558 822410 |

Butcher; organic meat/Welsh black beef

| | Dewi Roberts, Llandeilo | 01558 822566 |
| Group tours | Tomos Watkin Brewery, Llandeilo | 01792 775333 |

CARMARTHEN & NEARBY
Cheese, poultry, bacon, ham, sewin, cockles, waffles

	Carmarthen Market	01267 228841
Farmhouse cheese	Nantybwla Farmhouse Cheese, College Rd	01267 237905
Welsh wildflower honey	Abergorlech Post Office	01558 685211
Salt marsh	Eynon's Family Butchers, St Clears	01994 230226
Farmhouse cheese, Caerphilly	Caws Ffermdy Cenarth, Pontseli	01239 710432
Handmade chocolates	Pemberton's Victorian Chocolates, Llanboidy	01994 448768

FISHGUARD & ST DAVID'S
Meat and fish	PM & B Butchers, Fishguard	01348 872394
Homemade preserves	Miranda's Preserves, Goodwick	01348 872011
Farmhouse cheeses	Llangloffan Farmhouse Cheese, Castle Morris	01348 891241

Organic farmhouse cheese/produce

	Caerfai Farm, St David's	01437 720548
Organic produce	The Pumpkin Shed, St David's	01437 721949
Ewes, goats cheese	Rhosygilwen Dairy, St David's	01437 721954

NEWPORT
| Takeaway | Fountain House Foods, Market St | 01239 820151 |

Health foods, organic wines, cheese

| | Bydydd Cyflawn, East St | 01239 820773 |
| Herbs | Cilgwyn Herb Garden, Cilgwyn | 01239 820398 |

CRYMYCH & NEARBY
Wholefoods	Bwyd y Byd, Prospect Pl	01239 831537
Bakery	JK Lewis & Sons, Preseli Stores	01239 831288
Organic produce	Pencrugia Organic Farm Shop, Felindre Farchog	01239 881265

Farmhouse goats and Caws Cerwyn cheese

	Pant Mawr Farm	01437 532627
Handmade speciality preserves	Wendy Brandon, Boncath	01239 841568
Own traditionally brewed ales	Nag's Head Brewery	01239 841200

CARDIGAN & ST DOGMAELS

Wholefoods	Go Mango, Cardigan	01239 614727
Honey	Life of the Hive, Cardigan	01239 810301
Organic Gouda cheese	Penbryn Organic Farmhouse Cheese, Sarnau	01239 810347
Stoneground flour, bread	Y Felin Mill, St Dogmaels	01239 613999

LLANDYSUL & NEARBY

Bakery	Popty Bach, Llandysul	01559 362335
Fish	Rhydlewis Trout Farm, Rhydlewis	01239 851224
Organic Gouda cheese	Teifi Farmhouse Cheese, Ffostrasol	01239 851528

TENBY & NEARBY

Butchers	JV Rowe & Sons, High St	01834 842465
Caldy Island produce	The Caldy Shop, Quay Hill	01834 842296
Coffee & deli	Cooks Corner, Tenby Market	01834 843637
Fish	Pembrokeshire Fish Farm, Llandissilio	01646 661393
Bakery	Pobyddion Beca, Efailwen	01994 419616
Deli	The Old Moat House, Narberth	01834 861491
Wine	Cwm Deri Vineyard, Martletwy	01834 891274
Bakery	White's Golden Crust Bakery, Lamphey	01646 672102
PYO/farm shop	Springfields Fresh Produce, Manorbier	01834 871746
Farmhouse cheese, Chesire type	St Florence Cheese	01834 871181
Farmshop, fruit and veg	Priory Farm Shop, New Hedges	01834 844662

MILFORD HAVEN & HAVERFORDWEST

Fish	The Fish Plaice, Milford Haven	01646 692331
PYO strawberries	New Creamson Farm, Creamson Rd, Haverfordwest	
		01437 763732
Organic meat	Meat Centre, Haverfordwest	01437 768877
Organic produce	Growing Concern, Camrose	01437 710384

South East Wales - Food List

ABERGAVENNY & NEARBY

Delicatessen	Vin Sullivans, Frogmore St	01873 856989
Butcher	H J Edwards, Flannel St	01873 853110
Wine	Sugar Loaf Vineyard, Llwyndu	01873 858675
Fishery	Trout Farm, Llanfihangel Crucorney	01873 890545
Organic meat, to order	Upper Pant Farm, Llanddewi Rhydderch	01873 858091
Pure apple, blackcurrent liqueur	Black Mountain Liqueur, Llanfoist	01873 852345
Natural Jersey cream, yoghurts	Bower Farm, Grosmont	01981 240219
Free range pork, Welsh Black beef, lamb	Blorenge Mountain Farm, Pontypool	01495 755557
Honey, honey products	Gwent Vale Apiaries, Upper Llanover	01873 880625
Rhea meat (ostrich family)	Pampas Poultry, Llanddewi Rhydderch	01873 840281

MONMOUTH AREA

Speciality sausages, butcher	Hancocks, Monnow St	01600 712015
Deli	Irma Fingal Rock Foods, Monnow St	01600 712372
Welsh Wine	Offas Vineyard, Llanivangel Ystern Llegwrn	01600 780241
WelshWine	Monnow Valley Wine, Osbaston	01600 716209
Organic fruit, veg, dairy, breads	Medhope Organic Growers, Tintern	01291 689797
Organic herbs	Wye Valley Plants, Tintern	01291 689253
PYO/farm shop	Great Tyrmynach Farm, Raglan	01291 690470

NEWPORT AREA

Butcher; salt marsh lamb/rose beef to order

	Graham Palfrey, Church Rd	01633259385
Delicatessen	William Baldocks Deli, Central Market	01633 257312
Butcher/deli	Dave Buckland, Bedwas	029 2088 5288

CARDIFF & NEARBY

Fish, cheese, meat	Cardiff Central Market	029 2087 1214
Health foods	Beanfreaks, St Mary St	029 2025 1671
Delicatessen	Wally's Deli, Royal Arcade	029 2022 9265
Delicatessen	Shelly's Deli, Cathedral Rd	029 2022 7180
Food hall/deli	Howells Food Hall, St Mary St	029 2023 1055
Indian shop	Madhav's, Lower Cathedral Rd	029 2037 2947
Chinese shop	Jim's Eastern Chinese Supermarket, Tudor St	029 2039 7148
Italian meat/deli	Gorno's Speciality Foods, Taffs Well	029 2081 1225
Welsh speciality foods	Museum of Welsh Life, St Fagans	029 2057 3500
Welsh speciality foods	Cegin Cymru, Caerphilly	029 2088 2882
Butcher	David Lush, Glebe Street, Penarth	029 2070 7007
PYO fruit & ice cream	Ices from the Fruit Garden, Peterston Super Ely	01446 760358
Organic dairy, wholefoods, herbs	Spice of Life, Roath	029 2048 7146
Ice cream	Minnoli's of Machen, Machen	01633 440551

COWBRIDGE & NEARBY

Welsh Black beef	I.G. Nicholas, High St	01656 772550
Delicatessen	Glyn T Jenkins, High St	01446 773545
Wine	Llanerch Vineyard, Llantrisant	01443 225877
Organic produce	Pencoed Organic Growers, Pencoed	01656 861956
PYO/farm shop, asparagus	Ton Fruit Farm, Merthyr Mawr, Bridgend	01656 650090
Local meat, own lamb occasionally		
	James Traditional Butchers, Bridgend	01656 652343
Organic cakes, breads, deli	Lewis' Delicatessen Porthcawl	01656 783300

A Welsh Cheeseboard

Produced on a number of farms in Wales, and some on larger dairy factories, Welsh cheeses are available throughout the year and offer enough variety of taste and texture to make up a splendid Welsh cheeseboard.

These cheeses are not cheap, because making small quantities by hand takes time, but the best Welsh farmhouse cheeses are among the finest made anywhere and deserve to be treated as such. Some are sold in Harrods, some are exported, and many are available at good delicatessens throughout Britain or at the cheese counter in supermarkets. Almost all hotels and restaurants in Wales now serve local cheeses, and here are some of the best.....

Aeron Valley
A range of pasteurised cheeses are made under this label and, although production is on a large scale, the flavour, texture and price makes them popular with chefs.

Acorn
Unpasteurised ewes' milk cheese, vegetarian. Natural rind, mild flavour with pleasant slightly crumbly texture.

Caerfai
Organically-produced, unpasteurised hard cows' milk cheese matured for at least four months. Fine flavour. Also with leek or spring onions with garlic.

Caws Celtica
Two good new ewes' milk cheeses, Lammas, a mild caerphilly-type and Beltane which has a fuller flavour and is made like a gouda. Also available smoked.

Caws Ffermdy Cenarth
Traditional unpasteurised Caerphilly, semi-hard with a crumbly texture. Mild, matured and smoked, plus various added flavours.

Celtic Promise
Medium-hard cheese with a washed rind, made from unpasteurised cows' milk. Strong individual character with powerful smell and flavour. Greatly acclaimed.

Gorwydd Caerffili
Traditional Caerphilly, with natural rind, exceptionally good.

Hen Sir
The name translates as Old Shire, and is a mature cheddar with a nutty flavour. Popular and reasonably priced.

Lady Llanover
Ewes' milk cheese which has its rind washed with a saffron solution. Fine flavour.

Llangloffan
A hard, pressed cheese made to an original Cheshire cheese recipe from the unpasteurised milk of Jersey cows. Good flavour. Also available with added garlic and chives.

Llanboidy
A hard, pressed farmhouse cheese with a rich nutty flavour made with unpasteurised milk from a herd of pedigree Red Poll cows. Laverbread Llanboidy also available.

Merlin
Unpasteurised hard goats' milk cheese, with a texture between cheddar and gouda and a creamy flavours. Natural, smoked, with olives, walnuts and other flavours, all in waxed covers.

Monks of Strata Florida
A range of flavoured cows' milk cheeses.

Nantybwla
Unpasteurised Caerphilly traditionally made and matured. Smoked variety also available and with garlic and chives.

Pantmawr
A cows/goats milk cheese make in the Preseli Mountains in Pembrokeshire. Available smoked also.

Pant ys Gawn
Soft organic goats' milk cheese available in natural and with herbs. Clean, fresh texture and taste.

Penbryn
Another fine hard gouda cheese made with organically produced cows' milk and matured for three to six months.

Rhosygilwen
An exciting new range of soft cheeses made from home produced ewes and cows milk. Caws Jemma and Barti Ddu are excellent.

Skirrid
An interesting semi-hard ewes' milk cheese, marinated in mead.

St. David's
A washed rind chaum-type cheese with lots of character when ripe.

St Florence
Firm cheese, based on a traditional Cheshire recipe. Unpasteurised cows milk, with a natural rind. Available also with chives and leeks.

St.Illtyd
A popular soft cheese made from mature Welsh cheddar milled with Welsh wine, garlic and herbs.

Teifi
Traditional unpasteurised gouda with excellent flavour and texture. Available in a range of flavours including, garlic, celery, nettle, sweet peppers, laverbread and cumin.

Tintern
A milled cheddar flavoured with garlic and leeks.

Y Fenni
Milled cheddar with Welsh ale and mustard seed. Very popular, and excellent for making Welsh rarebit.

A Welsh Wine List

The wine industry in Wales is in remarkably good health. With more than a dozen vineyards in production, there are now enough Welsh wines to make a wine list. Despite the fact that it takes only a late frost, dull summer, hailstorm or wet autumn to write off most of the crop, and that once Customs and Excise taxes are added the retail price seems high compared to the mainly imported wines, Welsh wines are holding their own.

Almost all the vineyards are found in the south, where the Romans planted one of the largest vineyards in Britain in the Vale of Glamorgan. The Normans encouraged viniculture by monasteries, and it was only the success of the Plantagenets in France that demoralised wine production in Wales. The Marquis of Bute challenged the French with his vineyard at Castell Coch, just north of Cardiff. In 1876 he sent his head gardener, Andrew Pettigrew, to Bordeaux for a year to study viticulture in order to produce red wine from a grape variety called Gamay Noir. By 1905 the total amount of vines planted exceeded 63,000 and the wines were sold commercially in London with prices higher than imported Burgundy wines (60 shillings per case for the Castell Coch 1893 vintage).

A new burst of wine-making enthusiasts emerged in the 1970s, and today the Welsh wine industry thrives. There are more than a dozen vineyards, some of whose wines achieve a quality equal to any made in the British Isles. These are mainly white wines, with a few light reds and some promising roses, as well as sparking wines. The grapes uses are generally hybrid Alsace varieties such as Madeleine Angevine, Seyval Blanc, Reichensteiner, Leon Millot and Triomph d'Alsace, which can withstand the Welsh climate. The Welsh wines are light, dry and fruity in character. Many of the vineyards welcome visitors and offer wine-tastings.

Glyndwr
Brothers Robbie and Richard Norris produce 3-6,000 bottles of white, red, rose and now a Glyndwr sparkling wine from their five-acre vineyard. Established in 1983 and set amid rolling hills with a small wood to the west, it enjoys a very mild maritime climate four miles from the sea. The vines are planted on limestone topped by loamy clay, with the vines trained on the double Guyot system in rows 6ft apart. Glyndwr has sold its wine to France and Switzerland.

Pant Teg
Cardiff's own vineyard was planted in 1986 on a south-facing field of Pant Teg Farm at Lisvane, to the north-east of the city. The vineyard has produced white wines since 1991 under the capable hands of Kynric Lewis and John Albert Evans. New from Pant Teg is a sparkling wine from Kerner and Kernling grapes.

Monnow Valley
The vineyards, now extending to four acres, were first planted in 1979 on the sheltered slopes of the Monnow Valley just outside Monmouth. Production includes 500 bottles of sparkling wine from Seyval Blanc grapes; the other grape varieties are Huxelrebe/Seyval.

Cariad
Planted on the slopes of the Ely Valley at Pendoylan, in the Vale of Glamorgan, Llanerch Vineyard has become perhaps the premier vineyard in Wales. Diana and Peter Andrews have perfected the skills of viticulture and viniculture since retiring as pharmacists, and produce a range of award-winning wines, from white and roses to a sparkling and even a fume. Visitors are welcome for wine-tasting and a cup of tea in the café.

Cwm Deri
This family-run vineyard is in Martletwy, Pembrokeshire where the Cowburns make four white and a light red on the farm. Fourteen grape varieties include Madeleine Angevine and Seyval Blanc. Country wines and liqueurs are also available. Visitors are welcome to look around and taste.

Ffynnon Las
A small, well-established vineyard of about an acre in the Aeron Valley, producing around 3,000 bottles a year. Martin Lewis now produces three still table wines from Madeleine Angevine, Schonburger, Reichensteiner and Seyal Blanc grapes. The wines are dry and medium dry, and there's also a red wine.

Offa's
At the end of the 1980s Peter Johnson planted 2,500 vines for white wine and 250 for red at Llanvihangel-Ystum-Llywern, near Monmouth. This two and a half acre vineyard now produces three wines; a blend of Bacchus and Faber white grapes, a blend of Fabe and Schonburger white grapes and a red made from Merlot and Cabernet Sauvignon.

Tintern Parva
Planted originally over 25 years ago, the current owners have spent the past two years restoring the vineyard to good health. With 17 varieties of grape, most wines are blends apart from Seyval and maybe some Pinot Noir this year. Visitors are welcome to take an unguided tour of the vineyard and taste the wine.

Wyecliff
The vineyard overlooks Hay Castle and was first planted more than a decade ago. The wine is made from Madeleine Angevine grapes.

Hiraeth
Planted in 1997, the vineyard at Oelynis farm just north of Cardiff occupies less than an acre. First vintage spring 2001, predominately Seyval Blanc, medium dry, and made with the help of winemaker Diana Andrews of Cariad wines.

Worthenbury Wines
This vineyard in Wrexham consists of an acre of vines grown in poly tunnels, with classic red and white grape varieties of Pinot Noir and Chardonnay. The award winning wine (at the UK vineyard association) is sold as single varieties and available at local restaurants. See more on www.worthenburywines.com.

North Wales Entries

1 Abergele

Kinmel Arms

St George
Abergele
Conwy
LL22 9BP
Tel: 01745 832207
Fax: 01745 832207

Situated just off the A55, this lovely old coach house is easily accessible to most travellers and is very popular with locals and tourists alike.

Chef Gary Edwards has now compiled just one menu to cater for both bar and restaurant customers, on which dishes like giant king prawns with a spicy chilli and garlic butter and a warm tartlet of creamy smoked haddock and leek sit alongside beef lasagne with chips and salad. Under the heading 'roasts', the Welsh lamb rack with herb crust and a red wine sauce is served pink and sweet and the roasted half-duck with a proper plum sauce works extremely well. Fish and vegetarian options are adequate, if a little uninspiring.

A short but carefully chosen wine list has a fair selection of half-bottles although only one red and two house white wines are available by the glass.

Desserts are well executed, the raspberry crème brulée light and creamy with a fine dusted glaze. A good selection of cheese with an even better choice of biscuits follows and coffee is good.

Service is efficient and the enthusiastic waitresses add colour to the slightly fading decor of the restaurant.

MEALS: L 12-2 from £5; D 7-9 from £13.50
Closed: Christmas Day
Cards: All major cards
CHEF/PROPRIETOR: Gary Edwards

LOCAL INTEREST: Walking, historic buildings, local shoot.

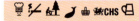

2 Abersoch

Porth Tocyn

Bwlch Tocyn
Abersoch
Gwynedd
LL53 7BU
Tel: 01758 713303
Fax: 01758 713538

e-mail:
porthtocyn.hotel@virgin.net
www.porth-tocyn-hotel.co.uk

'Less than a mile to go', a sign in the hedgerow encourages seekers of this secluded haven. Labyrinthine lanes descend on to an oasis of calm and serenity. Palms lend a Mediterranean aura to startling views over Tremadog Bay to the mountains of Snowdonia.

Nick Fletcher-Brewer greets his guests personally with unflappable, friendly confidence, seating them in calming nooks to study the mouth-watering menu.

Diners wander into the comfortably traditional dining room when they wish, seating themselves informally at their choice of antique oaken tables, where young, capable and friendly staff take orders and the kitchen produces swiftly.

A first course of seared foie gras with buttered spinach, blackberry jus and apple sorbet competes with toasted brochetta with ratatouille, Parmesan and olives, and a seafood terrine dressed with smoked salmon and dill.

From five choices of substantial main courses decisions are not easy. Will the baked loin of venison wrapped in a wild mushroom and coriander pancake with a redcurrant sauce be a wiser choice than a generous hunk of grilled cod on English mustard mash with caramelised onions and red wine jus?

One could justifiably call "enough" at this stage and sit by the fire to enjoy excellent coffee and home-made petit fours, but true trenchermen will bravely find room for an exquisite Bailey's Cream cheesecake with blackcurrant coulis or generous spoonfuls of perfect Stilton excavated from the whole round.

MEALS: L 12.15-2; Sunday L £8; D 7.30-9 £25.50-£32
Closed: Mid November – Mid March
Cards: All except Amex and Diners
CHEFS: Louise Fletcher-Brewer and Gary Moreton-Jones
PROPRIETOR: Nick Fletcher-Brewer

LOCAL INTEREST: Plas yn Rhiw, Lloyd George Museum at Llanystumdwy, Criccieth Castle, Talhenbont Hall, Plas Gyn y Weddw Historic House and Art Gallery, boating

3 Bangor

Goetre Isaf Farmhouse

Caernarfon Road
Bangor
Gwynedd
LL57 4DB
Tel: 01248 364541
Fax: 01248 364541

e mail: wer@fredw.com
www.fredw.com

'Now, does everyone know all these Welsh cheeses?' enthuses Fred, as he produces one of the most comprehensive cheese boards in Wales. An evening meal, cooked by Alison and served by Fred Whowell, will showcase the very best of local produce, often from the garden of this charming old farmhouse.

Notching up 143 years between them, this mature team of hosts obviously enjoys guests, and the two are full of stories of travel and adventure themselves. "Do try this crab apple and lavender jelly, or the green tomato jam" says Alison from the kitchen.

The dinner menu, possibly the best value in Wales, might include artichoke soup (made from home-grown artichokes) smoked mackerel pâté, avocado or melon starters.

For main course, a casserole of pork and coriander or a choice of fish, served with no less than four vegetable dishes such as boiled Pembrokeshire potatoes, baked root vegetables in the Finnish style, oven-baked peppers and sprouts cooked with bacon. Puddings might be summer fruit meringue or pears poached in wine.

And so back to the cheeseboard, which includes a locally-made buffalo milk Brie, Welsh goat's, ewe's, smoked Caerphilly and the splendid Celtic Promise from Carmarthenshire.

MEALS: D As and when £10.50
Closed: Please call
Cards: None accepted
CHEF: Alison Whowell. PROPRIETORS: Alison and Fred Whowell
WTB: 2 ★★
Rooms: 3, £18 S, £32 D, £40 Suite

LOCAL INTEREST: Extensive garden, Snowdonia, Anglesey and the Lleyn Peninsula

4 Bangor

Herbs

162 High Street
Bangor
Gwynedd
LL57 1NN
Tel: 01248 351249
www.herbsrestaurant.co.uk

Herbs has moved. No longer constrained by its back-street, crammed-into-every-nook-and-cranny, dilapidated terraced house, its faithful and ever-growing clientele now step from Bangor's main shopping street into a vibrant, brisk, business-like interior. Polished storm lanterns shine down on to a serving counter alive with exotic lilies. Modern prints adorn the walls.

The menu is a massive, double-sided laminate offering a bewildering choice of refreshment from 10am to 9pm with a 'take-out' service available at 10% reduction.

Your mood may be to breakfast on a bagel with smoked salmon and scrambled egg (and why not chase that down with a litre of freshly squeezed orange juice and champagne at £25.75), or perhaps you would favour a ciabatta with Mozzarella, black olives and sun-dried tomatoes.

Some may call by for their daily fix of hot chocolate with Maltesers and leaf through one of the complimentary newspapers, whilst their table companions munch steadily through respective choices of Thai green chicken curry with fragrant rice, a Caesar salad rich with the taste of anchovies, crisp bacon and Parmesan, or foil-baked salmon with hollandaise sauce.

Others simply settle for fresh scones with home-made jam and thick cream, just to watch the unflappable young waiters as they juggle two-score orders simultaneously, clear and lay tables, open wines and perculate fragrant coffee, serving and chatting pleasantly whilst computing bills.

It is a humming dynamo of a place, yet, when one is seated, pleasantly tranquil and soothing.

MEALS: All day; 10am until 9pm £3-£10.50
Closed: Sunday and Bank Holidays
Cards: All major
CHEF/PROPRIETOR: Sue Marchant

LOCAL INTEREST: Bangor Cathedral, Penrhyn Castle, Anglesey

5 Bangor

Rosie Lafin runs a very good restaurant here, making the perfect resting spot from a tour of the castle and encouraging visitors to enter into the spirit of Penrhyn. She has put together a menu that captures the flavour of Penrhyn's Victorian past, when the castle had an international reputation for the quality and range of its vegetables and

National Trust Tearoom

Penrhyn Castle
Bangor
Gwynedd
LL57 4HN
Tel: 01248 353084
Fax: 01248 371281

exotic fruits – its kitchen gardens covered more than six-and-a-half acres. Fresh dairy produce and home-grown meat came from Penrhyn's own farm and game from its extensive estates.

Today's menu is based on recipes from Penrhyn archives, information from the servants who worked here and traditional Welsh fare – for example, potted Welsh cheese with walnuts and sage, cheese and leek bread-and-butter pudding, lamb hotpot with rosemary-flavoured Victorian Doughboys or Gardener's Pie. This is made in honour of Walter Speed, who was head gardener at Penrhyn for 58 years and served under three Lords Penrhyn.

Puddings include a fashionable Victorian bavarois au café et chocolat, a steamed sponge pudding known as Gentleman's Pudding or even mucky-mouth pie, which was given to the children after they gathered bilberries.

As with all National Trust restaurants, baking is a strength. Choose from cinnamon-iced ginger cake, Victoria sponge, a Penrhyn Welsh cream tea or the full monty with Lady Penrhyn's afternoon tea.

MEALS: L 11-5 approx £7.50
Closed: November to April and Tuesdays
Cards: Visa and Mastercard
CATERING MANAGER: Rosie Laflin

LOCAL INTEREST: Penrhyn Castle and Penrhyn Bay

6 Barmouth

Bae Abermaw

Panorama Raod
Barmouth
Gwynedd
LL42 1DQ
Tel: 01341 280550
Fax: 01341 280346

e-mail:
bae.abermaw@virgin.net
www.abermawr.com

An American architect has converted this well-positioned small hotel overlooking sea and estuary at the southern end of Barmouth into a stunningly beautiful place with marvellous unity of style. It has all-white walls, bleached wood, blond-polished wood floors, and splashes of colour in dramatic modern rugs, abstract paintings and kelim cushions on the plentiful beige settees. The theme is carried through into 14 bedrooms and the whole house is a triumph of restful minimalist modernity.

The teething problems of a new operation are apparent in the kitchen, which has not had time to shake down. Rough edges mar food that cannot yet be wholeheartedly recommended although the aspirations seem to be there. Bae Abermaw could well be a new Welsh star and is worth watching (and visiting for its interior alone).

There are all-day bar snacks, a three-course dinner and Sunday brunch. Service is friendly

MEALS: L 12-2.30; Sunday L 12-3; D 7.30-10
Closed: Christmas Day and Boxing Day and two weeks January
Cards: All major cards
MANAGER: John Clarke
WTB: 4 ★★★★
Rooms: 14, £65D

LOCAL INTEREST: Golf course, horse riding, Harlech Castle, canoeing, walking.

7 Barmouth

Indian Clipper Balti House

2 Church Street
(next to Save the Children)
Barmouth
Gwynedd
LL42 1EW
Tel: 01341 280252

It seems appropriate that "Birmingham by the sea", as Barmouth is sometimes called, should boast this very good family-run Balti house. As you would expect it is noisy, basic and thoroughly good-natured. A traditional Pakistani family business, unlicensed (but bring your own), it makes a speciality of vegetarian dishes and uses only Halal meat.

Sip a delicious glass of mango or passionfruit lassi (made with yoghurt and fruit juice) as you decide on your meal. Advice if required is knowledgably and genially provided by host Alyas. The six vegetarian dishes are worthy of note; for example Ajwain Mooli with crisp slices of white radish and mixed peppers in a light coconut sauce – both subtle and delicious.

Fish, chicken and lamb feature in various guises, from the ultra-hot Achar Balti to Macchi Sebz, using white fish with crisp aubergine and broccoli in a mild sauce of fennel, coriander and sesame seeds.

Start with a samosa or pakora but leave room for the made-to-order naan, either garlic, coriander or, perhaps best of all, Peshawari with layered sultanas and almonds which help you mop up the sauces in the sizzling Balti dishes placed on the table.

Those with really serious appetites might attempt a pudding – but few do! For the few, there is halva, zarda and sayvian (the last two served hot) or ice creams.

Masala tea to a family recipe is an aromatic post-prandial pleasure.

You eat well here. Portions are generous and reasonably priced. All dishes are additive and preservative-free and all vegetarian dishes contain only fresh vegetables.

MEALS: D from 6
CHEF: Mrs Hussain. PROPRIETOR: Mr Hussain

LOCAL INTEREST: Cambrian Coast Railway, Fairbourne and Barmouth Steam Railway, Llfeboat Museum and Ty Gwyn in Barmouth

8 Barmouth

When you arrive at this ancient farmhouse, above the Harlech road north of Barmouth and look down on the sea breaking below, you feel almost on board ship until the warmth of the place envelops you with its oak panelling, beams, and huge fireplaces, along with the tempting smells from the kitchen.

Since 1985 Peter and Paula Thompson have been welcoming many returning guests who come to stay awhile or simply stop for Peter's hearty but skillful cooking.

The three-course dinner (with a two-course option for the faint

Llwyndu Farmhouse

Llanaber
Barmouth
Gwynedd
LL42 1RR
Tel: 01341 280144
Fax: 01341 281236

e-mail: intouch@
llwyndu-farmhouse.co.uk
www.llwyndu-farmhouse.co.uk

hearted) always offers an interesting soup such as butter bean, coconut and cumin, along with the renowned Llwyndu starter of Welsh Tintern cheese with garlic mayonnaise wrapped in ham, grilled gently and served on a bed of dressed leaves of herbs. Chicken livers with grapes pan-fried in butter with sherry is a popular alternative.

Vegetarians are catered for at the main-course stage too. Local fish may come perhaps in a pancake filled with salmon, prawns, smoked haddock and mussels in a mild curry cream sauce. Local lamb is excellent, as is the Welsh Black beef appearing in innovative dishes like the stir fry with peppers and a haunting cream sauce scented with cardamom.

Puddings stretch from hefty banana pancakes or pineapple fritters with sharp plum sauce to hazelnut meringues and home-made ice creams.

There is a compact and keenly-priced wine list.

MEALS: D 7-8.30
Closed: Christmas
Cards: Mastercard, Visa
CHEF: Peter Thompson. PROPRIETORS: Peter & Paula Thompson
WTB: 3 ★★★
Rooms: 7, £32-36 D

LOCAL INTEREST: Cambrian Coast Railway, Fairbourne and Barmouth Steam Railway, LIfeboat Museum and Ty Gwyn in Barmouth

9 Beaumaris

Ye Olde Bull's Head

Castle Street
Beaumaris
Anglesey
LL58 8AP
Tel: 01248 810329
Fax: 01248 811294

This fine old coaching inn on the high street has moved stylishly into the 21st Century. The traditional bar and comfortable chintz lounge are still there but the newly refurbished restaurant glows in its new decor of soft blue, pink and purple, and the modern brasserie in the courtyard is beautifully appointed, using local wood and slate.

Eat pasta, sandwiches, salads and side orders in the brasserie, from a short menu full of favourites such as baked potato gnocchi with leeks, gruyere cheese and cream and bacon, lettuce and tomato sandwiches.

In the dining room upstairs start with home oured bresaola with basil oil and shavings of fresh Parmesan, salt cod fish cake with rocket leaves and dill mayonnaise or salad of smoked goose breast with fresh fig and roasted hazelnut dressing.

Main courses offer pan-fried fillet of Welsh beef with pancetta, black pudding and Conwy mustard sauce, pan-fried noisettes of Welsh lamb with a thyme risotto and red port jus, and roast breast of Hereford duck with stir-fried pak choi leaves, sesame and ginger. The fish is magnificent: steamed turbot fillet with spinach tagliatelle and saffron sauce, grilled whole lemon sole or pan-fried fillet of sea bass with a fine ratatouille and trompette mushroom sauce.

Service is charming and runs like clockwork – drinks in the lounge where you select your menu choice, clear direction to the upstairs

dining room, just catching the buzz from the bar and brasserie, and back to the lounge for coffee and sweetmeats.

This team of two families has stood the test of time and Ye Olde Bull's Head has grown bigger and better gracefully, with careful management. While Keith heads the culinary team, David masters the wines and the list is worthy of note; house selections are especially good at the price.

MEALS: L 12-2 £5-£10; Sunday L 12-2 £6.95; D 7-9.30 £27.50
Closed: December 25 - 26
Cards: All major cards except Diners
CHEFS: Keith Rothwell, Ernst Van Halderen and Jamie Williams
PROPRIETOR: David Robertson
WTB: 3 ★★★
Rooms: 15, £53 S, £83 D, £96 Suites

LOCAL INTEREST: Beaumaris Castle, Court House, Gold, Walking, Fishing, (wheelchair access to Brasserie)

10 Caernarfon

Courtenay's Bistro

9 Segontium Terrace
Caernarfon
Gwynedd
LL55 2PH
Tel: 01286 677290

Caernarfon boasts the grandest of the Norman castles in Wales, but the town has a 21st century attraction as well. Tucked away in Segontium – the Roman name for Caernarfon Terrace overlooking the dock is Courtenay's Bistro.

At lunchtime, a short but varied menu offers soup, several rice dishes and a selection of baked and casseroled dishes, some without meat.

The menu for dinner changes monthly and autumn appetisers include celery and Stilton soup, local mussels with bacon, creamed mushrooms or crispy choux pastry buns stuffed with large chunks of smoked salmon in soft cheese.

To follow there is venison pie, perfectly cooked rack of lamb in a Madeira sauce and beef stew complemented by tangy mustard dumplings. There is always a choice of two fish dishes, varying from day to day, and Anglesey eggs, a well known local favourite. All these are accompanied by a selection of carefully selected fresh vegetables.

Waistbands adjusted, round off with a rich, home-made gooey chocolate and brandy truffle, orange cheesecake or nut nutters flan. There is a selection of Welsh cheeses for those lacking a sweet tooth and for the over-full there is a selection of ices and sorbets – the coffee ice cream being a perfect ending to the evening.

MEALS: L 12-1.45 £7; D 6.30-9 £13.50
Closed: Sundays - Mondays in off peak season
Cards: All major cards
CHEF: Cynthia Gilbey. PROPRIETORS: Derek Norton and Cynthia Gilbey

LOCAL INTEREST: Caernarfon Castle, Welsh highland railway, Caernarfon Victoria dock and marina.

11   Caernarfon

Ty'n Rhos Country House

Seion
Caernarfon
Gwynedd
LL55 3AE
Tel: 01248 670489
Fax: 01248 670079

e-mail:
enquiries@tynrhos.co.uk

Lynda Kettle is the lynchpin of this warm and friendly hotel. A perfectionist, she cares passionately that her establishment offers visitors the best that Wales has to offer. From the lilting local accents of her staff to the files of local interest, here visitors can enjoy a real taste of Wales.

Every ingredient in the kitchen is sourced locally if possible, but not when it compromises quality. Catch of the day is phoned direct to the kitchen from the fisherman on the boat, local beef is well matured, the chicken organic and the cheeses are Welsh. When the quality of vegetables, salad and herbs failed in the shops recently, Lynda planted her own vegetable patch.

To start, perhaps, panfried Welsh lamb and leek sausage on garlic creamed potato and onion sauce or home-made salmon and haddock fishcakes – with fresh coriander and lemon. Main courses might be seabass on home-made noodles with fresh herb sauce or rib eye steak of Welsh beef with a wild mushroom sauce served on a leek potato cake. And to finish, roasted pineapple with a lime syrup and home-made coconut ice cream or warm chocolate tart with bitter chocolate sauce and poached pear.

MEALS: L 12.30-1.30; D 7-8.30 from £19.95
Closed: one week Christmas
Cards: Visa, Mastercard, American Express
CHEF/PROPIETOR: Lynda Kettle
WTB: 4 ★★★★
Rooms: 14, £55 S, from £85 D, £150 Suite

LOCAL INTEREST: Caernarfon Castle, Anglesey, Snowdon, Bodnant Gardens, Portmeirion, Lleyn Peninsula

12   Capel Garmon

Tan y Foel

Capel Garmon
Nr Betws-y-Coed
Conwy
LL26 0RE
Tel: 01690 710507
Fax: 01690 710681

e-mail: enquiries@tyfhotel.co.uk
www.tyfhotel.co.uk

Up the wooded hillside towards Capel Garmon, off the busy Betws-y-Coed to Llanrwst road, hides this peaceful old stone house set in a mature garden. It now has a brilliant modern interior of pale wood, hessian and halogen lighting, unfussy and restful, although some might find it a trifle incongruous in this setting. The comfortable dining room extends into a conservatory, all pale green, with immaculate tables and beautiful glassware.

Dinner offers three courses with a two-course option, sensibly limited to two choices at each stage. Janet Pitman's cooking has grown more confident with the years, thoughtfully striving for

excellence in all its parts. Hot brown bread rolls flavoured with dried figs and fennel seeds are very good indeed, as are the hot canapés served in the lounge.

Start with a crab cake of startling freshness on a confit of peppers spiked with sweet chilli sauce or perhaps tian of diced avocado and smoked chicken on chicken rillettes.

Typical main-course dishes are ragout of sea bass, mussels and prawns in a rich creamy sauce or noisettes of near-perfect venison fillet on discs of green cabbage, black pudding and potato cakes with a smoky rowanberry sauce. Raw materials are mostly local and it shows in the freshness.

Finish perhaps with panetone bread-and-butter pudding or the selection of Welsh and French cheeses with warm cheese scones.

There is a wide-ranging wine list, but eight well-chosen house wines available by the glass shine sensibly.

MEALS: D 7.30 8.15 from £25
Closed: Christmas, New Year, January
Cards: All
CHEF: Janet Pitman. PROPRIETORS: Peter and Janet Pitman
WTB: 4 ★★★★
Rooms: 7, £70-£90 S, £90-£150 D

LOCAL INTEREST: Bodnant Garden, Conwy Castle, Swallow Falls, Penrhyn Castle, Capel Garmon Neolithic Burial Chamber, Penmachno Woollen Mill, Trefriw Wells Spa.

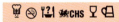

13   Chirk

National Trust Tearoom

Chirk Castle
Chirk
Clwyd
LL14 5AF
Tel: 01691 777701
Fax: 01691 774706

The National Trust has gone to great lengths to tie the flavour of their restaurants into the history of the venue, and the tea room at Chirk Castle follows this line. The menu reads of a time when Sir Thomas Myddleton in 1660 wrote of his garden at the castle "When first I did begin to make this garden – I knew not what it would cost, but I repent not, for ye poore doe there finde work".

Today, the Welsh Garden Tea offers a pot of tea served with home-made bara brith and scone with Welsh butter and strawberry jam. The Woodman's Savoury Tea is named after Thomas Parks, who was a woodman in the Castle park in 1751 and was paid 20 shillings a year. The tea includes two savoury scones with Welsh cheese, butter and Welsh onion relish, a slice of home-made cake and a pot of tea.

More substantial dishes include spiced onion tart and Welsh cheese and leek flan. The spice is cinnamon, the menu noting that on one of the voyages financed by Sir Thomas Myddleton in 1592 he brought back 21,700 cwt of 'sinamon' which was sold for the huge sum of £3,616.13/d.

Puddings are equally imaginative, with an 18th-century tart made of oranges and apples, and Chirk Castle apple pie served hot with fresh cream or Welsh dairy ice cream.

MEALS: L 11-5 approx £7.50
Closed: November–April
Cards: Visa, Mastercard
CATERING MANAGER: Jamie New

LOCAL INTEREST: Chirk Castle

14   Colwyn Bay

Café Nicoise

124 Abergele Road
Colwyn Bay
Conwy
LL29 7PS
Tel: 01492 531555
Fax: 01492 531555

The deep-blue Parisienne-style frontage of this busy restaurant would not be out of place in the artists' quarter of Paris. Inside, a varnished wooden floor, soft terracotta walls and tables covered with white linen give the impression of warmth and space.

The menu touristique, available during the week, is good value at £14.95 for 3 courses – it offers a short choice, perhaps salad of bacon, avocado and pine nuts followed by supreme of chicken in a Thai-style sauce and finishing with crème brulée and blackberry compote.

The à la carte menu might offer a carpaccio of tuna à la Nicoise or onion, Teifi and nettle tart with pesto and melt-in-the-mouth pastry. To follow, roast sea bass with marinated vegetables (a triumph) or fillet of Welsh beef, cooked to perfection, served with roasted shallots and sauté potatoes.

Inviting puddings could include a summer-fruit strudel with home-made mango ice cream or chocolate nemesis with fudge sauce. An assiette du chef offers three or four tasters from the menu, possibly a baby crème brulée, some fresh strawberry ice cream in a brandy snap basket and a slice of the gooey chocolate concoction.

The selection of Welsh and French cheeses includes Llangloffen with garlic and chives, St Aubrey, Teifi and blue Brie, and will arrive in perfect condition.

There is a balanced wine list with good house choices, while the good, plentiful coffee, home-made truffles, happy smiling faces of the staff and some jolly customers would definitely encourage a return visit.

MEALS: L 12-2 from £7.25; D 7-10 from £7.25
Closed: All day Sunday and Monday and Tuesday lunch
CHEF: Carl Swift. PROPRIETOR: Lynne Swift

LOCAL INTEREST: Conwy Castle, Colwyn Bay Zoo, Bodnant Gardens, Eirias Park

15   Colwyn Bay

The views from Michael and Wendy Vaughan's hotel over the estuary to Conwy Castle and down the River Conwy to the mountains of Snowdonia are stunning.

The Old Rectory Country House

Llanrwst Road
Llansanffraid Glan Conwy
Colwyn Bay
Conwy
LL28 5LF
Tel: 01492 580611
Fax: 01492 584555

e-mail:
info@oldrectorycountryhouse
www.
oldrectorycountryhouse.co.uk

Once inside, diners are shown through the dining room to the wood-panelled lounge where menus, appetisers and pre-dinner drinks are dispensed by mine host, from a disguised bookshelf bar. The walls abound with paintings, mainly landscapes but one or two of a seafaring nature, and a grand piano is covered in reference books of all sorts, including a long history of good food guides.

There is a certain precision to the order of the evening and, whilst the menu descriptions are brief, Michael gives a fuller description as the food is served.

This is seriously good food; Wendy is a magician in the kitchen. Spiced seared monkfish might be served on a vanilla risotto with red wine sauce – a delicious mix of just-cooked fish with a creamy, delicate risotto and a rich sauce with flawless presentation and exquisite taste.

This might be followed by a perfectly cooked loin of mountain lamb from the Conwy Valley with spinach parcels, and for dessert a deliciously tangy passion fruit tart. The Welsh and Celtic farm cheeses are always excellent and can be exchanged for the pudding or taken as a extra course.

After-dinner coffee and petits fours are served back in the lounge with a wonderful array of ports and brandies; so expect to enjoy a truly memorably evening!

MEALS: D 7.30-8.15 £29.90
Closed: A month over Christmas
CHEF: Wendy Vaughan. PROPRIETOR: Michael Vaughan
Cards: All major
WTB: 5 ★★★★★
Rooms: 6, £79-£99 S, £119-£149 D

LOCAL INTEREST: Historic Conwy, Victorian Llandudno, the Conwy Valley and Betws-y-Coed.

16 Criccieth

Tir-a-Môr

1-3 Mona Terrace
Criccieth
Gwynedd
LL52 0HG
Tel: 01766 523084
Fax: 01766 523049

Although commonplace around much of continental Europe, a restaurant offering well-cooked, genuinely fresh local fish and shellfish is sadly a rarity on the British coast. Every reason, therefore, to happen with gratitude upon Tir-a-Môr, where chubby local scallops seared in butter with sage and capers on home-made tagliatelli is a typical offering; it is all about freshness.

The Vowells have certainly found their niche having changed direction from landscape gardening and child-minding to building up this admirable place. They rely totally on local catches of the day, rejoicing if a clutch of rod-caught sea bass are offered at their door, dishing them up stuffed with herbs and butter or filleted with a tomato and basil concasse.

Grilled turbot with a velouté sauce competes with the scallops in the popularity stakes. All this after being first tempted with antipasti of marinated mackerel with potato and chive salad or intensely flavoured

salmon and crab rolls (baked, not fried) with a spicy harissa sauce.

Vegetarians are customarily well-catered for and meat-eaters' temptations include fillet of Lleyn roast beef, rump of local salt-fed lamb, Gressingham duck breast and foie gras on an apple pancake.

Puddings are simple and light, perhaps a pannacotta with raspberry purée or spumoni amaretto. It is all backed up by a wide-ranging and intelligently compiled wine list and amongst the delights is the Dog Point Sauvignon from New Zealand.

While service might be slow at times, the food is well worth waiting for.

MEALS: D from 7 approx £22.50
Closed: Sunday and January also weekdays in the winter
Cards: Visa, Mastercard and Switch
CHEF: Clare Vowell. PROPRIETORS: Martin and Clare Vowell

LOCAL INTEREST: Criccieth Castle, Snowdonia, local beaches, Lloyd George Museum, Portmeirion village and steam trains

17 Deganwy

La Paysanne

147 Station Road
Deganwy
Conwy
Gwynedd
LL31 9EJ

Tel: 01492 582079
Fax: 01492 583848

It is best to book in advance at this popular restaurant that overlooks the stunning Conwy estuary.

Warm terracotta walls covered in a variety of prints, photographs and paintings, a collection of corkscrews and Bob Ross's beloved jazz all help to set the scene at this typical French bistro.

Bob and Barbara offer two three-course menus at 150 French francs and 175 French francs. The former has slightly less choice but is equally varied. Starters might include marinated Conwy mullet with herbs, a tasty Mediterranean-style fish soup with rouille or individual Bury black pudding with apples and mustard. Main courses include half a roasted Gressingham duck with kumquat sauce and a succulent rack of lamb, roast with herbs and spices, served with a rich red wine sauce. Fish choices depend on the day's catch with a variety of sauces and preparations. Vegetables are simple and precisely cooked – including perhaps crisp cabbage, with plenty of black pepper.

From an almost exclusively French wine list purchased from small unknown vineyards that the Rosses have discovered themselves, select perhaps a delicious 1995 Vacqueras – Domaine la Garrigue.

The mobile blackboard offers classic puddings such as crème caramel, apricot and almond tart with brandy, plump profiteroles coated in a rich chocolate and Grand Marnier sauce and tempting home-made ices – toasted almond and honey or fruits of the forest served in a brandy snap basket. A balanced cheese board of, say, Vignotte, St David's and Saint Agur is followed by good coffee.

MEALS: D 7-9.30 £17.50
Closed: Sunday, Monday
Cards: Access, Visa, Switch

CHEF: Barbara Ross. PROPRIETORS: Bob & Barbara Ross

LOCAL INTEREST: Conwy Castle, Conwy Harbour, Llandudno

18 Dolgellau

Bontddu Hall Hotel

Bontddu
Dolgellau
Gwynedd
LL40 2UF
Tel: 01341 430661
Fax: 01341 430284
e-mail: reservations@bontdduhall.co.uk
www.bontdduhall.co.uk

This grand Victorian house above the Mawdach Estaury between Barmouth and Dolgellau has one of the very finest hotel views in Wales – through old pine trees to Cader Idris beyond the river. For all its high neo-Gothic style, it is a surprisingly quiet and unpretentious place. The comfortable dining room has a wall of picture windows which, like the bar, maximise the view.

Dinner is three courses with Welsh cheeses as an alternative to puddings or as a supplement. Each course is beautifully presented but the food is certainly not just pictures on plates. Hot and cold canapés appear once orders for dinner have been taken, for example little seafood tarts and kebabs of duck pâté with tomato and chutney.

Starters may be asparagus with herby hollandaise, a roulade of smoked salmon and spinach with salmon and prawns or French onion soup with Gruyère croutons.

Main courses come on large plates covered by silver domes which are lifted ceremoniously after the vegetables have arrived. This is not risible but done with quiet pride and the food revealed well presented. Rack of local lamb, Gressingham duck on red cabbage, salmon on roast vegetables and a vegetarian alternative. Vegetables are especially good and come in generous portions.

Puddings are justly praised and a delight to the eye. Baked Alaska with autumn fruits, perhaps, or crunchy lemon pie with strawberries, or the hotel's definitive bread and putter pudding often appear.

A wine list of 80 bins covers all needs, with a good smattering of halves.

Lunch on Sundays is a carvery.

MEALS: L 12-2.30 £15; Sunday L 12-2 £15; D 7-9.30 £25
Closed: November to March
Cards: All cards
CHEF: David Murphy. PROPRIETOR: Mike Ball
WTB: 4 ★★★★
Rooms: 20, £61 S, £100 D, £160 Suite

LOCAL INTEREST: Harlech Castle, Cader Idris, Bala Lake, little railway

19 Dolgellau

Entering straight off the street into the tiny bar and reception area, you could be forgiven for imagining yourself in a take away – a fear

Dylanwad Da

2 Ffos-y-Felin
Dolgellau
Gwynedd
LL40 1BS
Tel: 01341 422870

speedily dispelled by the warm welcome from local girls and the glimpse of a busy kitchen and attractive restaurant beyond. Dylan Rowlands has been cooking cheerfully and generously here since 1988 and as befits such places, the dining-room is packed with locals out of season.

Changing regularly, the à la carte menu, with five or six offerings at each stage, always includes interesting vegetarian options – perhaps a mildly curried cream of vegetable soup or tomato, cumin and lentil pâté, with sundried tomato relish, followed by poppyseed pancake with roast vegetables in a herb and cheese sauce. Amongst the many starters, salmon fishcakes and lemon pork and mushrooms with saffron rice have won much praise.

Dylan has a sure hand with lamb, whether it be a crisp, tender rack with rosemary sauce or a delicate casserole with vegetables lifted by the addition of rowan jelly. Welsh Black steak is ever-present and fish according to local availability – perhaps fillet of monkfish braised in red wine with bacon, shallots and mushrooms.

Pudding ranges from orange and apricot sponge and chocolate and ginger truffle cake to home-made ice creams. A generous platter of Welsh cheeses is always proudly on hand.

There is a wide-ranging wine list, with interesting tasting notes and a page of house wines available by the glass or for £9.40 a bottle.

MEALS: D 7-9 £15-£25
Closed: February and March
CHEF/PROPRIETOR: Dylan Rowlands

20 Dolgellau

George III Hotel

Penmaenpool
Dolgellau
Gwynedd
LL40 1YD
Tel: 01341 422525
Fax: 01341 423565

e-mail: reception@
george-3rd.co.uk
www.george-3rd.co.uk

This is a hotel of many parts, sitting gleaming and white by the tidal pool created by the River Mawddach, as it loops on its way to the sea at Barmouth. Across from the hotel, the Rhinog mountains stare grandly down. The George III boasts a fine old pine panelled pub downstairs but there is also an atmospheric hotel bar upstairs. Both serve first-rate hot and cold snacks for most of the day. It is a comfortable place, busy and well run.

Dinner in the hotel's fine new dining room with tall windows taking in that view is an à la carte affair. Starters of seafood pancake and smoked haddock and leek soup, a warm salad of queen scallops and bacon and the very good home-made gravadlax seared and served on a hot plate with a mustard and dill sauce have all earned praise.

Main courses embrace fish, fillet steak au poivre, chicken stuffed with ham and gruyère and served with asparagus, roast duck with red cabbage and orange sauce and a generous rack of lamb. Vegetables are simple but fresh and the hotel's own breads are very good indeed.

Puddings include date, sticky toffee and bread and butter along with a gingernut and orange cheesecake and pear Belle Helene.

There are good real ales and a comprehensive and reasonably priced wine list.

MEALS: L 12-2.30 from £2.50; D 6.30-9.30 £20-£25
Cards: All except Amex and Diners
CHEF: Elen Pugh. PROPRIETORS: John and Julia Cartwright
WTB: 3 ★★★
Rooms: 11, £55 S, £94 D, Suite

LOCAL INTEREST: Local walks, Cader Idris, Mawddach trail and bike hire, pony trekking, fishing free to guests, Fairbourne minature railway.

21 Dolgellau

Penmaenuchaf Hall

Penmaenpool
Dolgellau
Gwynedd
LL40 1YB
Tel: 01341 422129
Fax: 01341 422787

e-mail:
relax@penhall.co.uk
www.penhall.co.uk

Welsh produce at its best

This is a quiet comfortable house above the Mawddach estuary, furnished with restraint and good taste with lovely trees and gardens all around. On entering, you are greeted by a log fire in the grand old fireplace with comfortable chairs around and you very much get the feel of visiting friends in their country home.

It is to be hoped that chef David Banks settles down here, and first indications are encouraging.

In the panelled dining room the no-choice table d'hôte is supplemented by a small à la carte menu.

Starters of excellent fresh local scallops, seared crisp and set on a lemon beurre blanc or a tart tatin of caramelised shallots with a sharp goat's cheese are typical. Follow with a small helping of soup, in autumn perhaps the noteworthy pumpkin and nutmeg.

Main courses might include local rack of lamb with lentils, seared tuna with wild rice or Welsh Black beef and local salmon and poultry. Vegetables are good, especially the creamy dauphinoise potatoes.

Puddings perhaps have been less successful although the marmalade sauce and custard with a steamed pudding and the white chocolate sauce with another have been admired.

Good home-made bread and excellent canapés before the meal indicate a serious intent and, in time, this confident cooking will add lustre to this hotel's long reputation for its cuisine.

There is an extensive, reasonably priced wine list with, commendably, 10 house wines all available by the glass. The service is warm-hearted and professional.

MEALS: L 12-2; D 7-9.30
Closed: 2 weeks January
Cards: All major
CHEF: David Banks PROPRIETORS: Lorraine Fielding and Mark Watson
WTB: 4 ★★★★
Rooms: 14, £70-£110 S, £110-£170 D, £170 Suites

LOCAL INTEREST: Ffestiniog railway, Centre of Alternative Technology, King Arthur's Labyrinth, Harlech Castle, Celtic Talyllyn railway, Portmeirion

22 Dolgellau

Pentre Bach

Llwyngwril
Nr. Dolgellau
Gwynedd
LL37 2JU
01341 250294
10341 250885

e-mail: info@pentreback.com
www.pentreback.com

Margaret Smyth is a winner – she was voted Mid Wales Cook of the Year in 2000 and she ran the Best Bed and Breakfast in 1996, according to Radio 4's Food Programme. Organic and locally sourced is the key to the business here, and although it is topical right now, the Smyths have been in business for a decade. Many of the ingredients are home-grown, with eggs, herbs and vegetables from the garden.

The only way to taste Margaret's fine cooking is to stay overnight. Guests eating in the slightly austere dining room can choose from a menu of seven starters and nine main courses, with many vegetarian options. Enjoy her perfectly prepared Glamorgan sausage with spicy apple sauce or grilled goat's cheese with walnuts and a salad of mixed leaves.

Fillet of sea bass in a light sauce delicately flavoured with tarragon, guinea fowl's leg set on a bed of crumbly couscous and perhaps a casserole of local Welsh lamb with apricots or Welsh Black beef steak pie with fresh herbs accompany at least two other fish dishes. Vegetables on a side plate are hot and innovative, especially the Jerusalem artichokes, roasted with caraway seed, pak choi and a purée of butternut squash and potato.

The selection of Welsh cheeses is as good as it gets, and indeed the Snowdonia from Llanrwst is worth tracking down.

Puddings are traditionally homely, and none the worse for it – for instance, a marmalade sponge with matching sauce.

MEALS: L packed lunch; D 7-8 £14.95-£16.95
Closed: December
Cards: All major
CHEF/PROPRIETOR: Margaret Smyth
WTB: 4 ★★★★
Rooms: 3, £54-£64 D

LOCAL INTEREST: Walking, beaches, Tal y Llyn railway, Harlech Castle, Portmeirion

 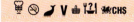

23 Dolgellau

This fine old house was the great love of William Maddocks, who created Porthmadog and Tremadog, and heartbrokenly lost in his bankruptcy. It stands in a forested river valley north of Dolgellau, backing up into the Rhinog mountains. It is very much a quiet place of peace, a comfortable country house to which you are welcomed by the twinkling, ever sprightly Jon Barkwith, whose daughter Joanna presides in the kitchen.

A daily changing menu of infinite variety through the year reflects what fresh and often local produce is available and choices are sensibly limited.

Plas Dolmelynllyn

Ganllwyd
Dolgellau
Gwynedd
LL40 2HP
Tel: 01341 440273
Fax: 01341 440640

e-mail: info@dolly-hotel.co.uk
www.dolly-hotel-co.uk

Order in the conservatory bar overlooking the garden and mature trees; excellent hot canapés and good black olives raise anticipations. Start, perhaps, with a perfectly poached egg in puff pastry with asparagus and hollandaise or a warm salad of roast vegetables and smoked duck breast accompanied by warm home-made bread rolls. Soup (cream of cauliflower and parsley is a favourite) or a sorbet follows.

Main courses feature fish and meat with innovative and successful partners – roast monkfish with a saffron risotto and wild mushrooms in a sherry cream sauce, for example, or roast Welsh Black beef fillet with a hazelnut and herb crust. There is always an interesting alternative for vegetarians.

Puddings embrace first-rate cheesecakes, crumbles, home-made ice creams and seasonal delights such as apple fritters with bramble and honey compote.

A long and enthusiastic wine list offers many delights at very reasonable prices.

MEALS: D 7-8.30 £26.50
Closed: November-February
Cards: All major
CHEF: Joanna Reddicliffe PROPRIETOR: Jon Barkwith
WTB: 3 ★★★
Rooms: 10, £50-£65 S, £90-£125 D, £115-£125 Suites

LOCAL INTEREST: Fishing, walking, mountain-bike centre, canoeing, riding, railways, castles, etc.

24 Erbistock

The Boat

Erbistock
Wrexham
LL13 0DL
Tel: 01978 780666
Fax: 01978 780607

It is well worth the detour down seemingly endless narrow lanes to the swirling river Dee and this lovely old pub and restaurant. The timbered bars remain, with snacks at lunchtime, while the restaurant has been given a makeover with polished wood floors and comfortable steel-and-cane chairs creating a thoroughly modern look conservatory while a row of French doors gives virtually every table a view of the river.

If the restaurant is modern and bright there is something reassuringly old-fashioned about the cooking. Eat your heart out Thailand and Mexico – here are starters of prawns in marie rose sauce, garlic mushrooms baked with tomatoes and cheese, smoked salmon and melon and grilled king prawns with a sharp lemon, garlic and cream sauce.

Main courses continue the theme with rack of lamb and roast vegetables; fillet of salmon and tarragon cream; and "Shropshire Chicken" – a supreme stuffed with mushrooms and blue cheese wrapped in bacon, grilled and served with a rich Shropshire blue cheese sauce. Nat King Cole tapes in the background similarly echo the time-warp.

Traditional puddings include apple pie, pecan toffee tart and ice creams. There are tempting draught beers and a short, keenly-priced wine list, with espresso or cappuccino to follow.

MEALS: L 12-2.30 £14; Sunday L 12-2.30 £14.95; D 6.30-9 £25
Closed: Sunday evenings in winter
Cards: All major
CHEF: Bill Jenkins. CONTACTS: Andrew Coke and Fiona Bell

LOCAL INTEREST: Erbistock ferry, Chirk Castle and Erddig National Trust property

25 Harlech

Castle Cottage Restaurant with Rooms

Pen Lleth
Harlech
Gwynedd
LL46 2YL
Tel: 01766 780479

e-mail: gh.roberts@talk21.com
www.lokalink.co.uk/
harlech/castlecottaage

The guides have not always done justice to Glyn Roberts's assured and hearty cooking at his cottage hotel in the shadow of Edward I's mighty fortress. Castle Cottage is a comfortable little place with an intimate bar and a pristine pink dining room. (Glyn and his wife Jacquie, who presides out front, have been here now for 11 years, providing outstanding food in this warmhearted setting).

It would be worth eating here for the hot canapés alone, yet the three-course dinner including coffee and home-made sweetmeats, also lives up to the expectations it arouses.

Good soups, perhaps wild mushroom or asparagus with gruyere, are always available, along typically with Welsh smoked salmon with hot potato cakes and sour cream and usually Carmarthen-cured ham with melon and fresh figs.

Local fish is a reliable option, depending on availability, and the seafood thermidor is a winner. Gressingham duck and other poultry feature as does wonderful game in season. Local Welsh lamb is a daily speciality – a generous rack, crisp yet pink and tender, comes with a red wine and rosemary sauce and garlic mashed potato. Local Welsh Black beef appears as fillet or rib-eye steak on cabbage with a brandy and green pepper sauce. Vegetables are plain and plentiful with an interesting potato dish in addition.

Puddings range from Glyn's definitive treacle tart to a lime and ginger syllabub. Home-made sorbets and ice creams are good and there is a cheeseboard of Welsh and English offerings and usually a savoury.

Wine comes by the glass or from a comprehensive list, with a special section of recommendations under £15.

MEALS: D 7-9.30 £23.50
Closed: 2 weeks February
Cards: Visa, Switch, Mastercard, Delta
CHEF: Glyn Roberts. PROPRIETORS: Glyn and Jacquie Roberts
WTB: 3 ★★★
Rooms: 6, £29 S, £62 D

LOCAL INTEREST: Royal St David's golf club, Harlech beach, Snowdonia, slate mines.

26 Harlech

Plas Café

High Street
Harlech
Gwynedd
LL46 2YA
Tel: 01766 780204

This handsome house on Harlech's high street, with its recently restored stable block and cobbled courtyard, serves meals seven days a week from breakfast to bedtime. There is an elegant dining room, a conservatory restaurant and a terraced tea garden with stunning views over Cardigan Bay, the castle, the Lleyn Peninsula and the mountains of Snowdonia. It is a romantic spot and once the summer home of the Finch Hattons of *Out of Africa* fame.

Breakfasts, home-made cakes, sandwiches and snacks are available for most of the day, with hot and cold lunches and in the evenings dinner with local lamb, beef and trout and house dishes such as the popular salmon and prawn garlic crumble and chicken supremes in tarragon and cream. Snacks such as baked potatoes and salads with a variety of fillings are available for most of the day.

This Harlech institution has no pretensions, no dress requirements and simply gets on with serving honest fare generously at reasonable prices.

There is a short wine list and good draught beers. Vegetarian dishes always available.

MEALS: L 12-3; Sunday L 12 onwards £7.95;
D until 8.30 summer from £5;
Closed: January 3rd - January 31st
Cards: All except Amex and Diners
CHEFS: Neville and Ken Brown. PROPRIETOR: Neville and Christine Brown

LOCAL INTEREST: Harlech Castle, great views of Tremadog bay and Lleyn peninsula from the conservatory.

27 Hawarden

The Brasserie

68 The Highway
Hawarden
Flintshire
CH5 3DH
Tel: 01244 536353
Fax: 01244 520800

Just into Wales and just into *The Red Book* this Hawarden Brasserie boasts an impressive menu of eight starters and nine main dishes, most with fashionable, cutting-edge accompaniments. However, they prove strangely bland in execution, although the raw materials are good. For example, in a starter of "Mexican marinated chicken on a Caesar salad with guacamole and croutons" there was no taste of chilli anywhere, though the chicken was delicious, the guacamole was simply avocado purée and the salad, though very good, was hardly Caesar's. Likewise, herb seared tuna with chorizo sausage and a red onion marmalade on garlic mashed potatoes with a spiced lentil salsa, was not seared and pink, rather, gently cooked through. The chorizo sausages won that one! Home-made chips were not crisp but other vegetables were well-nigh perfect.

Because the skills and imagination seem to be there, can it be that, in deference to readers of *Cheshire Life* who named it Restaurant of the Year 2000, the chef feels he should tone down his flavours?

Notwithstanding our constructively intended comments, it obviously pleases many, and puddings such as the raspberry ripple cheesecake,

the sticky toffee pudding and the upmarket version of a nursery favourite, champagne and passion fruit jelly with citrus fruits, are highly praised.

Alas, no Welsh cheese but really excellent espresso coffee.

MEALS: L 12-2; D 6.45-9
Closed: Saturday L
Cards: All except Diners and Amex
CHEF: Mark Jones. PROPRIETORS: Neal Bates and Mark Jones

LOCAL INTEREST: Historic city of Chester, Hawarden Castle.

28 Holyhead

Lobster Pot

Church Bay
Holyhead
Anglesey
LL65 4EY
Tel: 01407 730241/588
Fax: 01407 730598

www.lobster.pot.net

Something of a Welsh national treasure this, tucked away in a remote corner of Anglesey and approached by a series of winding lanes. It is light years from the busy A5 with its fast-food outlets, and nestles between the church and little village up the hill and the lovely beach below. Family-run since its creation in 1946 and now presided over by Lindy Wood, it is sourced by the fish-retailing business they run, with tanks of local crab, lobster, oysters and scallops guaranteeing uniquely fresh raw materials.

It is a homely, cottage place with bar and neighbouring rooms supplying snacks and lunch and a large dining-room with a log fire. Everything is utterly straightforward and informal and comfortable.

Start dinner with half-a-dozen local oysters and move on to a dressed crab with lemon mayonnaise or a plate of freshest whitebait.

Catch your breath (and thank your good fortune) with a glass of good white wine and contemplate a whole fresh lobster cooked in any of a variety of ways, perhaps best of all simply grilled with garlic butter, or some wonderful chubby scallops, Dover sole grilled on the bone or a superb platter of fruits de mer. Determined meat-eaters can satisfy themselves with pâté and duck or a variety of steaks.

After all this splendour, a perfect fresh fruit pavlova, just as it should be, crisp on the outside and sticky within with rich Anglesey cream, or try the raspberry shortcake amongst other offerings.

A good colection of wines and fine ales accompanies this wonderfully simple operation run with abundant good nature.

MEALS: L 12-2 £3-£10; D from 6.30 £10.30
Closed: November - April, Sunday and Monday except Bank Holidays
Cards: Switch, Visa
CHEF: Steffan Coupe. PROPRIETOR: Lindy Wood
WTB: 3 ★★★ and 4 ★★★★
Rooms: 2 self-catering units

LOCAL INTEREST: Two minutes from a sandy cove; coastal walks, sailing and golf, local thatched cottage open as a living museum of life at the beginning of the last century.

29 Llanarmon Dyffryn Ceiriog

West Arms

Llanarmon Dyffryn Ceiriog
Nr Llangollen
Wrexham
LL20 7LD
Tel: 01691 600665
Fax: 01691 600622

What every country inn should be is this 16th-century treasure 11 miles from Chirk, down the idyllically pastoral Ceiriog Valley. Warm and welcoming, full of old beams, slate floors, crackling fires and decent old oak furniture it is also the setting for Grant Williams's deft cooking. He has a lightness of touch that is both refreshing and enjoyable. In the bar fresh pasta and feta cheese salad feature amid more usual offerings.

Dinner in the fine old dark green and pink dining room is a three-course meal with limited choice. Freshness and lightness is the theme – a warm salad of smoked chicken or a surprisingly successful combination of water melon, rocket, smoked salmon and mandarin sorbet to start.

Tender medallions of local venison with port sauce or herbed rack of the splendid local lamb with ratatouille may feature, or a successful combination of sea bream fillets steamed with strips of leek and Carmarthen ham on a tarragon butter sauce.

Puddings likewise eschew heaviness in favour of a warm cherry and kirsch tart or a saffron poached pear with chocolate mousse in an almond tuile basket with a beguiling toffee sauce. Welsh cheeses and the honorary Welshman, Shropshire blue, are always on offer.

A hotel since 1670 this place knows what it is about and provides a hearty cooked breakfast.

MEALS: L 12-2 approx £15; Sunday L 12-2 approx £15;
D 7-9 approx £21.90;
Cards: All major
CHEF: Grant Williams. PROPRIETOR: Geoff Leigh-Ford
WTB: 3 ★★★
Rooms: 16, £46.50 S, £41.50 D, £51.50 Suites

LOCAL INTEREST: Waterfalls, all outdoor pursuits.

30 Llanberis

Y Bistro

43/45 High Street
Llanberis
Gwynedd
LL55 4EU
Tel: 01285 871278
Fax: 01285 871278
e-mail: ybistro@fsbdial.co.uk
www.ybistro.co.uk

Perhaps a little incongruously on the main street in Llanberis, Y Bistro's plate-glass windows boast an impressive gallery of awards and plaudits from discerning foodies. Choose from the à la carte or daily set three-course menu, which includes 25cl of French red wine, for £15.50.

Front-of-house is run by Danny Roberts, whilst wife and chef Nerys prefers to stay in the kitchen. The bilingual menu draws heavily on local suppliers who have been cultivated to reliable dependability over the past 20 years.

To start, try caws a cenin – deep-fried cheese and leek croquettes with onion marmalade – coes cyw iâr – five-spice chicken leg confit with ginger and sesame dressing or reis cranc – Anglesey crab and

Welsh produce at its best

leek risotto, which is skilfully constructed and precisely cooked, although the portion is small.

Oen Iafant – best end of Welsh lamb with rosemary and potato rosti crust, is served with a lavender-scented sauce, ffrwyth y môr provencale translates to scallop, mussels and squid in provencale tomato, basil and olive sauce on spaghetti, and there are another eight main courses to choose from.

Pwdin – or sweets – range from pot sioc, a rich dark chocolate pot, to pwdin taffi glynnu – sticky toffee pudding, served warm with caramel sauce – or teisen afal a sinamon – a warm apple cake with cinnamon cream.

Wines are recommended by Danny from a short, intelligent list.

MEALS: D 7.30-9.30 from £15.50
Closed: Occasional days in winter
Cards: Visa, Mastercard, Switch
CHEF: Nerys Roberts. PROPRIETORS: Danny and Nerys Roberts
WTB: Awaiting grading
Rooms: 3, self-catering apartments £150 x 2 nights, £450 x7 nights

LOCAL INTEREST: Snowdon Mountain Railway, Llanberis Lake Railway, Star Pleasure Cruises, Electric Mountain, Welsh Slate Museum, Vivian diving centre, hill walking, mountain climbing.

31

Pale Hall

Pale Estate
Llandderfel
Nr Bala
Gwynedd
LL23 7PS
Tel: 01678 530220
Fax: 01678 53022

e-mail: palehall@fsbdial.co.uk
www.palehall.co.uk

Llandderfel

Completed in 1871, this Victorian neo-Gothic mansion is as grand as they come in Wales and looks very romantic in its lovely parkland setting in the upper Dee valley. It has been lovingly restored by its owners and the splendid high rooms all with beautiful ceilings have been sensitively redecorated. For all its splendour, it is surprisingly comfortable, even in the vast inner hall, with its voluptuous settees beckoning by a huge log fire.

The three-course dinner with vegetarian options is straightforward and generally good, with the kitchen achieving best results in the starters and puddings.

Starters run from a hearty terrine of ham hock and foie gras with onion marmalade or beef marinade with chilli and coriander to a prawn and salmon mousse wrapped in marinated salmon.

Rack of local lamb with a fricassée of leeks, fillet of Welsh rosé beef, roast fillet of pork stuffed with prunes and wrapped in bacon or tuna steak with a salad Nicoise are typical main-course offerings, in generous portions.

Amongst the puddings, thoroughly decadent chocolate pie and a sharp lemon tart have won praise, as has the eclectic cheeseboard.

A short wine list covers most wine-producing areas with the notable exception of Alsace. There are some attractive bottles, including, several halves.

MEALS: L 12-1.45 £15.95; Sunday L 12-1.45 £15.95;
D 7-8.30 £24.95;

Cards: Visa, Mastercard, Switch
CHEF: Philip Nahed. PROPRIETOR: Mr Saul Nahed
WTB: 4 ★★★★
Rooms: 17, from £69 S, from £95 D

LOCAL INTEREST: Bala lake, lake railway, white water rafting, Llangollen railway, Erddig house.

32 Llandegla

Bodidris Hall

Llandegla
Nr Wrexham
Denbighshire
LL11 3AL
Tel: 01978 790434
Fax: 01978 790335
e-mail: bodidrishall@fsnet
www.bodidrishall-fsnet.co.uk

This is the genuine thing – a well preserved 15th-century Tudor manor house, now owned by publishing boss William Fardon of Seattle, who bought the hotel when on a shooting trip. Its location is magical, with a tree-lined drive through parkland, where you almost expect a nobleman with ruffs and rapier to greet you.

The table d'hote, even though some might think it expensive, as an occasional treat of high quality is justifiable. Four courses include six starters, of which seared scallops wrapped in bacon with cauliflower cream and sweet chilli dressing or langoustine and saffron soup or duck and foie gras confit, wrapped in Parma ham and served with toasted brioche, plum compote and puy lentil dressing are typical.

Following a sorbet the seven main courses cover most eventualities such as fresh sea bass, turbot, breast of duck, pheasant supreme served with a parsnip purée, deep-fried celeriac and soft peppercorn sauce (watch out for the shot), lamb and peppered venison tenderloin sliced on to savoy cabbage with bacon, redcurrant and port wine sauce and cheese beignets. Vegetables are served on the plate and might include small onions, baby leeks, asparagus and french beans.

Sweets are spectacular: vanilla brulée, served in a biscuit basket with chocolate-dipped cape gooseberry, a mixed-nuts nougat praline with three flapjack dumplings or perhaps pear tart topped with marzipan.

Coffee in the lounge is accompanied by home-made truffles.

MEALS: L 12-2; D 7-9
Closed: 27, 28, 29 December
Cards: All major
CHEF: Kevin Steel. PROPRIETOR: Ken Roberts
WTB: 3 ★★★
Rooms: 9, £85-£99 S, £105-£155 D

LLOCAL INTEREST: Town of Llangollen, outdoor pursuits

33 Llandrillo

The food here is very good indeed. It is not fashionable, trendy or fussy but plain cooking carefully and deliciously composed and shorn of all extraneous components. Flavours sing out clearly the self-

Tyddyn Llan

Llandrillo
Corwen
Denbighshire
LL21 0ST
Tel: 01490 440264
Fax: 01490 440414

e-mail: tyddynllanhotel@
compuserve.com
www.tyddynllan.co.uk

discipline of the cuisine as something of a surprise.

The setting for Matthew Haines's justly-praised endeavours is the lovely, comfortable, relaxed hotel created by Peter and Bridget Kindred from a lovingly restored and extended old stone house in this gentle Welsh valley. Peter's joyous paintings hang throughout the hotel. The dining room is bright and beautiful in yellow and blue.

Dinner is a no-choice three-course affair, with a soup or sorbet, or an à la carte menu enabling one to have starters such as terrine of duck confit and foie gras with a pretty delicious compote of onions and sun-dried tomatoes or a light goat's cheese soufflé with a pickled walnut salad.

Main course fillets of freshest sea bass on a vegetable ragout in a prawn and tomato sauce or pan-fried rib-eye steak with honey drizzled sautéed root vegetables and caramelised shallots well illustrate the syle of cooking, with its accuracy and clarity of flavour.

Puddings show a sure hand in a sharp lemon tart with lemon parfait and dark chocolate topped Baileys cheesecake.

A savoury and a board of farmhouse cheese with home-made biscuits is always available.

A sensible, thoughtfully constructed wine list has a good range of house selections and wines by the glass.

MEALS: L 12.30-2; D 7-9 £27
Closed: Two weeks in January
Cards: All major
CHEF: Matthew Haines. PROPRIETORS: Peter and Bridget Kindred
WTB: 4 ★★★
Rooms: 10, from £67 S, from £105 D

LOCAL INTEREST: Bodnant Garden, Portmeirion village, slate mines

34 Llandudno

Bodysgallen Hall

Llandudno
N. Wales
LL30 1RS
Tel: 01492 584466
Fax: 01492 582519

e-mail:
info@bodysgallen.com
www.bodysgallen.com

This lovely distinguished old house is a reassuring place, furnished with quiet elegance and stunning floral arrangements. It is set just outside the town, in fine gardens and wooded parkland. The staff are unobtrusively efficient and charming.

The food has faltered sometimes in the past few years, but the new chef, David Thompson, has raised standards encouragingly. Starters and puddings have pleased particularly although recent visits have indicated that there is still some way to go as far as main courses are concerned.

The three-course dinner offers starters ranging from lobster salad with chilli couscous and chilled lasagne of marinated halibut to quail ravioli. They are beautifully presented and flavours are good.

Main courses feature pan-fried calf's liver with asparagus and a caramelised onion sauce, grilled fillet of salmon on braised fennel, seafood tortellini and caviar sauce, medaillons of monkfish wrapped in Parma ham with langoustines and saffron noodles, roast fillet of cod

with pickled cucumber, scallops and cherry tomatoes, roast rump of Welsh lamb with a pesto dauphinoise and shallot purée, or roast guinea fowl stuffed with tarragon forcemeat and served with its own leg braised. Vegetable accompaniments can be rather sparse.

Puddings really shine, from excellent ice creams and sorbets to bara brith and butter pudding with Calvados by way of a particularly successful chocolate fondant pudding with crème anglaise to caramelised bananas on a rice pudding tart with honey ice cream.

Coffee and house chocolates are good and the wine list is comprehensive and interestingly presented. A popular good-value lunch is served daily.

MEALS: L 12.30-1.45 from £15.50 Sunday L 12.30-1.45 £19.50; D 7.30-9.30 from £33.90
Cards: Visa and Mastercard
CHEF: David Thompson. MANAGER: Matthew Johnson
WTB: 5 ★★★★★
Rooms: 35, from £109 S, from £145 D, from £180 Suite

LOCAL INTEREST: Llandudno and Snowdonia

35 Llandudno

Empire Hotel

Church Walks
Llandudno
Conwy
LL30 2HE
Tel: 01492 860555
Fax: 01492 860791

e-mail:
reservtions@empire.hotel.co.uk
www.empirehotel.co.uk

Situated at the top end of Llandudno, with the Great Orme as its backdrop, the Empire Hotel is a testament to the Maddocks family's desire to please their clientele. Len and Elizabeth are gradually making way for their daughter Elyse and son-in-law Michael Waddy to run the business.

Guests arrive to a warm welcome and are encouraged to enjoy a pre-dinner drink in the elegant lounge, surrounded by antiques, while perusing an exceptional-value five-course table d'hote menu that offers a wide choice of dishes.

To start, choose between perhaps salmon and prawn fishcakes with a Thai dressing and a mushroom and hazelnut pâté. Oat-crusted grey mullet is voted a hit, and the flat mushrooms and king prawns in garlic butter also work well.

From a choice of more than 12 main courses, five are local fish and two vegetarian. The Cajun-style sea bass shows chef Michael's American roots. Good use of local beef and lamb includes Welsh fillet steak with a leek, bacon and onion ragout and garlic mash.

From the selection of puddings on offer, a sweet and creamy white chocolate and pear tart, is particularly delicious and a light lemon meringue roulade wins applause. Three or four Welsh farmhouse cheeses are also available. Home-made bread of the day might be roast onion or courgette and walnut, both delicious and sliced at the table.

The staff at this elegant restaurant, with its grand piano and curtained booths for secret assignations, are aided by a computerised

system that tells the kitchen when diners are ready for their next course – clever stuff.

The wine list is so extensive one probably needs to be a resident to do it justice. Coffee is plentiful. Back in the lounge is there time for a dance?

MEALS: L 12-2 from £5; Sunday L 12.30-2 £14.50
D 6.45-9.30 £24.50;
Closed: Christmas
Cards: All major
CHEF: Micheal Waddy. PROPRIETORS: Elizabeth Maddocks and Elyse Waddy
WTB: 4 ★★★★
Rooms: 58

LOCAL INTEREST: Conwy Castle, Caernarfon Castle, Snowdonia National Park, Bodnant Garden.

36 Llandudno

Martin's

11 Mostyn Avenue
Llandudno
Conwy
LL30 1YS
Tel: 01492 870070
Fax: 01492 876661

e-mail: martins@walesuk4.freeserve.co.uk
www.smoothhound.co.uk/hotels/martins2.html

Situated in Craig-y-don, Llandudno, Martin's is a few minutes' walk from the North Wales Theatre and is very convenient for pre- or post-theatre dinners. The restaurant is clean and attractive, with two downstairs rooms having been knocked together with a small bar in one corner.

The menu offers a small selection of starters. Choose between a pastry case topped with wild forestiere mushrooms served with a pommery mustard sauce or leek, potato and smoked bacon soup with cheese croutons, venison and cogniac terrine with Cumberland sauce and hot toasted bioche, locally hot-smoked salmon with a herb and potato sauce with a tomato mayonnaise.

Two fish options might be fillet of wild salmon and local sea bass, both served with creamy well-seasoned sauces and well garnished. The loin of Welsh lamb with onion marmalade in red wine jus can be lovely and tender, if cooked slightly beyond pink. Vegetarians might be offered a puff pastry pillow with stir-fried vegetables, cheddar and tomato and herb butter sauce.

For pudding, the lightly baked crème brulée with raspberry coulis is nicely executed. A selection of cheeses is available, as well as a hot pastry pillow filled with Stilton served with poached pear and salad garnish.

The wine list is well chosen but quite limited. This is an expensive evening but with a cafetière of good coffee, chocolates and a walk along the promenade should add up to a special occasion.

MEALS: D 6-late from £17.95
Closed: Sunday and Monday
Cards: All major
CHEF: Martin James. PROPRIETORS: Martin James and Jan Williams
WTB: 4 ★★★★
Rooms: 5, £30-£45 S, £50-£58 D

LOCAL INTEREST: Castles, mountains, lakes

37 Llandudno

Richard's Bistro

7 Church Walks
Llandudno
Conwy
LL30 2HD
Tel: 01492 875315
     01492 877924

Head along Llandudno's unspoilt Victorian promenade, opposite the pier, turn left up Church Walks and Richard's is 200 yards on your left. This bistro/restaurant has a more formal upstairs, with tablecloths and plush seating, while downstairs is wood and stone with open fires, bench seating and a view of the cooking area.

Gone is the 365-day opening with three chefs on shifts. Richard now cooks five days a week and it shows. Starters include spicy Thai salad of beef fillet with a great list of spices and pickled vegetables, Welsh leek and lentil pâté with apple chutney, and a wide choice of fish and vegetarian options.

For main course, there is a spectacular fish platter (salmon, turbot, brill, grey mullet and hake) with spinach and black pepper sauce. Also, a roast breast of Shropshire duckling served boneless with a crispy skin and a fresh and very fruity plum sauce, or a succulent medallion of roast lamb, slow-cooked in a rich red wine, redcurrant and Calvados gravy and served with poached apricots.

A pancake filled with roasted vegetables and cheese served with a herby tomato sauce would satisfy most vegetarians.

Puddings follow with perhaps rhubarb and vanilla crème brulée, a chocoholics delight consisting of slices of dark and light chocolate terrine, with chocolate ice cream and two sauces, or a lighter option of fresh and tangy lemon ice cream with raspberry coulis and crisp brandy-snap basket.

A good cheese platter with up to eight varieties of Welsh and French cheeses is served with fresh fruit, celery and biscuits.

MEALS: D 5.30-11
Closed: Sunday and Monday
Cards: All major
CHEF/PROPRIETOR: Richard Hendey

LOCAL INTEREST: Castles, mountains, lakes

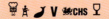

38 Llandudno

At the Great Orme end of Llandudno's promenade, this hotel has long been one of the best places to eat in this part of Wales. The hotel is owned and run by the Bland family who have worked tirelessly to maintain their justified reputation over a quarter of a century.

On arriving for dinner, the friendliest, efficient staff offer drinks and delicious appetisers before ushering diners through to the garden restaurant – all greenery and trellis. Chef David Harding creates a

St Tudno Hotel

Promenade
Llandudno
North Wales
LL30 2LP
Tel: 01492 874411
Fax: 01492 860401

e-mail:
sttudnohotel@btinternet.com
www.st-tudno.co.uk

seasonal menu of five or six choices over three courses and a smaller daily table d'hote which can be mixed with the à la carte.

Duck-liver parfait with crushed walnuts in the shape of a pear tastes as good as it looks, served with chunky apricot chutney and toasted brioche. A flavoursome hot pot of creamy curried mussels is another fine starter.

Follow with rich, gamey saddle of hare with spicy red cabbage and apple, or perhaps breast of Trelough duckling with its confit of leg and lemon sauce. Fish might be salmon with couscous, roasted tomatoes and deep-fried courgettes.

For dessert, a poached pear with a dark chocolate sauce and Drambuie parfait is rich but light. The selection of Celtic cheeses arrives in good condition with generous accompaniments of celery and grapes.

Petits fours and coffee round off the evening and can be enjoyed in the comfortable residents' lounge or the bar.

MEALS: L 12.30-1.45 £13-£16; Sunday L 12.30-1.30 £16.50;
D 7-9.30 from £35
Cards: All major cards
CHEF: David Harding. PROPRIETOR: Mrs J A Bland
WTB: 4 ★★★★
Rooms: 19, from £78 S, from £55 D

LOCAL INTEREST: Snowdonia, Great Orme mines, Conwy Castle, Bodnant Garden, Snowdon mountain railway.

39 Llandudno Junction

Queens Head

Glanwydden
Llandudno Junction
Conwy
LL31 9JP
Tel: 01492 546570
Fax: 01492 546487

The Queens Head, owned and run by Robert and Sally Cureton, nestles comfortably in the small village of Glanwydden, a few minutes drive from each of Llandudno and Colwyn Bay. This is a busy pub with a special emphasis on its food. The décor is basic but functional. A small public bar on entering opens out into a dining area where the kitchen is visible through a hatch for those who like to sneak a peek!

Lunch might be a 'tasty bap' split open and topped with grilled cheese and bacon, a salmon and pasta bake or a more substantial plate of gammon steak with pineapple salsa.

The dinner menu offers a large selection of hot and cold starters including moist and crispy duck leg on a bed of tangy red onion marmalade or a more traditional smoked trout and smoked salmon mousse. Main dishes range from pizzas and pasta to chef's specials, including a rich and tasty steak and mushroom pie, served with fresh vegetables and new potatoes, or a more adventurous grilled marinated orange and chilli-glazed chicken with roasted Mediterranean vegetables.

The wine list offers excellent value and is easy to read.

Hot puddings are rich and tempting – sticky toffee pudding (an excellent interpretation), bread and butter pudding or hot sticky pecan pie. Cold puddings – on display in a chilled dresser – include blackberry cheesecake, chocolate and nut fudge pie and fresh fruit pavlova to name but a few.

Dessert wine is available by the glass and good coffee comes with delicious home-made mint chocolate fudge – a box of which can be bought for a small sum.

MEALS: Pub opening hours
Closed: Christmas Day
Cards: All major cards apart from Amex or Diners
CHEF: N. Mackenzie. PROPRIETOR: Robert Cureton

LOCAL INTEREST: Conwy Castle, Royal Cambrian Art Gallery, Great Orme Tramway and mines, LLandudno Pier, the Rabbit Hole, Welsh Mountain Zoo at Colwyn Bay

40 Llanfairpwll

Anglesey Sea Zoo

Brynsciencyn
Llanfairpwll
Anglesey
LL61 6TD
Tel: 01248 430411
Fax: 01248 430213

e-mail: fishandfun@seazoo.demon.co.uk
www.angleseyseazoo.co.uk

This is undoubtedly one of Wales' top visitor attractions, offering visitors the chance to see fish from around the coastal waters of Wales in family-friendly surroundings. Right beside the Menai Straits, the Lee-Wilsons also produce highly praised sea salt of top quality; with an enviable balance of minerals and trace elements.

The cafe can suffer from all the problems posed by a substantial clientele demanding a variety of food, particularly at the cheaper end of the market. Home-made soup, local bread and salads are generally good, and the range of filled baps reflects a commendable level of commitment by the staff.

Coffee and home-made cakes are the highlight, however, and are well recommended for freshness and flavour.

MEALS: L 11-2 £5.95
Closed: November - April
Cards: All except Amex
PROPRIETOR: Alison Lee-Wilson
WTB: 5 ★★★★★ attraction

41 Llanfairpwll

Plas Newydd National Trust Tearoom

Olas Newydd
Llanfairpwll
Anglesey
LL61 6DQ
Tel: 01248 714795

The country seat of the Marquis of Anglesey, Plas Newydd has beautiful gardens which overlook the Menai Straits, with Snowdonia's majestic mountains as a backdrop.

The tea room, sited in the early 19th-century dairy, is well worth a visit, perhaps for just a cup of tea and slice of home-made cake or bara brith, although it would be a shame to miss out on the good, wholesome lunchtime fare. Freshly made soup such as celery and bramley apple might tempt, or a simple salad of local ham. More substantial dishes might include Welsh Cottager's Pie, filled with a

tasty chicken, bacon and mushroom mixture and served with seasonal vegetables, or a casserole of Welsh steak topped with a root vegetable mash – 'stwmp'.

Vegetarians do well, with a Welsh leek, potato and cheese pie or root vegetable crumble served with a fresh, crisp side salad.

A short, reasonably priced wine and beer selection is available, and traditional Welsh mead may also be bought by the glass.

Home-made hot puddings are worth indulging in; the lovely sticky treacle tart is a favourite with lashings of creamy custard.

Afternoon tea packages include Welsh Garden Tea – a pot of tea served with home-made bara brith and home-baked scone, Welsh butter and home-made jam – a more substantial high tea or simply a scone with jam and cream.

MEALS: L 11-5 approx £7.50
Closed: Thursday and Friday - November - March
Cards: Visa/Mastercard

42 Llangefni

Tre-Ysgawen Hall Hotel

Capel Coch
Llangefni
Anglesey
LL77 7YR
Tel: 01248 750750
Fax: 01248 750035

e-mail:
enquiries@treysgawen-hall.co.uk
www.treysgawen-hall.co.uk

Those who wish to refine their navigation skills and who relish a challenge will rejoice in the task of finding this Gothic mansion buried in the heartland of the island. A ghostly glimmer of light glimpsed through an avenue of mighty-trunked oaks burgeons into a splendidly proportioned edifice, protected from the world by jungly gardens and sweeps of scrunchy gravel.

One enters into a vaulted and panelled interior more grand than possibly imagined; a calming stillness and peacefulness pervades.

Close attention to detail continues into the pink-clothed dining room, swagged and marbled and glittering with polished glassware, gleaming cutlery and crisp damask napery. Confident, professional service delivers simple yet competent cawl of leek and potato, tender prawns with earthy mushrooms and salad leaves. Main dishes of tenderloin of Welsh lamb resting on a reduction of sweet red peppers, or fillet of wild salmon with a herb and butter sauce, are revealed, from beneath gleaming cloches. Drivers would be advised to enjoy the chocolate terrine with an orange caramel sauce, and avoid the Bailey's Cream cheesecake!

For those with deep pockets, the wine list rises to dizzying heights of hundreds of pounds for sought-after clarets and burgundies though most will be satisfied with fairly priced bottles chosen with care from reputable sources such as a Sauvignon Blanc from New Zealand's Marlborough estate that proved excellent and robust enough to match the style of cooking.

Generous cafetières of coffee are served in the peaceful drawing room.

MEALS: L 12-2 £15.95; D 7-9.30 £22.50-£32.50
Closed: The week between Christmas and New Year

Cards: All
CHEF: M. Evans. PROPRIETOR: T. Rowlands
WTB: 4 ★★★★
Rooms: 19, from £74 S, from £96 D, from £147 Suite

LOCAL INTEREST: Snowdonia mountains, Anglesey coastline and beaches, Beaumaris, Conwy, Caernarfon and Bodelwyddan Castles, Llanfair PG railway station, Bodnant Garden

43 Llangollen

Bryn Howel Hotel

Llangollen
Denbighshire
LL20 7UW
Tel: 01978 860331
Fax: 01978 860119

e-mail:
hotel@brynhowel.co.uk
www.brynhowel.co.uk

In many ways, the star of this rather grand hotel's restaurant is Mr Seddon, its manager who, holding the fort past retiring age on a Saturday night with a large wedding bagging his waiters, runs the entire front of house in exemplary style, with no one wanting for anything. Let us hope that they are able to find a replacement who can hold a candle to him!

The restaurant has aspirations and most of the dishes are a catering student's examination nightmare; yet if they come off, they can be very good. For example, a starter of fried whiting in a light batter with a delicious salmon roulade and fromage frais with gherkins comes out a winner.

Some main courses suffer from over-complication and an otherwise delicious ballotine of local rabbit, wrapped in ham and stuffed with white cabbage mousse on a good parsley and potato purée, finds itself at odds both with the loin wrapped round pickled kumquats and at war with a watercress coulis. A confit of guinea-fowl leg with its supreme in a chestnut cream sauce works better, as does sautéed chicken breast with oyster mushroom sauce. Vegetables, by contrast, are plain.

Puddings, too, are complex – the simplest a stunning light vanilla soufflé with a crisp poached pear.

The wine list of a hundred bins, sparse on halves, covers all areas with a full page of house-wines available by the glass.

The hotel, mock Tudor with more contemporary additions, is very comfortable and beautifully situated.

MEALS: L 12-2; D 7-9
Cards: All major cards
CHEF: Dai Davies. PROPRIETORS: John and Anne Lloyd
WTB: 4 ★★★★
Rooms: 36, £47.50 S, £95 D, £125 Suites

LOCAL INTEREST: Chirk Castle, Erddig, Llangollen steam railway, Telford's aqueduct, Valle Crucis abbey, International Eisteddfod

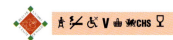

44 Llangollen

Cornmill

Llangollen
LL20 8PN
Tel: 01978 869555
Fax: 01978 869930

A new star has arrived in Llangollen in this dramatic conversion of an old cornmill on the River Dee just down from the bridge. Almost every table has a view of the river in this, airy, multi-level, three-storey restaurant serving food from noon until 9.30pm. There is outside seating on decking by the riverside and the impressive finish of this excellent building extends to stunning loos.

The food is trendy but well executed, with starters of Thai chicken and rice noodle salad, Greek salad with deep-fried feta cheese or, nearer home, a warm salad of crispy smoked bacon with black pudding and poached egg. There is a good twice-baked smoked salmon soufflé set off by rocket salad and basil crème fraiche.

Main courses can be hefty for hikers – a half shoulder of lamb, braised with mushrooms and onions and with roast vegetable mash, or braised venison haunch steak with chorizo sausage and suet crust, while the faint-hearted can find solace in grilled fillet of sea bream or Shetland mussels (which may be very good but so are Conwy ones!). There are good chips and innovative sandwiches available all day.

Things are rounded off with a Welsh cheeseboard and puddings ranging from the fashionable lemon tart to the almost extinct sherry trifle.

There is good espresso or cappuccino coffee, a short wine list with a goodly number of wines by the glass and good cask beers.

MEALS: L From 12 £8.50; D until 9.30 approx £13
Closed: Christmas Day and Boxing Day
Cards: All major
CHEF: Tim Watts

LOCAL INTEREST: Castles, river, local shops, trout farm and abbey

45 Llangollen

Gales of Llangollen

18 Bridge Street
Llangollen
Denbighshire
LL20 8PF
01978 860089
01978 861313

e-mail:
richard@galesofllangollen.co.uk
www.galesofllangollen.co.uk

It is difficult to believe you are not in a quiet corner of Paris as you sit down here with a glass of crisp wine and the chef's splendid hors d'oeuvre platter! It is a friendly, intimate, clubby little place with lots of locals. Order at the bar from blackboards listing food, wines and lagers of the day.

Restaurants and fashions in food come and go in this bustling town on the river but Gales has long been a fixture here for many years now.

From noon at lunchtime and in the evening, there are daily specials – braised shoulder of lamb, salmon in sorrel sauce, or Thai-style chicken, for example, along with a vegetarian dish, perhaps ricotta and Parmesan-filled pasta parcels in a tomato and basil sauce.

Starters are commendably simple – smoked salmon, potted shrimps, good soups and pâtés while at night steaks and other beef main dishes will appear.

There are Welsh cheeses, along with Stilton and Brie and puddings

such as apple crumble with real custard, cassis cheesecake or home-made ice creams.

The French house wines at £1.50 a glass are an object lesson in what a house wine should be, and there are many other bargains, along with good beers and lagers.

There is accommodation and parking for residents.

MEALS: L 12-2 £6; D 6-10 £12
Closed: 24.12-2.1
Cards: All
CHEFS: John Gosling and Grant Davies. PROPRIETOR: John Gosling
WTB: 3 ★★★
Rooms: 15, £45 S, £48 D, £50 Suites

LOCAL INTEREST: Llangollen town centre and canal.

46 Llangollen

Jonkers

Hadyn House
9 Charles Street
Llangollen
Denbighshire
LL20 8NN
Tel: 01978 861158

Llangollen has become rather like Mont St Michel in the tourist season – full of restaurants. Every street around the central Castle Street seems to have a clutch and Jonkers gets more than fair its share of admirers with its pubby atmosphere, and the smallness of just two rooms with eight tables. Run by Heather Petrie and John Spice, supervision is close but gentle and customers have a good time.

Heather's five starters might include pâté from the local Patchwork company in Ruthin, a leek and cheese soup, garlic mushrooms with granary bread and smoked salmon.

Main courses include venison, redcurrant and port sausages, served on a bed of potato mash with fresh vegetables, leek and Caerphilly gratin, Welsh lamb cutlets with a leek and white wine sauce, or cod and courgette bake. Vegetarians are well served with stuffed aubergine, filled with sliced onion, tomatoes, peppers and mushrooms and finished under the grill with breadcrumbs and melted cheddar, or a potato, apple and celery bake.

Puddings are spectacular as in a banana meringue, which drew the comment "I didn't know whether to eat or wear it!"

MEALS: D 7 to midweek, 5pm on Saturday approx £15
Closed: Sunday and Monday, please phone.
Cards: All major
CHEF: Heather Petrie PROPRIETORS: Heather Petrie and John Spice
Rooms: 2 £20 S, £18 D

LOCAL INTEREST: Ladies of Llangollen house, Plas Newydd, River Dee and Horseshoe falls, Shropshire Union canal, Llangollen steam railway, International Eisteddfod, jazz festival.

47 Llanrwst

La Barrica

21 Ancaster Square
Llanrwst
Conwy
LL26 0LD
Tel: 01492 642297

e-mail: labarrica@aol.com

A continental coffee bar and bistro is not your regular run-of-the-mill establishment for an old market town in the heart of the Conwy Valley. Primarily a daytime operation open for coffee, pastries and light lunches, they do, however, open on Thursday and Friday nights, when it is vital to book.

Alan and Adrian's love of travel has enabled them to refine their art at this highly individualistic venue. The bar has been designed to hold tapas dishes of the day with additional items on the menu and it is great fun to go and make up your own combination of dishes.

During the day there is a wide choice of filled crisp baguettes. Two that catch the eye are hot and spicy chicken and tzatsiki on salad leaves, houmus and salsa.

Pastries and desserts go down wonderfully well with some of the best coffee served in the area.

For dinner, starters might range from Thai fish 'Tom Yam' – fish poached with rice in a spicy stock – to baked feta parcels with tomato and herbs.

For main course you might choose, arni lemonata – a tangy and unusual Greek dish of lamb braised with lemons, mushrooms and herbs or a marmitako - a Basque fisherman's stew. Vegetarians are equally well looked after.

MEALS: L all day; D from 7
Closed: Sunday, Monday, Tuesday and Wednesday evenings, all December and January

LOCAL INTEREST: Not licensed – bring your own wine.

48 Llanrwst

Amser Da

Heol yr Orsaf
Llanrwst
Conwy
LL26 0BT
Tel: 01492 641188
Fax: 01492 642215

e-mail: deiniol@blasarfwyd.com
www.blasarfwyd.com

Still finding its feet in the busy valley town of Llanrwst, this restaurant has great potential. It is run by Deiniol and Chandra ap Dafydd, who also own the justifiably well-known Blas ar Fwyd delicatessen across the road.

The modern interior has an interesting wooden feature in the centre, carved with a Welsh poem. Welsh music plays in the background and chattering in Welsh can be heard from the kitchen, all pointers to the regionality of the establishment.

The bilingual menu, however, is truly cosmopolitan – and offers meals, snacks and beverages of a many and varied nature throughout the day.

At lunch, choose 'The Big Soup' – leek and potato, home-made and a substantial portion served with a cold baguette and several packs of Welsh butter, or perhaps a Welsh salad of local bacon and cheddar cheese, served on mixed leaves with a tangy mustard vinaigrette.

For dessert try brandied chocolate mousse, served in a sundae glass topped with an inch of thick cream or lemon tartlet, sharp and lemony.

Welsh produce at its best

The evening menu is more sophistocated, offering a plate of tapas for starters or Parma ham and figs. Pizza and pasta are on offer, as well as lots of local fish, or Thai baked red snapper. Duck, venison and a full range of meat dishes follow, whilst vegetarians must decide between cashew and porcini strudel, mushroom stroganoff with couscous or coconut and masala curry. Naturally, the cheese board is excellent, with the best of the day's choice from the deli over the road. Wines also cover a splendid spectrum from Deiniol's fine wine shop.

Waitress service is friendly; coffee fresh and good.

MEALS: L from 10am £2.50-£12; Sunday L 11-6 £10.95;
D until 10pm £10-£19
CHEF: Gwenda Evans. PROPRIETOR: Deiniol ap Dafydd
Closed: Mondays and Tuesdays
Cards: All major

LOCAL INTEREST: Traditional market town, Welsh delicatessen, walking, cycling.

 V CHS

49   Mold

Belvedere

85 Wrexham Street
Mold
Clwyd
CH7 1H8
Tel: 01352 753229

This is a little bit of Naples in Mold. Giuseppina and Jaetano Sciarrillo set up their restaurant 14 years ago and the menu has not changed. "I am still learning," says Jaetano, who resembles the famous Italian chef Anton Carluccio. The eight green-clothed tables, a tiny bar in the corner and small spotless kitchen, make a cheerful setting and platform for this devoted-to-southern-Italy couple.

Zuppa casalinga (soup of the day), stracciatelle (egg and cheese soup), Parma ham with melon, grilled asparagus with butter and Parmesan or antipasto misto make up the starters, with three specialities of pepperoni farciti, (baked stuffed sweet pepper with prawns, cheese and herbs), baked stuffed aubergine with Parma ham, and a mixed seafood salad. Hunks of crusty white bread accompany.

Much of the pasta is home-made for the 13 dishes covering favourites such as lasagne al forno, canneloni, penne arabiata (with chilli, bacon and garlic) tagliatelle al funghi and spaghetti bolognese or siracusana (with aubergines, courguettes, sweet peppers and vegetarian sauce). There is a range of pizzas too.

Main courses encompass steak, chicken and trout, with four specialities such as sogliola alla positano, (fillet of sole with ham, cheese and herbs cooked in wine, cream and fresh grapes) or melenzani parmigiana, (baked aubergines with parmesan, mozzarella and ham cooked in a rich tomato and béchamel sauce).

Italian puddings include favourites such as tiramisu.

The warmth and friendship of the Sciarrillos undoubtedly brings the sun of south-west Italy to Metropolitan Mold.

MEALS: D 6.30-10.30 £10-£20
Closed: Sunday and Monday

CHEFS/PROPRIETORS: Givseppina and Jaetano Sciarrillo

LOCAL INTEREST: Market town, Clwydian hills and country parks.

---

50   Mold

The Stables Restaurant and Paddock Bar

Soughton Hall Hotel
Northop
Mold
Flintshire
CH7 6AB
Tel: 01352 840577
Fax: 01352 840382

e-mail:
soughtonhall.co.uk

This highly enjoyable conversion of stable-block to a restaurant seems to have changed direction a little towards middle Britain and the middle-aged but it remains on the whole good value. The Stables is approached down a magnificent carriage row with fine old trees on either side framing the Hall (an impressive building – either very French chateau or Victorian waterworks, depending on your mood!).

The fare is hearty and occasionally heavy and inconsistent. Starters from black pudding with caramelised apple soufflé to salmon filo pastry with salad leaves and salsa precede calves' liver and bacon, lamb shanks, cod and monkfish with mushy peas and good chips, roast salmon on buttered courgettes and steaks ranging from 8 to 32oz sirloins and fillets.

Puddings take in a classic tarte au citron, summer pudding, banana and custard pie or an excellent cheese board of three named varieties from each of Wales, England, Scotland and Ireland.

Beer drinkers have a treat of a choice and the Wine Shop has a daily list of bargains and some by the glass.

The à la carte menu is available at both lunch and dinner in the Racecourse Restaurant upstairs, while in the Paddock Bar downstairs are blackboard extras and sandwiches.

MEALS: L 12-2.30; Sunday L 12-3 £7.95; D 6.30-10
Cards: All major
CHEF: Paul Wright. PROPRIETOR: Rosemary Rodenhurst

LOCAL INTEREST: Chester, Theatre Clwyd, Welsh mountains.

---

51   Porthmadog

Yr Hen Fecws

15/16 Lombard Street
Porthmadog
Gwynedd
LL49 9AP
Tel: 01766 514625

This atmospheric rather noisy bistro serves excellent food in a converted corner cottage behind Porthmadoc's High Street. It is full of interesting old photos and prints of the town with stone walls, beams and candles in bottles on well-spaced tables.

The printed menu is best ignored, as the real business of the evening is set out on blackboards detailing the day's dishes. Strong in all departments, portions are generous and prices reasonable. Starters of warm salads (scallops and bacon or grilled goat's cheese and walnuts for example) are of a quality unique for some miles around while chicken liver pâté, smoked salmon and Thai fish cakes with chilli sauce also win praise. Seared fillets of local sea bass on a crisp ratatouille with pesto dressing is a typical main course, along

with duck breast and plum sauce, chicken casserole, goulash with garlic and mash, aubergine, tomato and Mozzarella gateau or perhaps a Welsh Black fillet steak with caramelised shallots and port and thyme sauce. Vegetables are good and plentiful, with world-class chips as an alternative to new or baked potatoes.

Standards are maintained with pudding such as crème brulée with strawberries and cream, bara brith and butter pudding with elderflower custard, toffee meringue torte and ice creams and sorbets.

The shining enthusiasm and generosity of the food redeems any rough edges in the service and almost makes one forget intrusive piped music.

Wines from a short list are remarkably priced from £7.50 to £11 a bottle.

MEALS: D 5.30-10 £12-£22
Cards: All except Amex or Diners
CHEF: Bryan Jones. PROPRIETORS: Helen Owen and Michael Hughes
WTB: 3 ★★★
Rooms: 4, from £25 S, £22.50-£25 D

LOCAL INTEREST: Portmeirion, Ffestiniog Railway, Snowdonia National Park

52 Portmeirion

Portmeirion Hotel

Portmeirion
Gwynedd
LL48 6ET
Tel: 01766 770000
Fax: 01766 771331

e-mail:
hotel@portmeirion-village.com
www.portmeirion.com

It is always a pleasure to be in this enchanting place of delight to the eye everywhere. The gardens are looking better than for years and the comfortable bedrooms possess great charm. It all looks loved and cared for. So more is the pity that the food does not always live up its surroundings, being occasionally uninspired and a little dull.

Lunch is very good value. The three-course dinner (with a two-course option) offers a respectable choice. Starters of splendid smoked salmon, crab and avocado, good soups and terrines, perhaps a trio of meats with marinated beef, game terrine and chicken liver parfait – are typical.

Main courses offer fish, local lamb, excellent Brecon venison, Welsh beef fillet and poultry, along with vegetarian dishes such as a tian of ratatouille or wild mushroom risotto.

Puddings range from sorbets and exotic fruit vacherin to pear and chocolate pudding with crème anglaise. A board of Welsh and other cheeses is always available.

The wine list is a remarkable one, with very reasonable mark-ups and offering a good selection of house wines. It is a minor work of art in itself, being written in Welsh with an English translation.

MEALS: L 12.30-2 £14; Sunday L 12.30-2 £16; D 6.30-9 £35
Closed: January 7th – February 14th
Cards: All
CHEF: Billy Taylor
WTB: 5 ★★★★★

Rooms: 50, £115-£180 S; £145-£230 D

LOCAL INTEREST: Ffestiniog Railway, Llechwedd slate caverns

53   Pwllheli

Plas Bodegroes

Nefyn Road
Pwllheli
Gwynedd
LL52 5TH
Tel: 01758 612363
Fax: 01758 701247

e-mail:
gunna@bodegroes.co.uk
www.bodegroes.co.uk

Chris Chown mans the galley, Gunna steers the ship with her elegant charm at the front of house, and Plas Bodegroes again sparkles in offering one of the most remarkable eating experiences in Wales. After sixteen years, the gardens are charming and mature, while the house is a relaxed haven, well off the beaten track, where the greatest care is taken over details from furnishings to art on the walls.

"We simply can't state where our ingredients come from on the menu, because it would read as 'local, local, local'. I source everything from here unless the quality is missing then I look further afield," says Chris.

His signature dishes are still on the menu – warm salad of monkfish, Camarthen ham and mushrooms, bara brith and butter pudding with rum and raisin ice cream, and a cinnamon biscuit of blackberry and apple with elderflower sauce. There are tempting additions, too, with wild mushroom tart with herb salad and balsamic dressing, seared John Dory with spicy tomato and anchovy salsa, braised mountain lamb chop with cannellini bean and garlic casserole, chargrilled rib-eye of Welsh Black beef with braised shallots and red wine sauce and Sunday lunch is remarkable value for money. Portions are not large, just as balanced as the flavours in the dishes. The wine list is one of the best in the country for range and care of choice, with input from a variety of sources. Service is elegant and unhurried.

It is good to see again the magic of Plas Bodegroes, epitomised by its unique combination of house and garden. A customer who had not been before was overheard in the garden to say "How remarkable to find such a beautiful place with such marvellous food and SUCH nice people. Even the other customers are nice!!"

MEALS: Sunday L 12 2 £13.50; D 7 9 £25
Closed: December – Mid March, Mondays
Cards: Mastercard and Visa
CHEF: Chris Chown. PROPRIETORS: Chris and Gunna Chown
WTB: 3 ★★★
Rooms: 11, £40 S, £80-120 D
LOCAL INTEREST: Pen Llyn, Pwllheli Marina,

54   Rhyl

This is the home of David and Elvira Barratt, both of whom have worked in catering for the past 20 years, having formerly created the

Barratts Restaurant

Ty'n Rhyl
167 Vale Road
Rhyl
Denbighshire
LL18 2PH
Tel: 01745 344138
Fax: 01745 344138
email: barrat@freeserve.co.uk

successful Buttonhole in Ruthin. Theirs is an elegant, serious restaurant, originally a Tudor hall. Its cosy lounge has a wonderful historical ambience, with carved wooden panels and coats of arms, although the dining room does not continue the Tudor theme.

Drinks are served with nibbles such as small quiches and tartlets, then first courses cover perhaps leek and pimento soup, tartlet of goat's cheese with home-made chutney, black pudding on a base of creamed potato, topped with roasted shallots and melon with smoked salmon and prawns.

Of five main courses, there might be sirloin steak with mushrooms, chicken liver pâté and sage and truffle sauce, roast honey-glazed Gressingham duck breast served with orange and whisky sauce, supreme of chicken marinated in rosemary, lemon and oil, a cutlet of pork served with apricots, or salmon and cod baked with spinach and mussels in white wine and cream.

Puddings include Pavlova with cream and fruits and bread and butter pudding laced with Grand Marnier. Coffee is accompanied by chocolates and almond biscuits.

David Barratt's cooking is skillful, giving a direct experience of fine ingredients and presented with care. He changes the menu weekly offering ingredients of the season, including seafoods from local fishermen.

MEALS: L 12.30-2.30 £12.50; D 6.30-9.30 £12.50-£25
Closed: Sunday evening and Monday
Cards: All major
CHEF: David Barratt. PROPRIETORS: David and Elvira Barratt
WTB: 3 ★★★
Rooms: 3, £35 S, £70 D

LOCAL INTEREST: Beaches, Snowdonia, Chester, golf, fishing, walking

55 Ruthin

DaVincis

Castle Mews
Well Street
Ruthin
Denbighshire
LL15 1AH
Tel: 01824 702200
Fax: 01824 702201

With Ruthins population hardly exceeding 4,000 the success of this restaurant is remarkable. Every day diners travel from Chester, Wrexham and Denbigh just to enjoy the cooking of Andreas Brunzel. In the first-floor restaurant, above historic Well Street, there is seating for 80 and booking is recommended, especially for dinner.

Lunch daily specials, chalked on the board, include bangers and mash with onion gravy and baked salmon in white wine and chive cream sauce. Baguettes and salads are available.

In the evening, starters might include mushroom and chive soup or black pudding and potato cake in apricot sauce. A grilled rib of beef in red wine sauce is typical of the four main dishes on offer as is roast breast of duckling incoise with an aubergine gateau in roast garlic sauce.

Puddings are sublime – perhaps a three-chocolate terrine with raspberry coulis and cream.

Although the cutlery is rather disappointing, the food comes hot from the kitchen on large plates full of the freshest flavours. Service is pleasant and prompt in a friendly fashion.

MEALS: L 11.30-3 £4-£7.50; D from 6pm £12-£20
Closed: Sunday and Monday
Cards: Visa and Mastercard
CHEF: Adrian Coles. PROPRIETOR: Andreas Brunzel

LOCAL INTEREST: Picturesque market town, local craft centre, Ruthin castle.

56 St. Asaph

Drapers Café, Tweedmill

Tweedmill Factory Outlet
Llanerch Park, Trefnant
St Asaph
Denbighshire
LL17 0UY
Tel: 01745 731005
Fax: 01745 731008

e-mail: dorothy@tweedmill.co.uk
www.tweedmill.co.uk

On the Denbigh side of St Asaph, part of the Tweedmill Factory Outlet complex that attracts hundreds of visitors daily, this is on the surface an unlikely place to find a restaurant of distinction. And at these prices it is no wonder that the dining-room – two pleasant freshly-decorated rooms with a patio outside for good-weather eating – is always busy, more often than not with golf players from the adjoining Llanerch course.

Paul Hollingsworth is in charge of the kitchen; previously at the Imperial Hotel, Llandudno, he certainly has made an impression. The emphasis is on fresh ingredients, varied fruits, creative salads and a menu that changes weekly with the seasons: ingredients are as local and fresh as possible, with the six special main courses changing weekly the range is spectacularly good value, generosity on the plate meaning not just quantity but quality and range, on hugely over-size plates.

Starters might include home-made vegetable soup and chicken liver pâté, followed by Welsh rack of lamb with hedgerow-berry sauce, with vegetables and salad or steak-and-ale cobbler with vegetables and salad. Dishes include five varieties of vegetables; and fresh varied salads, including fruit as well as the usual ingredients.

Round off with tiramisu and coffee ice cream or Tweedmill chocolate heaven with chocolate ice cream.

MEALS: L 9.30-5.30 from £3.95
Closed: Christmas Day
Cards: All major
CHEF: Paul Hollingsworth
CONTACTS: Tracey O'Connor and Dorothy Ainsworth

LOCAL INTEREST: Retail outlet on site, marble church, St Asaph Cathedral, Vale of Clwyd

57 St Asaph

Just off the A55 exit, on the road into St Asaph, Simon Rodenhursts ambitious Stables at the Plough Inn is a dramatic conversion, with

The Plough

The Roe
St Asaph
Denbighshire
LL17 0LU
Tel: 01745 585080
Fax: 01745 585363

large alcove rooms off a long bar downstairs with chunky, dark wood furniture and lamps.

Upstairs are the Racecourse Restaurant, with one wall given over to an enormous mural in relief of Chester racecourse viewed from above, and an elegant, all black-and-white, glass-and-chrome and glass Italian restaurant, "Graffiti".

The Racecourse boasts an eclectic menu, with favourites like prawn chow mein or black pudding for starters and main dishes of lamb shank with honey and mustard sauce, excellent calf's liver and smoked bacon with sage gravy and sirloin and fillet steaks with very good chips. There is a Chinese section offering dim sum and crispy duck pancakes, and there is a children's menu.

Graffiti offers pasta dishes, starters of king prawns, fried squid and Parma ham and melon and main courses comprising a variety of meat and poultry such as chicken breast stuffed with Mozarella on noodles and medallions of veal on rice.

Everything in this complex operation here is straightforward good value. The place has a happy buzz to it and the staff are efficient and good-natured.

A second Graffiti opened in Wrexham last October, offering bed and breakfast.

MEALS: from 12 noon until 11pm £5-£15
Cards: All except Amex
CHEF: Steve Cregg. PROPRIETOR: Simon Rodenhurst

LOCAL INTEREST: St Asaph Cathedral

58 Tal-y-Bont

The Lodge

Tal-y-Bont
Conwy
LL32 8YX
Tel: 01492 660766
Fax: 01492 660534

e-mail:
bbaldon@lodgehotel.co.uk
www.lodgehotel.co.uk

The Lodge Hotel at Tal-y-Bont in the Conwy Valley is a pleasant drive on the B5106 from either Conwy or Betws-y-Coed. The hotel, with its mainly wooden exterior is extremely popular as a lunch venue, its lounge dominated by a huge slate fireplace with brass chimney.

Barbara runs the front of house with bubbly enthusiasm. The kitchen is Simon's domain, although both are likely to turn up anywhere, such is their flexibility.

Extraordinary good value prevails. The table d'hote menu, written daily, is strongly influenced by available local produce.

On a cold December night, it might include locally smoked duck with a delicious home-made redcurrant jus and a salad garnish, lightly dressed. Locally baked crusty bread rolls are splendid and arrive warm at the table.

A grilled fillet of sea bass served with a sharp lime hollandaise, works well. Pork fillet with caramelised apples and cider sauce also featured alongside Conwy lamb cutlets with glazed shallots and red wine. Plentiful vegetables are served in rather dated stainless steel dishes.

The home-made puddings are simple and very good. Lovely walnut tart with brandy icing and hot apple pie are both served with local

double cream. A selection of cheeses is also on offer, mainly Welsh.

Plentiful coffee with lots of crisp after-dinner mints served in the lounge in front of the blazing fire makes the winter's evening complete.

MEALS: L 12-2; D 7-9
Closed: Monday lunch, some evenings during winter
Cards: All
CHEF: Simon Baldon. PROPRIETOR: Barbara Baldon
WTB: 3 ★★★
Rooms: 14, £35 S, £35 D, £60 Suites

LOCAL INTEREST: Bodnant Garden, Conwy Castle and walled town

59 Trefriw

Prince's Arms Country Hotel

Trefriw
nr Betws y Coed
Conwy
LL27 0JP
Tel: 01492 640592
Fax: 01492 640559

enquiries@princes-arms.co.uk
www.princes-arms.co.uk

Drive up the Conwy Valley towards Betws-y-Coed on the B5106, with stunning views of the river and the mountains, to Trefriw. Here you will find the Prince's Arms Country Hotel, recently refurbished by Lindsay and Anne Gordon and now boasting a brasserie.

The restaurant, with its soothing cream decor and crisp linen, offers a good-value table d'hote menu of five starters, main courses and puddings, followed by coffee and petit fours. The traditional Sunday menu is also served in the brasserie whose sizeable menu offers starters such as hot avocado pear with a tomato salsa or a port and Stilton pâté served with slices of good home-made walnut and chive bread.

Main courses include a braised lamb knuckle with rosemary and root vegetables which would satisfy the hungriest walker. Pan-fried sea bass with ratatouille is the printed fish choice, although there are further blackboard specials, such as a succulent salmon steak with a mango salsa.

Desserts might include 'light as a feather', steamed syrup sponge with fresh cream anglaise or a rich and creamy crème brulée with strawberries encased in a crisp caramel cage.

The brasserie wine list is available by the glass, large or small and is exceptional value. The restaurant's short, well chosen list offers wine at a fractionally higher price but still offers amazing value.

Good coffee, friendly staff and a wonderful view over the river Conwy make this an ideal stop for lunch or dinner.

MEALS: L 12-3 £5; Sunday L 12-3 £9.50; D 6-9.30 £10-£20
Cards: All major
CHEF: Anne Gordon. PROPRIETORS: Lindsey and Anne Gordon
WTB: 3 ★★★
Rooms: 14, £38 S, £33 D, £36 Suite

LOCAL INTEREST: Next to old quay where paddle steamers drop off visitors, spa and woollen mill in village, scenic lakes and woodland around hotel

60 Tremadog

The Golden Fleece Inn and Bistro

Market Square
Tremadog
Gwynedd
LL49 9RB
Tel: 01766 512421
Fax: 01766 513421

e-mail: roger@
thegoldenflece.freeserve.co.uk

This old coaching inn retains its popularity with both visitors and locals, serving excellent beers and bar snacks at lunchtime with good humour and warmth.

At lunchtime, go for sandwiches made to order, grilled gammon and egg or honey roast ham cut generously, both with very good chips, or try the fish cake, which is a salmon and broccoli shanty with dill. When available, fresh local crab and whitebait are worth a detour; keep an eye on the blackboard listing special dishes of the day.

In the evening, the bistro behind the pub in the old stable block serves (weekends only in winter) a variety of straightforward fish, poultry and steak dishes, in a large comfortable candlelit room.

In the summer, Roger Glyn Jones goes down the Lleyn Peninsula to Uwchmynydd, near Aberdaron to his simple little restaurant, Pen Bryn Bach (tel: 01758 760216) that serves only local crab, lobster and a variety of fish. Ask first at the pub to avoid disappointment.

MEALS: L 12-2 from £2.95; D 6.30-9 £8.10
Cards: Visa and Mastercard
PROPRIETOR: Roger Jones
WTB: 2 ★★
Rooms: 3, £28.50 S, £40 D

LOCAL INTEREST: Birthplace of Lawrence of Arabia, Ffestiniog and Welsh Highland Railways, Maritime Museum, Portmeirion, Criccieth and Harlech Castles

61 Wrexham

National Trust Restaurant

Erddig
Wrexham
Clwyd
LL13 0YT
Tel: 01978 355314

The Yorke family estate of Erddig is a great place to visit, with its historical detail of life in the 17th Century. From the gallery of photographs to the complete contents of the kitchens and relics of farm mechanisation, there is a lot to see.

Refreshment is a treat, too. The restaurant, well run by Pat Bodymore, offers a menu of dishes using recipes and details from the Yorke family archives. Some of the recipes have been adapted to suit today's taste, but there is still a flavour of simple Georgian and Welsh fare.

Home baking of Welsh butter shortbread, honey and ginger slice and bara brith always fits well with a cup of coffee or tea or even Lady Abesses biscuits. For lunch the menu offers Erddig carrot soup, Welsh cawl or lobscouse, Philip Yorke mushroom and vegetable crumble or ham or Welsh Cheddar sandwiches made from bread with flour grown and milled on the estate and baked in scuffle ovens in the bakehouse.

Puddings and desserts also have a historical touch to them such as

Louisa Yorke's Chester pudding or Sir Watkin Williams Wynne's steamed lemon pudding.

The restaurant is licensed and is happily situated right above the well-stocked shop. During the summer season, visitors to the restaurant must pay the entrance fee for the property first. During the winter, access is free.

MEALS: L 11-5 approx £7.50
Closed: November - April
CATERING MANAGER: Pat Bodymore

LOCAL INTEREST: Erddig Country House

62 Wrexham

Pant-yr-Ochain

Old Wrexham Road
Gresford
Wrexham
Clwyd
LL12 8TY
Tel: 01978 853525
Fax: 01978 853505

A bright update to this elegant house offers a remarkably pleasant rendezvous for lunch or dinner or just good sandwiches, all served from noon until 9.30pm.

Pant-yr-Ochain, once a 16th-century inn, is found down a lane by the side of one of the small lakes hereabouts and has outdoor seating for summer drinking. Take the exit unpromisingly signposted "Wrexham Industrial Estate" from the A483 and, a few hundred yards on the left, turn at a sign marked The Flash – not a factory to be seen!

The daily menu offers interesting new dishes and variations on old ones. For example, Shropshire Blue replaces Caerphilly with leek in sausages and rillettes of salmon and smoked salmon are dressed with red pepper crème fraiche. Well-judged grilled bream fillets come with wilted spinach on a creamy risotto with lemon and Mascarpone and roast salmon with watercress sauce on sun-dried tomato linguine.

Traditionalists would be happy with braised shoulder of lamb with parsnip and potato purée, creamed cabbage and rosemary sauce, and vegetarians with pumpkin and potato curry or a gratin of vegetables and goat's cheese with tomato and basil sauce.

Puddings range from profiteroles and lemon crème brulée to roast pineapple crepes and glazed rice pudding with honeycomb ice cream.

Coffee comes all ways, there is a compact wine list, special wines of the month and a seductive range of cask beers with listed on blackboards.

MEALS: Served from 12 noon to 9.30pm £15-£20
Cards: All except Diners
CHEF: James Elwood
PROPRIETORS: Graham Arathoon and Lindsey Prole

LOCAL INTEREST: Erbistock ferry, Chirk Castle and Erddig National Trust property

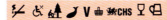

Mid Wales Entries

63   Aberaeron

Hive on the Quay

Caedwgan Place
Aberaeron
Ceredigion
SA46 0BU
Tel: 01545 570445

Perched on the wharf between the inner and outer harbour in the coastal town of Aberaeron, there is rarely a dull moment at this restaurant. With a fresh fish stall on one side, the honey bee exhibition on the other and Sea Aquarium just down the quay, there can't be a better spot to visit with the family during the summer months.

Sarah Holgate and her family have been here for more than 25 years and the menu tells of all the best ingredients in the region, organic, local and fresh in a kitchen where Welsh recipes are legion.

There is something for everyone from an eclectic menu. Crab and lobster salad follow boiled egg with soldiers on the menu or a portion of home-grown potatoes with grilled local mackerel, toad-in-the-hole, salad of roasted red pepper and feta cheese, cod fish cakes, lamb shank pie and twice baked cheese souffle. Dinners are served only in August.

The cooking is sophisticated, the fish sublime and cakes all home-made and moreish. And that's before we mention the unique honey ice cream. The limited wine list includes organic mead and elderflower wine.

The Hive on the Quay is a welcome haven from the madding crowd and none can argue with Sarah's policy of 'mobile phones unwelcome!'

MEALS: L 12-3; D 6-9 August only
Closed: Mid Sept - Spring Bank Holiday
Cards: Visa and Mastercard
CHEF/PROPRIETOR: Sarah Holgate
LOCAL INTEREST: Georgian harbour town, sea aquarium, Llanerchaeron walled garden, lobster boat trips.

64   Aberdovey

The Bear of Amsterdam

9 Sea View Terrace
Aberdovey
Gwynedd
LL35 0LW
Tel: 01654 767684

This tiny fish and chip shop is proudly declared by happy locals to serve the best for miles around. Named after a ship and not a mammal, it almost hides away on the front at Aberdovey with a cheerful dining room of pine tables and chairs and a window looking out across the estuary, probably only yards from where its namesake moored.

It serves all-day breakfast, soup of the day and various sandwiches, plain or toasted.

But its pride is fresh cod and chips which are both excellent. No more to be said, except perhaps that every town and village should have one!

MEALS: All Day; approx £5
Closed: Monday
CHEF: George Smith. PROPRIETOR: Anna Smith
LOCAL INTEREST: Water sports and golf.

65 Aberdovey

Panteidal Organic Garden Restaurant

Aberdovey
North Gwynedd
LL35 0RG
Tel: 01654 767322
Fax: 01654 767322

e-mail:
office@panteidal.co.uk
www.panteidalorganics.co.uk

Make no mistake! This is not a garden centre cafe but a delightful and outstanding restaurant in a bewitching small garden of winding paths and secret ponds. It is probably unique in Wales, being 100% organic in all it offers from sherry, gin, cider and beer to marvellous salads and vegetables and cooked in winning style by Sheila Mathias and her assistant.

The restaurant is housed in a converted barn with immaculate tables covered in dark green cloths, modern bird prints on the walls and down one side windows and French doors onto the garden.

There is comfortable pine seating and a new rough-slate floor.

It is a special joy on a mild day to come here for lunch, gaze at the garden through the open doors, sip a glass of champagne and await perhaps a spinach and Stilton crepe or a platter of smoked fish, both with salads of just-picked leaves and herbs. Follow these with sliced chicken breast cooked in white wine, cream and tarragon or a special of the day such as brisket cooked in red wine, accompanied by up to seven fresh vegetables and potatoes cooked two ways.

Puddings range from banana and apricot crumble with thick cream to cappuccino ice cream with cinnamon wholemeal shortbread. Welsh cheeses are of course on offer.

The wine list is extensive with a good number available by the glass.

It bears repeating that everything is organically produced, which is a remarkable achievement, and nearby, are an organic food shop, garden centre and self-catering chalets.

MEALS: L 12.30-3 from £4; D 7-9.30 from £4
Closed: Monday, Tuesday and all November
Cards: All major
CHEF: Fleur Wells. PROPRIETOR: Sheila Mathias
WTB: Awaiting grading
Rooms: 3 self catering chalets, £50 S, £65 D

LOCAL INTEREST: Sandy beaches, Aberdovey golf club, sailing, walking, bird watching, steam railways, fishing.

66 Aberdovey

Robert and Sally Hughes have made famous this black-and-white old inn by the Dovey Estuary, where the sea laps almost at the doors. It is both a traditional pub with excellent beers and snacks and hotel with a serious restaurant. Every year it plays host to locals and visitors from all over the world – a relaxed and informal place.

Restaurant dinners offer three courses, with cheeses of Welsh and English origin as an optional extra. As you would expect, the freshest fish features strongly, for example in crab and avocado or melon with prawn starters and in four or more main-course offerings of the day's catch – perhaps baked cod with a roast pepper, haddock with prawns

Penhelig Arms Hotel and Restaurant

Aberdovey
North Gwynedd
LL35 0LT
Tel: 01654 767215
Fax: 01654 767690

e-mail:
penheligarms@saqnet.co.uk

and velouté sauce and seared salmon or tuna fillets. Admirable Gressingham duck, local lamb and Welsh Black beef are usually available as well as vegetarian options all in generous portions. Delicious puddings range from poached pears and ice cream with butterscotch sauce to bread and butter pudding and lemon tart. This is not fussy nor cutting-edge cuisine but simple and skillful use of good fresh ingredients and local produce wherever possible.

Whilst the quality of raw materials has not faltered, the menu has somehow become a little unadventurous; the skills are there and we should be able to peruse the dinner menu with a sense of excitement! Staff remain as pleasant, welcoming and skilled as ever.

The wine list is one of the finest in the country, with 300 items, including 40 half-bottles and ten or a dozen house wines for under £10 (or by the glass) – reflecting Robert's great enthusiasm and knowledge.

MEALS: L 12-2 from £3.95; D 7-9 £21
Closed: 25–26th December
Cards: Visa, Mastercard, Switch
CHEF: J Howkins. PROPRIETOR: Robert Hughes
WTB: 3 ★★★
Rooms: 10, £39.50 S, £52 D, £55 Suites

LOCAL INTEREST: Water sports, Snowdonia National Park, narrow guage railways.

67 Aberystwyth

Conrah Country House Hotel

Rhydgaled
Chancery
Aberystwyth
Ceredigion
SY23 4DF
Tel: 01970 617941
Fax: 01970 624546

e-mail: hotel@conrah.freeserve
www.hotel@conrah.co.uk

A family-run concern, this hotel has an easy-going charm. Set amidst beautiful rolling hills, the dining-room has a magnificent view. Peaceful in the extreme, from the cosy bar and its rattan furniture, to a lounge with large comfortable furnishings, it would be simple to book in here and never move on.

Stephen West has cooked for a decade and his modern British style sits well with local ingredients and produce, with fresh fish, Welsh beef, lamb and venison to the fore.

Sunday lunch is good value and has become a great favourite with locals; featuring melon, Carmarthen ham and cranberry dressing, followed by a medley of fish, perhaps salmon, monkfish and brill on a lobster bisque. Vegetables are crisp with the cauliflower coated in a mustard and Y Fenni cheese sauce.

Puddings cover old favourites like apricot sticky toffee pudding with butterscotch sauce, pineapple fritters with dark chocolate sauce and brandy snap basket with roasted figs and honey ice cream.

Well worth reading, an extensive wine list offers some fine choices by the glass.

Coffee, taken in the lounge with the papers to read and abundant peace and quiet, is excellent.

The Conrah suits everyone and is a particular favourite for special occasions, from birthdays to weddings.

MEALS: L 12-2 £4 £12; D 7-9 £24 £30
Closed: Christmas week
Cards: All major
CHEF: Stephen West. PROPRIETOR: Mr F. J. Heading
WTB: 4 ★★★★
Rooms: 17, £70-£80 S, £100-£135 D

LOCAL INTEREST: Rheiddol railway, National Library, golf, horse riding, Ceredigion coatline.

68 Aberystwyth

Harry's at Swn-y-Don

40-42 North Parade
Aberystwyth
Ceredigion
SY23 2NF
Tel: 01970 612647

Come to Harry's on a Saturday night and there is a real buzz. The dining-room is full to the brim, the chatter animated and the pace metropolitan (possibly slightly too much for those wishing to linger). Lunches are served as well as an early evening menu bistro-style.

Starters may include soup, rillettes of duck and pork with an onion marmalade and crispy prawns in batter with garlic mayonnaise dip.

Main dishes offer classic Tournedos Rossini on a crouton topped with pâté, grilled goat's cheese on herb-roasted flat mushrooms with a hot salad of potato gnocchi and vegetables, or a navarin of king prawns and seafood (fillets of smoked and unsmoked white fish and salmon) in a saffron sauce.

Desserts are a dream, from comforting bread and butter pudding with a zingy apricot sauce, deliciously moist warm cherry and almond tart (with excellent pastry) and served with a beautiful pale-green pistachio ice cream, or a good old-fashioned knickerbocker glory. Some may find the wine list a little disappointing, especially if relying on its descriptions – the Gewurztraminer is amazingly sweet!

A menu devoid of any mention of local or Welsh produce is peppered with sometimes misleading Gallicisms, as in "navarin" of seafood – the French for 'mutton stew'. A pity, for French usage is no more "à la mode!"

MEALS: L 12-2.30 £9.00 for 2 courses; D 6-10 £18 for 3 courses
Closed: Monday
Cards: All major
CHEF/PROPRIETOR: Harry Hughes
Rooms: 14, £17.50 S, b&b

LOCAL INTEREST: Castle, Devils Bridge Falls.

69 Aberystwyth

There was a time when good places to eat were few and far between in Aberystwyth but a number of good eateries have recently sprouted here and Serendipity is one of them.

The cool clean look of the striking deep-blue and white interior and the conservatory-like extension proclaim Serendipity's allegiance to its

Mid Wales

Serendipity

14 Cambrian Place
Aberystwyth
Ceredigion
SY23 INT
Tel: 01970 625777

up-to-the-minute world-cuisine menu. The dishes have been drawn and fused from North Africa, Greece, South-East Asia, India, Mexico and Scandinavia – to name but a few – and Welsh lamb and local mussels also stand shoulder to shoulder with the other UN delegates.

The world tour can begin with dolmades filled with rice, pine nuts and feta served on a minted tomato salsa, Malay chicken satay or gravadlax of salmon roulade with fresh herbs and cream cheese. The next port of call might be a Moroccan chicken parcel with lime and coriander dip served with sesame sautéed potato wedges, duck breast in plum and elderberry sauce served with honey-roast root vegetables and fresh broccoli, or rack of lamb with a watercress and mint oil served with couscous and ratatouille.

The chef's own vegetarian platter is served with dips, salsa and dressed salad. A cooling trio of fruit sorbets in a brandy basket, rich chocolate and Tia Maria truffle cake, or a wholesome-sounding prune, apple and port wine cake with almond streusel topping might be your choice for desert.

All will be delivered promptly – a little too much at times, but then it is better to ask the waitress to return than fail to get her attention at all!

MEALS: L 11.45-2 £8; D 7-9 £18
Closed: Sunday, Monday, Tuesday, Wednesday evenings and Sunday and Monday.
Cards: All major
CHEF: Rant Kurdi. PROPRIETOR: Julie Roberts

LOCAL INTEREST: Centre for Alternative Technology, seaside town of Aberystwyth.

70 Aberystwyth

The Treehouse

14 Baker Street
Aberystwyth
Ceredigion
SY23 2BT
Tel: 01970 615791

e-mail:
jane@treehouse12freeserve.co.uk

The Treehouse is something of an institution in Aberystwyth. More than a shop-cum-restaurant, it is an ambitious project exploring another way of living – an attempt "to find real solutions for food, farming, the local community and the countryside" and "committed to fair trading principles, sustainable business practices and to supporting the local economy".

The food provided for the bustling shop, as well as the restaurant, is organic, non-GMO and much of it local; some is grown in the Treehouse's own market garden and meat comes from Graig Farm in Powys.

The restaurant upstairs attracts a mixed crowd: stern-looking politicians, instant-media-pundits, reflexologists and landladies-who-lunch. The standard lunch menu offers several types of hearty soup with home-baked roll and butter, vegeburger in a bap, Indian appetiser selection, pizza, quiche and baked pitta bread and rolls with various fillings. A selection of specials might include lentil bake topped with leek and mushroom cream sauce served with side salad, coriander and Welsh pork meatballs served with ratatouille or leek and

mushroom sauce on a bed of organic buckwheat fettuccini and a spicy Moroccan chickpea wrap with salad.

Organic sparkling drinks, beer, wine, tea and coffee are available.

The restaurant is also open three evenings a week, when there are usually more meat and fish dishes on the menu. The emphasis on the quality of the ingredients is not always matched by the care taken in preparation and lunch often represents better value than dinner.

MEALS: L 12-4 £5; D 6.30-9 £15
Closed: Dec 25-Jan 1
Cards: All major
CHEF/PROPRIETOR: Jane Burnham

71 Brecon

Brecon Beacons Mountain Centre

Libanus
Brecon
Powys
LD3 8ER
Tel: 01874 624979
Fax: 01874 624515

e-mail:
andrew.powell@breconbeacons

A bonus on a fine day and a refuge on a wet one, the café at the National Park mountain centre in the Brecon Beacons will revive any flagging spirits. It offers a full range of snacks and meals in a bright, cheerful setting with the most wonderful views of Pen-y-Fan, the highest mountain in southern Britain.

Under the competent management of Andrew Powell, the 'Welshness' of this small restaurant is well-researched and authentic. All the snacks, cakes and meals are home-made on site, with Welsh wines, beers and a range of jams and preserves also on sale.

Fresh soups, toasted sandwiches, jacket potatoes, quiches; aubergine and red lentil moussaka, pies made from local beef and lamb faggots in a rich onion gravy can be supplemented by these exemplary home-made cakes and scones.

Versatility is the key to success here; any number can be catered for; private parties, barbecues and packed lunches. Children have their own menu and Sunday lunch is generally packed too!

MEALS: L 12-3.30 from £3.75
Closed: Christmas Day
Cards: All major
CHEF/MANAGER: Andrew Powell
LOCAL INTEREST: Great views of Pen y Fan, good walks.

72 Brecon

An imposing town house that dates back to the 17th Century, Cantre Selyf, amongst Brecon's most historic buildings, is certainly one of the town's best-known properties, with its large walled garden edged by the Norman town wall. Inside, the owners have created a comfortable atmosphere with stylish decor, Georgian fireplaces, oak

Cantre Selyf

5 Lion Street
Brecon
Powys
LD3 7AU

Tel: 01874 622904
Fax: 01874 622315
e-mail:
enquirie@cantreselyf
www.cantreselyf.co.uk

beams, moulded ceilings, antique furniture and old family portraits. The three guest bedrooms are charming, the welcome is warm (even from the elderly dog) and the hosts take pleasure in sharing their unique home. Even though it is situated in the town centre, it has an air of tranquillity that makes for a restful break.

The food is home-cooked using local produce. Breakfast can be traditional Welsh, with home-made muffins and pancakes or locally baked croissants and bread. Picnickers' and walkers' packed lunches include fresh bread, home-made soup and locally produced cheese, ham, pasties and pies.

Dinner is an optional extra for guests (and good value too) and, when she is cooking for residents, Helen Roberts is happy to accept bookings from non-residents. A typical three-course meal might start with roasted red pepper soup or prawn, mango and avocado salad. Follow with pork fillet stuffed with plums on creamy wilted spinach, pan-fried cod with lime and coriander dressing or spinach and ricotta pancakes with tomato and basil sauce.

For dessert, there might be twice-baked chocolate soufflé with Irish cream or passion fruit tartlet with mandarin ice cream.

To accompany the meal, a selection of quality wines is very fairly priced.

MEALS: L; Packed on request. D 7.30 £15
Closed: December and January
Cards: None
CHEF/PROPRIETOR: Helen Roberts
WTB: 4 ★★★★
Rooms: 3 en-suite £56 D

LOCAL INTEREST: Brecon Beacons, Llangoise Lake.

73 Llyswen

Llangoed Hall Country House

Llyswen
Brecon
Powys
LD3 0YP
Tel: 01874 754525
Fax: 01874 754545
e-mail:
llangoed_hall_co_wales_uk@compuserve.com
www. llangoedhall.com

One of Wales's great bargains is the set lunch at this lovely house; it is an irresistable combination! Llangoed Hall is one of Clough William Ellis's most successful creations – full of space and light and elegantly filled with good furniture and interesting paintings. The kitchen is in excellent form, the staff charming and unobtrusively skilled.

An encyclopaedic wine list, including many half-bottles also offers a useful page of house selections and champagne by the glass. Throughout there are very useful tasting notes.

Dinner offers choice between a set three-course no-choice meal with an intervening sorbet, or an impressive "gourmet menu" with wider options.

The set lunch offers a choice at each stage – perhaps chicken liver and foie gras parfait or the excellent house gravadlax of salmon with a stunning orange and cardamom sauce, followed by rump of lamb or polenta and herb-coated cod on spring onion mash with a remarkably subtle Pernod and chive velouté.

Finally, in all cases a pudding or selection of cheeses in prime condition. The cafetière of coffee with house chocolates does not come much better, either.

The dining room, with its yellow-green decor sets off the food wonderfully and amid the grandeur are one or two beguiling small food paintings – one of oysters open on a plate and another amusing one of fish and a lemon on a napkin.

MEALS: L 12.15-2 £16.50; Sunday L; 12.15-2 £23.50,
D 7-9.30 £37.50 / £42.50
Cards: All major
CHEF: Daniel James. MANAGER: Graham Steel
WTB: 5 ★★★★★ Country Inn
Rooms: 23, from £110 S, from £145 D, from £295 Suites

LOCAL INTEREST: Brecon Jazz Festival, Hay Festival of Literature, walking, riding, shooting, fishing, golf, scenic drives to Powis Castle and other Mid Wales locations.

74 Brecon

Waterfront Bistro

Theatre Brycheiniog
Canal Wharf
Brecon
Powys
LD3 7EW
Tel: 01874 611866

Take a short stroll from the centre of the busy market town of Brecon and appreciate the delightful setting of this café-cum-bistro. Its home is the theatre, which overlooks the attractively restored basin at the north end of the Brecon and Abergavenny canal.

A café by day, it offers cakes, snacks and lunches such as soup, vegetable or meat lasagne, nut roast, stuffed pancakes and vegetable strudel. A blackboard announces with pride that all the food is home-made using local suppliers and producers and that coeliacs, vegans and vegetarians can be catered for.

In the evening, the Waterfront becomes a bustling pre-theatre bistro, where dishes are imaginative and well cooked, portions are generous and service is friendly and efficient. Dining takes place between 6pm and the final call to theatre at 7.30pm (but phone first to check).

Starters might be salmon pâté with thick melba toast, broccoli mousse or smoked chicken with bacon lardons and raspberry vinaigrette.

To follow, try pork steak and button onions with triple mustard and brandy sauce, spinach and feta cheese cannelloni, or Y Fenni cheese and asparagus tartlet with tomato vinaigrette. Desserts include traditional favourites – chocolate fudge pudding, lemon meringue pie and sticky toffee pudding – or a trio of Welsh ice creams.

There is a limited choice of draught beers, some bottled continental lagers and a short wine list with a global selection that provides particularly good value.

MEALS: L 11-4 £6-£12; D 5.30 £9-£15
Closed: Sundays except July and August
Cards: All major
CHEF/MANAGER: Clare Graham

LOCAL INTEREST: Brecon and Abergavenny canal, Theatre Brycheiniog.

75 Brecon

Three Cocks Hotel and Restaurant

Brecon
Powys
LD3 0SL
Tel: 01497 847215
Fax: 01497 847339

Situated on the A438 between Brecon and Hay-on-Wye, this 15th century inn is reputedly built around a tree. Outside is a cobbled forecourt with an old mounting block, whilst its interior exudes an air of calm elegance, with old oak beams, open fires and a comfortable light-wood-panelled lounge. The spacious restaurant has tapestries hanging on stone walls, an enormous armoire and classical music playing in the background. Service is charming and unobtrusive, and if the style of its classic French cooking has a Belgian influence, it comes from the owners' Anglo-Belgian roots.

There is no bar so instead relax in the lounge with drinks and complimentary canapés and peruse the menu.

To start, there might be a soup of wild mussels with small vegetables, served from large tureens, followed by wood mushrooms with soured cream in puff pastry, Scottish king scallops with garlic butter, or fish from the market.

For main course choose from loin of Welsh lamb on a cake of cauliflower, roast red-legged partridge on cabbage or cassoulet of wild boar with seasonal fruits.

Dessert might include apple mousse on a cinnamon biscuit with ginger caramel sauce, iced nougat with blackcurrant sauce, and a creamy savoury of grilled goat's cheese on a croute with honey.

The wine list is predominantly French with a superb choice including St Emilion, St Estèphe and a classic Pauillac. Belgian beers include Leffe, Galoise, Chimay and Rochfort.

MEALS: L 12-1.30 £28; D 7-9 £28
Closed: Tuesday, December, January
Cards: Visa
CHEF/PROPRIETOR: Mr and Mrs Winstone

LOCAL INTEREST: Walking, canoeing, browsing in Hay bookshops.

76 Brecon Beacons

On arriving at this family-run hotel, pause to admire the vast expanse of lawn and the stylishly arranged garden furniture. Inside, the atmosphere is informal, with a bar at the front of the building and a comfortable bistro-style restaurant decorated in sunny, Mediterranean colours at the rear. The same menu applies throughout.

Starters include Cajun sweet potato fries with cream cheese and chive dip, marinated herring fillets with new potato and dill salad,

Nant Ddu Lodge Hotel

Cwm Taf
Nr Merthyr Tydfil
Brecon Beacons
Powys
CF48 2HY
Tel: 01685 379111
Fax: 01685 377088

e-mail: enquiries@
nant-ddu-lodge.co.uk
ww.nant-ddu-lodge.co.uk

Jamaican prawn cocktail with toasted pine nuts, and seared guinea fowl in sweet potato and saffron mash.

The day's specials might be grilled fish in bouillabaisse broth with rouille, pan-fried pigeon breasts on honey-roasted parsnips and Madeira and thyme sauce, or chargrilled king scallop and bacon brochettes with caper and olive salsa, and for vegetarians focaccia pizza with wild mushrooms, spinach, mozzarella and Parmesan. Old favourites such as chicken supreme stuffed with Stilton, shank of Welsh lamb braised with beer, garlic and thyme and chargrilled steaks come with a choice of potatoes; vegetables are extra and can be unimaginative.

If you can find room for dessert, try Swiss apple and almond cake with honey and Calvados Mascarpone, or chocolate and hazelnut torte with praline custard. Or choose Welsh cheese with bara brith.

The wine list – it is carefully chosen and good value, with a selection of half-bottles.

MEALS: L 12-2.30 £7-£15; Sunday L 12-2.30 £10 £20;
D 6.30-9.30 £10-£20
Cards: All
CHEF: Mark Coniron. PROPRIETOR: Daniel Robson
WTB: 4 ★★★★
Rooms: 22, £55-£67.50 S, £69.50-£89.50 D

LOCAL INTEREST: Brecon Beacons National Park and waterfall country.

77 Builth Wells

Trericket Mill Vegetarian Guest House

Erwood
Builth Wells
Powys
LD2 3TQ
Tel: 01982 560312
Fax: 01982 560768

e-mail:
mail@trericket.co.uk
www.trericket.co.uk

An overnight stay is necessary to enjoy the excellent vegetarian food served at this Grade 2 listed water corn mill overlooking the River Wye on the A470, just south of Erwood. Accommodation includes en suite bed and breakfast (wooden beds are hand-made by a local craftsman), a bunk room and camping. It is a regular stop-off for walkers and cyclists, as tiles and flagstones line the ground floor. The furnishings – a pleasing mixture of comfortable and utilitarian – are perfectly in keeping with the industrial history of the building.

The owners are committed to a way of life that includes organic, free-range and whole foods. Breakfast in the dining room, complete with its original milling machinery, is self-service. There are cereals, juices and yogurt, followed by a cooked platter (try the bean, basil and tomato sausage), fresh hot croissants and baguettes with Welsh cheese and home-made jams, and perhaps a boiled or scrambled duck egg.

In the evening, residents can sample the great-value, three-course meal, starting perhaps with mushroom and hazelnut pâté or carrot and orange soup followed by Glamorgan sausage with port and orange sauce with rosemary potatoes or gabanzo (chick pea) and apricot stew with wild rice.

Finish with a hearty slice of Aberskithwin apple cake (apples from the

mill's brook-side orchard), home-made Baileys liqueur ice cream or chocolate fudge cake.

An extensive range of soft drinks and herb teas is available and the tap water comes from their own borehole. The mill is not licensed so guests are encouraged to bring their own wine.

MEALS: D 7-8 ish £12.50
Cards: None
CHEF/PROPRIETORS: Nicky and Alistair Legge
WTB: 2 ★★
Rooms: 3, £30-£32 S, £40-£44 D

LOCAL INTEREST: Walking, cycling, canoeing, pony trekking.

78 Crickhowell

The Bear Hotel

High Street
Crickhowell
Powys
NP8 1BW
Tel: 01873 810408
Fax: 01873 811696
e-mail: bearhotel@aol.com
www.bearhotel.co.uk

The Bear is a former coaching inn at the centre of Crickhowell, a delightful small market town on the banks of the River Usk between Brecon and Abergavenny. Its comfortable bars welcome you with cheering log fires in winter and coffee, real ales, good wines (most available by the glass) and excellent service all year round.

Blackboard bar meals might include home-boiled ham a freshly-made curry or Moroccan spiced lamb. The regular menu is extensive, with something for everyone – soup, sandwiches, baguettes, steaks, omelette with wild garlic and mushrooms, Caesar salad, Welsh rarebit on toasted olive bread with grilled bacon, baked fresh mackerel with rhubarb and sage crust and fishcakes of locally smoked haddock.

There are two restaurants, one small and cosy and the other in altogether grander style. Begin with a pot of cockles, mussels and laverbread baked with a puff pastry top, honey-roast parsnip and pancetta soup or gravadlax with a salad of cucumber, gherkins, capers and dill. To follow may be braised hock of Welsh lamb, fillet of Welsh Black beef with artichoke ravioli, or oven-baked breast of free-range chicken on home-made fettuccini.

Then you may be tempted by the house speciality – bread-and-butter pudding with bananas in flaming brandy and brown bread ice cream – or hazelnut parfait with a warm cassis-poached fig, home-made apple and whinberry pie, or a selection of good Welsh cheeses.

MEALS: L 11-2; D 7-9.30 Sunday Lunch 12-2
Cards: Amex, Access, Visa
CHEF: Anthony Jones. PROPRIETOR: Steve Hindmarsh
WTB: 3 ★★★
Rooms: 34, £49.50-£94 S, £65-£120 D, £120 Suites

LOCAL INTEREST: All outdoor activities.

79   Crickhowell

The Farmer's Arms

Cwmdu
Crickhowell
Powys
NP8 1RU
Tel: 01874 730464
e-mail: cwmdu@aol.com
www.thefarmersarms.com

This friendly roadside inn, now better known for its good food, consists of a small, cosy bar, a simply furnished restaurant and a beer garden. The bar has a typically Welsh feel with its flagstone floor, piano and large fireplace and you will be offered the usual range of beverages, including some Welsh real ales. On a busy evening, locals playing cards or a game of darts jostle with restaurant-goers in an atmosphere that is bustling and friendly.

Lunchtimes, as well as a ploughman's with Welsh farmhouse cheese, you may be offered braised pork belly in a plum sauce on mash, roast topside of local beef with Yorkshire pudding or fresh fish pie.

Evening options are chalked up on large blackboards in the restaurant. While making your choice, try a glass of their very palatable house wine. Start with baked flat mushrooms in garlic and chive butter, Greek-style salad or chicken liver pâté with redcurrant glaze. Steak-lovers are unusually spoilt for choice with several cuts of Welsh beef on offer, including T-bones. Alternatively, you may prefer braised shank of local lamb, chargrilled tuna topped with pesto or pan-roasted duck breast on a Thai stir-fry. There are usually a couple of vegetarian dishes, such as vegetable, herb and Brie puff parcels with red pepper sauce, or roast pepper, spinach and cheese tart (with crisp, buttery pastry) on Provencale sauce.

A choice of desserts rounds off a hearty meal or choose the Welsh cheeses served with celery, grapes and walnuts.

MEALS: L 12-2 from £4.95; Sunday L 12-3 £9.50; D 7-9.30 from £8.95
Closed: Monday lunch, Tuesday lunch October – March
Cards: All major
CHEF/PROPRIETOR: Andrew Lawrence
Rooms: 3, £15-£25 S, from £35 D, from £45 Suites

LOCAL INTEREST: Walking, trekking, Hay on Wye, Tretower Court, Brecon Beacons.

Mid Wales

80   Crickhowell

After a woodland drive (when it may be necessary to make way for a pheasant or two), visitors are rewarded with the sight of a spectacular Italian-style building in extensive grounds with breathtaking views over the River Usk. The Brabner family has run this comfortable mansion as a hotel for more than 50 years and the third generation has set about the task recently with renewed vigour.

The clientele returns often to enjoy fishing, golf, tennis, croquet or

Gliffaes Country House Hotel

Crickhowell
Powys
NP8 1RH
Tel: 01874 730371
Fax: 01874 730463
e-mail: calls@gliffaeshotel.com
www.gliffaeshotel.com

walking, and to enjoy, particularly, afternoon tea which can be taken outside overlooking the river.

The bar, with its large fireplace, is cosy and there are elegant drawing-rooms, although the wood-panelled restaurant has a slightly more solemn atmosphere. Expect to find starters such as Gressingham duck and juniper sausage with fried quail's egg, straw potatoes, and truffle oil, or glazed red pepper and goats' cheese roulade with smoked avocado sorbet and gazpacho sauce.

Main courses might include seared sea bass on a wild mushroom risotto with melting foie gras, Jerusalem artichoke and vanilla cream, pot-roast supreme of guinea fowl with garlic, thyme and rosemary, and double-baked polenta cake with aubergine caviar, roast red pepper coulis and mesclun leaves.

For dessert, there may be Eton Mess with strawberries, raspberries and Mascarpone or vanilla pod crème brulée with lavender ice cream and a tuile.

Dinner, although it can be fairly rich, is well balanced by a good selection of wines.

MEALS: L 12-2.30 from £8; Sunday L from 12.30 £18.50;
D from 7.30 £23.50
Cards: All major
CHEF: Iain Sampson. PROPRIETOR: Susie Suter
WTB: 3 ★★★
Rooms: 22, from £50-£60 S, from £61.20 D

LOCAL INTEREST: Tretower Court and Castle, Brecon Museums, local castles and Gliffaes's 33 acres of grounds and private fishing.

81 Crickhowell

Nantyffin Cider Mill Inn

Brecon Road
Crickhowell
Powys
NP8 1SP
Tel: 01873 810775
Fax: 01873 810775
e-mail: cidermill.co.uk

This 16th-century drovers' inn, a working cider mill until the 1960s, overlooks the river Usk, just west of Crickhowell. A sympathetic extension houses the restaurant, while the two bars have a welcoming pubby atmosphere. Fittingly, cider and scrumpy are well worth trying and real ale enthusiasts enjoy the fine range on tap. The wines, too, are innovative and good value, all available by the glass; each month one wine is featured and offered at a special price.

The Mill's reputation for good food holds true lunchtime or evening, for a snack or for two or three courses. An à la carte menu is supported by a list of blackboard dishes, many of which boast Welsh origins. Starters might include grilled Welsh goat's cheese on a toasted crouton with leeks and red wine dressing, naturally smoked haddock rarebit with leeks and Mozzarella, Moroccan spiced lamb, vegetable risotto, baked stuffed plum tomatoes, and pork black pudding terrine. Follow with roast rack of Old Spot pork, chargrilled rib-eye of Welsh Black, saddle of salt marsh lamb with a herb crust, wild mushrooms with feta and blue cheese, or a simply grilled whole lemon

sole. Finish with individual whinberry torte with Belgian chocolate sauce, caramelised rice pudding timbale with fresh cherry compote or lemon tart with lemon sorbet.

Service is informal – and sometimes too relaxed, when it can fail to live up to initial expectations.

MEALS: L 12-2.15; D 6.30-9.30
Closed: Monday
Cards: All
CHEF/PROPRIETOR: Sean Gerrard

---

82 Crickhowell

Ty Croeso

The Dardy
Llangattock
Crickhowell
Powys
NP8 1PU
Tel: 01873 810573
Fax: 01873 810573
e-mail:
tycroeso@
ty-croeso-hotel.freeserve.co.uk
www.wiz-to/tycroeso

Ty Croeso certainly lives up to its Welsh name (House of Welcome) and it is difficult to imagine that it was originally part of an austere Victorian workhouse. Situated on the steep hillside at Llangattock the views over Crickhowell are splendid.

The bar, with its log fire in winter, and restaurant, with its low lighting, light classical music and a Welsh dresser, contain a host of ornaments that would surely make the room looked cluttered if they weren't so tastefully arranged. In summer you may find yourself dining on the flower-filled terrace.

For those who like simple, honest food that is not over-garnished, the table d'hote "Taste of Wales" menu is well worth trying. For starters there may be Anglesey eggs, Black Mountain smoked duck breast, St Illtyd soft cheese mousse with apple and walnut salad, or oak-roasted salmon and leek cocotte. To follow, you may be tempted by Welsh salt marsh lamb shank braised in red wine, Welsh Black rump steak with Brecon blue cheese and leek and walnut sauce, or fillet of cod with laverbread herb crust and wine and laverbread sauce. Warm spiced pears with honey and lemon syllabub may follow or perhaps apple and blackberry crunchy nut crumble laced with Black Mountain liqueur. There is also an extensive selection of Welsh cheeses and wines. To finish, coffee comes with home-made fudge; all making for a very good value Welsh eating experience.

MEALS: L by appointment, please call; D 7-9 £16.95
Closed: 2 weeks, January
Cards: All major
CHEF: Karen Moore. PROPRIETORS: Ian and Mandy Moore
WTB: 3 ★★★
Rooms: 8, £35 S, £60-70 D

LOCAL INTEREST: Walks in Black Mountains and Brecon Beacons, red kite country, close to Hay on Wye and Big Pit.

83 Elan Valley

Elan Valley Hotel

Elan Valley
Nr Rhayader
Powys
LD6 5HN

Tel: 01597 810448
Fax: 01597 810448

e-mail:
hotel@elanvalley.demon.co.uk
www.elanvalleyhotel.co.uk

Wacky perhaps...zany certainly! This fine old, rather scruffy house by the river, almost in the shadow of the great dam, gives the odd sensation that you have wandered on to a rather shaky movie set yet it is a warmly welcoming place and you soon feel a member of the cast!

Food and drink are taken seriously – good beers in variety and well-chosen wines with good house selections.

If the pink-and-purple dining room is a stage set, the adjoining bar, for those who can remember, is Scottish west highland 1950s! What is provided in both is well worthwhile – good bar snacks at lunchtime and a daily-changing à la carte dinner.

Vegetarians are well catered for in starters of celery and Stilton soup, or roasted fennel with Parmesan and in main courses of Mediterranean vegetable ragout with coconut and coriander or chestnut and mushroom pie in red wine gravy.

Carnivores are treated to daube of Welsh Black beef, local lamb and chicken dishes and huge chargrilled tuna steaks with good fresh salsa.

Puddings range from sorbets and ice creams to banoffi pie and amaretto cheesecake.

The cooking does not pretend to great finesse but is wholesome and generous in its use of fresh ingredients – a boon to travellers to this beautiful and remote part of mid-Wales.

MEALS: L 12-2.30 £2.50-£8.50; D 7-9 £15-£25
Closed: One week in January
Cards: All except Amex and Diners
CHEFS: Anthony Ollman, Martin Ritchie, Pippa Boss.
PROPRIETORS: Pippa Boss and Louise Osborn
WTB: 2 ★★
Rooms: 11, from £32 S, from £55 D, from £70 Suites
LOCAL INTEREST: Gierinfarm kite centre, Welsh Royal Crystal, Elan Valley for walking, cycling, bird watching and other outdoor pursuits.

84 Felin Fach

The Griffin

Felin Fach
Nr Brecon
Brecknockshire
LD3 0UB
Tel: 01874 620111
Fax: 01874 620120

e-mail:
enquires@eatdrinksleep.ltd.uk
www.eatdrinksleep.ltd.uk

This country inn, the outside of which is painted brick red, is situated on the A470 just north of Brecon. Inside are open log fires, haphazard terracotta floors and an eclectic mix of old and new furniture, some pieces of which are more comfortable than others. Church pews, a school desk, an old filing cabinet, an enormous wooden chest and a piano are to be found dotted around the ground floor. From the bar are local ales and plenty of carefully selected wines, many of which are available by the glass, including a pudding wine. The restaurant has a cosy atmosphere, simply laid tables and terracotta-painted stone walls.

A short menu changes only occasionally (you get the feeling that each dish has been perfected), with contemporary and uncomplicated

food served simply but elegantly on large white shallow dishes.

For starters, try beetroot tarte tatin with crème fraiche, salmon and leek tart with sun-dried tomato mayonnaise, wood pigeon with wild mushrooms and puy lentils, celeriac soup and soda bread, or roast turbot with creamed leeks and truffle and chive oil.

To follow, choose from roast hake with grilled fennel and grain mustard cream, navarin of lamb with autumn vegetables and new potatoes, rib-eye of beef with chips and bearnaise, warm couscous salad with roast pepper dressing, or chicken breast with pearl barley, lemon and thyme.

Desserts are simple but superb – try the glazed lemon tart, chocolate mousse or crème brulée. Alternatively, opt for the selection of fine Welsh cheeses, which are served with mini celery sticks and good-quality biscuits.

MEALS: L 12-2.30 £7-£8; D 7-9.30 £16
Closed: Mondays
Cards: All
CHEF: Charles Inkin
PROPRIETORS: Hugh Evans Bevan and Charles Inkin
WTB: 4 ★★★★
Rooms: 7, £49.50-£73 D b&b

LOCAL INTEREST: All outward bound activities such as walking, climbing, fishing, shooting. Visits to Brecon and Hay.

85 Lampeter

Dremddu Fawr Creuddyn Bridge

Lampeter
Ceredigion
SA48 8BL
Tel: 01570 470394

Take a busy person like Ann Williams-Jones and ask her to fit yet more into her day, and what do you get but a positive answer? "We need to refurbish the farmhouse and I want to cook for more people and keep up the part-time job in Aberswyth."

Ann trained as a cook, spent some years in Switzerland and now cooks like a wizard for her guests, often trying out new recipes and yet turning her hand to the favourites that regular customers request. The farmhouse has, at the moment, just one guest bedroom, so she prepares meals both for locals and visitors staying nearby.

Dinner might begin with a Welsh cheese soufflé served with salad, or grilled goat's cheese followed by quails stuffed with rice, apricots and cranberries followed by roast Welsh lamb marinated in orange juice, mint and mead. Puddings are rich and delicious, such as the syrup cake with poached pears and raspberry coulis.

Welsh breakfast contains all the usual ingredients as well as muesli based on a Swiss recipe in which the oats are soaked overnight in apple juice. Scrambled eggs might be served with locally smoked salmon, cockles and laverbread together with home-made marmalade, jams, rolls and honey from the local honey farm.

Ann is a champion of local foods and has recently added locally made sausages and organic bacon to her shopping list.

93

MEALS: L; D 6.30-8
Closed: End December - March
Cards: Most
CHEF: Ann Williams-Jones
WTB: ★★
Rooms: £42 D

LOCAL INTEREST: Cheesemaking on local farms, sheep dog drials, red kite area, woollen mills and museum, market towns.

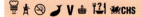

86 Llandrindod Wells

Guidfa House

Crossgates
Llandrindod Wells
Powys
LD1 6RF
Tel: 01597 851241
Fax: 01597 851875
e-mail:
guidfa@globalnet.co.uk
www.guidfa-house.co.uk

Expect a warm welcome from charming host Tony Millan, runner-up in the AA's Landlord of the Year Award 2000, on arrival at this elegant Georgian guest house, conveniently located three miles north of Llandrindod Wells at the junction of the A44 and A483.

Thoroughly deserving his accolade, Tony offers tea and biscuits in the lounge, dispenses pre-prandial drinks from the bar, discreetly waits on tables in the dining room and finds time to turn down your bed and pop a chocolate on your pillow while you relax over coffee and mints in front of the crackling log fire.

His wife Anne, a Cordon Bleu-trained chef, uses fresh local produce in creating an interesting blend of modern and traditional dishes. Her set, three-course dinners might offer warm smoked chicken salad with pesto dressing, grilled Pencarreg cheese with redcurrant relish, or smoked salmon roulade with hollandaise for starters, followed by rack of Welsh lamb with orange, port and cranberry gravy, pork tenderloin stuffed with prunes and almonds and served with apple gravy, or crispy duck breast with green peppercorn sauce. Accompanying fresh vegetables, often including dauphinoise potatoes, are well chosen to complement each dish.

Home-made puddings are deliciously naughty; so try her memorable lemon mousse cake with mango coulis or, perhaps, the rum and banana bread-and-butter pudding.

There's one catch; that to sample Anne's cooking, you will have to stay the night!

MEALS: L; D 7-8 £17.50
Cards: Visa, Mastercard
CHEF: Anne Millan
WTB: 4 ★★★★
Rooms: 6, £31 S, £53 D

LOCAL INTEREST: Elan Valley, RSPB Red Kite feeding centre, golf course, indoor and outdoor bowling, rally driving courses.

87 Llandrindod Wells

The Herb Garden

Spa Road
Llandrindod Wells
Powys
LD1 5EY
Tel: 01597 824737

e-mail:
ann@herbgardencafe.co.uk
www.herbgardencafe.co.uk

Llandrindod Wells is the ideal meeting place for travellers from north and south Wales and it seems that most meet in this lively vegetarian cafe, jostling for table space with the locals. Fridays are particularly busy after the early morning market.

Solid wooden tables, bare board floors and friendly, efficient service offer confidence that the food will be good too; and it is.

From breakfast through to tea, and open two nights as well, the flexible menu is based on fresh ingredients. The vegetarian breakfast consists of beans, toast, sausages, mushrooms, egg and tomatoes. A range of cakes such as lemon drizzle, apricot slice, apple cake and chocolate and walnut brownie tempt throughout the day.

Sandwiches made from organic white, malthouse and granary bread are available with a choice of margarines, low-fat or non-dairy.

The lunch menu offers a good choice of baked potatoes, falafel or houmus and salads, with daily options chalked up on the board.

Soup might be red pepper served with an organic roll, followed by ratatouille pancakes with tomato or white sauce, a special salad and sandwich of the day, filled for example, with pan-fried halloumi, basil and tomato. Soft drinks and fruit juices are offered in abundance.

MEALS: L 12-2.30 from £3.95; D 7.30-10 £12 approx
Closed: All evenings except Saturday, Sunday all day
Cards: None
CHEF/PROPRIETOR: Ann Stevenson

LOCAL INTEREST: Heart of Wales, Elan valley, Hay on Wye, Welsh show ground, historic spa town and lake, kite feeding centre.

88 Llandysul

Penbontbren Farm Hotel

Glynarthen
Nr. Cardigan
Llandysul
Ceredigion
SA44 6PE
Tel: 01239 810245
Fax: 01239 811129

New owners Miles and Jackie Glossop intend to keep faith with the well established traditions of this pleasantly converted farm. Its museum still contains many artefacts used here over the years and the restaurant, once a hay barn, now sports re-pointed stone walls and a cheerful atmosphere.

Welsh produce features heavily and is imaginatively used, as in laverbread pancakes with asparagus and cheese and Black Mountain smoked salmon served with fennel mayonnaise. Smoked chicken and goose breast with crab-apple and redcurrant shows adventure and the choice for vegetarians is impressive. Port and Stilton pâté and wild mushrooms in a creamy sauce are among the options.

Chicken breast with prune and bacon cream sauce, lamb cutlets, Halibut with dill sauce and Welsh Black fillet Diane all describe the traditional side of the menu, while vegetarians get a whole page of imaginative choices to themselves.

The dessert trolley hovers nearby, perhaps too close for comfort, displaying a tempting variety; lemon layer cake, meringues with fruits of the forest and fruit crumble and custard with Welsh cheeses an available alternative.

Easier to find than you might expect, the hotel is well worth a trip through country lanes north of Cardigan.

MEALS: L by prior arrangement; D 7-9 £15
Closed: please call
Cards: All
PROPRIETORS: Miles and Jackie Glossop
WTB: 3 ★★★
Rooms: 10 en-suite
LOCAL INTEREST: Farm Museum and Cardigan Coast.

89 Llanfihangel yng Ngwynfa

Cyfie Farm

Llanfihangel yng Ngwynfa
Nr Llanfyllin
Powys
SY22 5JE
Tel: 01691 648451
Fax: 01691 648363

Hospitality to strangers lies at the heart of any civilised society and George and Lyn Jenkins epitomise this in rural Wales. Cyfie Farm has been their home for 40 years, and for the past 20, they have been welcoming guests here, adding to its facilities for visitors year by year.

The guest suites are warm and comfortable, with immaculate bathrooms and furnishings. You eat both dinner and breakfast in the house with your hosts in their simply elegant dining room. Dinner is a set four-courses although Lyn always checks to see if you have any special requirements or dislikes.

Start perhaps with a light soufflé, perhaps asparagus and Stilton and move on to rack of lamb or seared chicken on an authentic salsa made from home-grown tomatoes with generous portions of flavoured vegetables.

Pudding might be a bread-and-butter special or a tower of shortbread rounds sandwiched with seasonal fruit, cream and ice cream. Finally, a plate of four Welsh cheeses arrives almost unnoticed while you have been enjoying the company and conversation of these gracious hosts.

Breakfast is all you could wish, with porridge, farm bacon and eggs from literally next door – all astonishingly good value!

MEALS: D 7 £16
Closed: January and February
CHEF/PROPRIETOR: Lyn Jenkins
WTB: 5 ★★★★★
Rooms: 4, £28 D, £30-£33 short breaks

LOCAL INTEREST: Lake Vyrnwy, RSPB centre, National Trust properties.

90 Llanfyllin

An astonishingly secret part of Wales, this is in fact an easy drive from Bala, Chester, Shrewsbury, Welshpool or Llangollen and remains largely

Seeds

5 Penybryn Cottage
High Street
Llanfyllin
Powys
SY22 5AP
Tel: 01691 648604

and unjustifiably unknown. Llanfyllin is a little gem of a town in the rolling countryside of the Berwyns and graced for the last decade by Mark and Felicity Seager's old pink brick, beamed cottage restaurant. Morning coffee is served and lunch from the blackboard offers home-potted shrimps, home-made soups, smoked salmon and warm salad of black pudding, followed by local lamb and beef.

Three course dinner includes excellent cafetière coffee in the price. Mark cooks simply without pretension and he produces good terrines, gravadlax and seductive warm salads. Local lamb and beef come with simple sauces as well as excellent fish – for example, seared tuna with Mediterranean vegetables.

Puddings encompass bread-and-butter, home-made ice creams, a fruit platter, treacle tart and classic crème brulée that is a lesson in perfection.

Seeds offers Welsh cheeses augmented by Stilton and Shropshire Blue because they feel Wales still needs to produce a more varied range. There must be an opening here for Berwyn Blue, and Finn from mid-Wales.

The short wine list is augmented by wines of the week and an impressive list of malt whiskies.

Seeds is an honest place and deserves better recognition in this under-rated part of the country.

MEALS: L 11-2; D 7-9 £19.95
Closed: Monday
Cards: Visa, Mastercard
CHEF: Mark Seager. PROPRIETORS: Mark and Felicity Seager

LOCAL INTEREST: Lake Vyrnwy, Myllins Well, Ann Griffiths Walk.

91 Llangammarch Wells

Lake Country House

Llangammarch Wells
Powys
LD4 4BS
Tel: 01591 620202
Fax: 01591 620457

e-mail:
info@lakecountryhouse.co.uk
www.lakecountryhouse.co.uk

"We are rather low key...don't show off," says owner Jean-Pierre Mifsud modestly about this star among Welsh country-house hotels. He and his wife run a very hands-on operation, albeit discreetly, and it certainly shows once one gets past the rather dated bar and hall to the splendidly understated elegance of the lounge and dining-room. It shows, too, in the excellence of the service from staff whose warm refrain is always "Welcome to the Lake".

Comfortable furniture, interesting paintings, fine flowers and immaculate tables set off the daily changing three-course dinner whose aspirations are clearly high. For the most part, Sean Cullingford and his team succeed admirably. Home-made breads are a great pleasure, particularly the stunning apricot and rosemary, just from the oven and sliced at your table, arriving with an unannounced amuse bouche, possibly a warm asparagus salad.

Starters of foie gras and leek terrine, roast Mediterranean vegetable soup with crab in pastry, or crisply seared meltingly tender scallops on an inspired sauce of carrot and cardamom all indicate a talented kitchen.

Main courses embrace local lamb and beef, imaginatively prepared, and often two fish dishes typified by beautifully presented pan-fried

John Dory fillets on a confit of red peppers with a tapenade sauce.

Puddings maintain the standard, notably the chocolate fondant while a board of tip-top cheeses is an alternative.

The majestic wine list is strong on clarets but with a goodly supply of half-bottles and a useful page of house recommendations.

Set in 50 acres of gardens and woodland, this excellent hotel is an inviting base from which to explore a wonderfully unspoilt area of Wales.

MEALS: L 12.30-1.45; Sunday L 12.30-1.45 £17.50-£22; D 7.30-9 £30
Cards: All major
CHEF: S. Cullingford. PROPRIETOR: Jean-Pierre Mifsud
WTB: 4 ★★★★
Rooms: 19, £90 S, £125-145 D, £175-205 Suites

LOCAL INTEREST: Elan valley, red kite feeding centre at Rhayader.

92 Llanidloes

Lloyds Hotel and Restaurant

Cambrian Place
Llanidloes
Powys
SY18 6BX
Tel: 01686 412284
Fax: 01686 412666

e-mail:
hayteroy@dircon.co.uk

The first town on the river Severn on its long journey to the sea is a jewel of a place, a proud borough since the 14th-century and site of a Saturday market since Edward I granted its charter in 1280.

Lloyds, a homely and characterful little hotel, is easily found near the centre of town, opposite the former train station. Built in 1872 of Buttington bricks brought on the new railway line from Welshpool it started life as "Humphreys Temperance and Commercial Hotel."

Partners Roy Hayter and Tom Lines welcome with a natural informal warmth. Discuss with Roy the menu for dinner, built around individual tastes, as local supplies permit.

Starters take in a platter of various Italian antipasti, monkfish kebabs and individual cheese soufflés stuffed with avocado slices wrapped in Parma ham.

Main courses of local free-range chicken, wild duck, venison and pork are imaginatively prepared, for example, local pork fillet with sliced nectarines, red peppers and balsamic vinegar. Young carrots cooked in honey, small potatoes roasted with garlic, white cabbage with apple and red onion, spinach with orange zest and toasted flaked almonds, crisp French beans, stuffed roast tomatoes and baby leeks cooked with currants and coriander all at one meal alone reflecting the enthusiasm of this self-effacing, skilled chef.

Puddings tends to the light and simple with some interesting additions – perhaps a fresh fruit salad with chopped hazelnuts and whisky in whipped cream or summer pudding with Drambuie cream.

Good breakfasts, include splendid local sausages and dry-cured bacon.

MEALS: L; D booking is essential £20
Closed: 14 January - 28 February
CHEF: Roy Hayter. PROPRIETOR: Tony Livies and Roy Hayter
WTB: 2 ★★ hotel

Rooms: 9, £19-£33 S, £20-£25 D

LOCAL INTEREST: Upper Severn and Wye Valleys, Clwedog and Elan Valley resevoirs, fishing, cycling and walking, Plynlimon range and Powis Castle.

93

Llanwddyn

Lake Vyrnwy Hotel

Llanwddyn
Montgomeryshire
SY10 0LY
Tel: 01691 870692
Fax: 01691 870259

e-mail:
res@lakevyrnwy.com
www.lakevyrnwy.com

Despite the grandeur of its position, this very relaxed, comfortable hotel immediately, puts one at ease. Its modern comforts are grafted seamlessly to the pitch pine, log fires and fishing prints of a traditional sportsman's retreat. Built around 1900 for the opening of the great dam by the Prince of Wales in 1910, its position high above the lake captures the most wonderful views around.

Shaun Mitchell, who did such admired work in the kitchen of Plas Bodegroes has recently taken over here as head chef; results will be worth watching and enjoying. His policy is to use wherever possible local raw materials and to use them simply without fuss; first indications are very encouraging.

The daily changing three-course dinner menu has just three or four options at each stage. Starters of cream of parsnip soup with parsnip chips, game terrine, a crab parcel with chilli salsa and braised oxtail with celeriac mash one evening were carefully crafted and the terrine was particularly good on the eye.

Main dishes are straightforward but with meaningful accompaniments; loin of pork comes with sage mash and cider sauce and fillet of bass with champagne rice and herb sauce. All the sauces are accurate and a red wine sauce with lamb Wellington was particularly good.

Puddings are colourful as well as delicious – a trio of chocolate with cherries and lemon posset with roast plums looking, as well as tasting, magnificent.

Wherever possible all ancillaries are made in the kitchens from bread and cakes to chutneys and preserves. The strength of the kitchen shows, too, in breakfasts of near-perfect poached eggs and grilled bacon.

As they embark on a planned series of improvements, the popular lunches will start again in spring.

MEALS: L 12noon £15.95; Sunday L 12noon £15.95; D 7pm £27
Closed: Weekday lunches during winter but tavern open
Cards: All major
CHEF: Shaun Mitchell. MANAGER: Anthony Rosser
WTB: 4 ★★★★
Rooms: 35, from £80 B&B S, from £110 D, from £125 Suites

LOCAL INTEREST: The lake and surrounding countryside.

94 Llanwrtyd Wells

Carlton House

Dolycoed Road
Llanwrtyd Wells
Powys
LD3 4RA
Tel: 01591 610248
Fax: 01591 610242

e-mail:
info@carltonrestaurant.co.uk
www.carltonrestaurant.co.uk

Quite simply, Mary Ann Gilchrist loves to cook and she cooks with boundless enthusiasm, great warmth of heart and dazzling skills. She is a real Welsh national treasure! The setting for her work, presided over with with quiet pride by husband Alan, is a dark-red painted house in this lovely little town of handsome buildings on the River Irfon.

Inside, the house has Italian glass light fittings and chandeliers and eclectic furnishings that are supremely comfortable. The dining-room gently lit with candles on crisp white table linen now has handsome new chairs, reminiscent of Rennie Mackintosh.

Dinner is either Mary Ann's table d'hote or à la carte, though you may move between one menu and the other. The menus change daily, constantly trying new ideas and flavours but always conditional on fresh and, where possible, available local produce. The mix of ingredients is innovative though never simply clever for the sake of being clever and works triumphantly.

A starter of seared marinated king prawns with a delicately balanced sauce of lime and ginger illustrates this well, the whole dish laid on stir-fried noodles and spiked with chopped coriander leaves.

Similarly, a main course of perfectly hung peppered fillet steak topped with black olive tapenade on a rich dauphinoise potato, with chopped smoked bacon and rocket adds a new dimension – the whole symphony laid on a coulis of fresh tomato and olive oil with roast fennel and tomatoes. An exemplary crisp filo basket of strawberries sitting on marzipan placed on a plate painted red and orange with raspberry and peach coulis again shows Mary Ann at her best.

Before your starter, comes not so much an amuse-bouche as another course, perhaps crisp, sharp, chicory-wrapped in Camarthen ham and baked in Parmesan sauce.

A cafetiere of coffee comes with very good home-made chocolates and there is a wide-ranging, reasonably priced wine list with four house wines available by the glass.

An exceptional dining experience here is greatly enhanced by the warmth and enthusiasm of the Gilchrists.

MEALS: D 7-8.30 £19.95 for 2 courses
Closed: Sunday and mid December
Cards: Visa, Mastercard
Rooms: 5, from £60 D
CHEF: Mary Ann Gilchrist. PROPRIETORS: Alan and Mary Ann Gilchrist
LOCAL INTEREST: Annual Royal Welsh Show, Brecon Beacons, historic spa towns including Llanwrtyd Wells.

95 Llanwrtyd Wells

On a square that would do handsome credit to many a larger town stands this 18th-century cottage house close by the bridge. It is one of

Drovers Rest

The Square
Llanwrtyd Wells
Powys
LD5 4RA
Tel: 01591 610264
Fax: 01591 610666
www.food-food-food-co.uk

those all-too-rare places in rural areas, an all-day brasserie with good food.

The day starts with breakfast, followed by morning teas and coffee with enormous toasted tea cakes, scones and a variety of cakes and bara brith all made on the premises. Snacks such as authentic Welsh rarebit with or without poached eggs are especially popular. At lunchtime, steaks, fish of the day and much more are there to tempt the traveller; and then full-scale afternoon teas and snacks continue.

In summer, dinner ends the day and every Friday and Saturday throughout the year a "Gourmet Dinner" is staged, featuring the likes of avocado and salmon gateau, potted queen scallops or smoked haddock and samphire to start, followed by Welsh Black fillet steaks, local lamb, or salmon with fennel. Chef Peter James's sister Paulette Reed produces tempting puddings and is also responsible for the daily choice of cakes. Vegetarians are not forgotten and there are bedrooms for those wishing to stay a while in this bright little rural town.

Whether you stay or not, the restaurant is an atmospheric place, with beams and chintz, so sit awhile and watch the local world go by (although it is more Elizabeth Gaskell than Dylan Thomas!).

MEALS: L 12-2.30 £10.50; Sunday L 12-2 £10.50; D 7.30-9.45 £14.50
Closed: Christmas Day
Cards: All major
CHEF/PROPRIETOR: Peter James
WTB: 2 ★★
Rooms: 4, £25 S, £40 D

LOCAL INTEREST: Abergwesyn Valley, Llyn Brianne reservoir, Black Mountains, annual Royal Welsh Show.

96 Llyswen

Griffin Inn

Llyswen
Brecon
Powys
LD3 0UR
Tel: 01874 754241
Fax: 01874 754592

email:
info@griffin-inn.freeserve.co.uk
www: griffin-inn.co.uk

The Griffin is a 15th-century sporting inn in the upper Wye Valley on the A470 just north of Brecon. It is a popular venue for fish and game enthusiasts and fishing and shooting trips can be arranged from here.

At lunchtimes, as well as The Griffin ploughman's of Welsh cheeses, there might be melon with bresoala and olives, crispy leg of duck with apple and onion compote and roasted vegetables, or smoked cod and Welsh cheese wrapped in bacon.

In the evening, the restaurant fills up quickly but, thankfully, the same menu is available in the bar. Start with duck liver and brandy pâté, a Greek-style salad or hot smoked salmon with Glanwye sauce (similar to hollandaise with dill). Follow with fillets of trout with smoked bacon and mushrooms, wild mushroom stroganoff with rice, corn-fed chicken supreme with cep risotto, or slow roasted crispy duck on root vegetables with cherry sauce. In winter the Griffin, with its large inglenook fireplace ablaze, specialises in hearty, warming fare, with lamb and beef that is slow-cooked to melt-in-the-mouth perfection – try braised knuckle of Welsh lamb on redcurrant and rosemary sauce or

Welsh Black beef daube. If all this is not enough, there are daily specials, too – perhaps a warm salad of duck fillets with orange sauce, fillet of lemon sole stuffed with smoked salmon, or roast local partridge with game jus.

The wine list is extensive, with good-value bottles from various countries (several available by the glass), a couple of organic varieties and helpful notes on which wines suit specific foods.

MEALS: L 12-2; D 7-9
Closed: 25th and 26th December
Cards: All major
CHEF: Andy Addis-Fuller. PROPRIETOR: Louise Gudsell
WTB: 3 ★★★ Inn
Rooms: 7, £45 S, £70-£80 D
LOCAL INTEREST: walking and fishing.

97 Machynlleth

Centre for Alternative Technology

Machynlleth
Pantperthog
Powys
SY20 9AZ
Tel: 01654 705967
Fax: 01654 702782
www.cat.org.uk

A tour of this fascinating living exhibition of alternative building techniques, power production, gardening and waste disposal is always thought-provoking. It is at the same time a restful, rather innocent place with a very useful vegetarian café at its heart.

Alternative methods are dramatically realised here, where 90% of the electric power for cooking and refrigeration is produced by solar and wind technology. "Fairly traded...locally organic... vegetarian" is the sourcing of raw materials. A wide variety of salads, such as bulgar and wild rice, is available at lunchtime, along with specials of the day listed on a blackboard; these may include vegetable lasagne, homity pie or a hotpot of home-grown vegetables.

All-day service of tea and coffee includes cakes such as chocolate and the winning carrot and coconut. Herbal teas, mineral waters and organic wines are also available.

The centre seems able to absorb large numbers of visitors without ever becoming noisy or losing its calm. You approach quietly by a water-powered furnicular and pass through the entrance to an artificial beach by a lake with large carp glistening in the water at your feet.

MEALS: L 12-3 or 4 from £4.60
Closed: 5 days over Christmas
Cards: All
CHEFS: Sandra Cutler and Kevin Price
LOCAL INTEREST: Enviromental Issues.

98 Machynlleth

The Wynnstay, a handsome 18th-century building, stands well on the broad main street of this elegant market town of interesting

Wynnstay Arms

Maengwyn Street
Machynlleth
Powys
SY20 8AE
Tel: 01654 702941
Fax: 01654 703884

e-mail:
info@wynnstay-hotel.com
www.whynstay-hotel.com

buildings rich in the history of Wales. The inn itself seems steeped in the aura of years past and very much a focal point of the town.

Cooking impresses with its use of much local produce.

The bar serves good beers and bar snacks and the three-course dinner comes in the charmingly idiosyncratic dining room. Starting impressively with the likes of tian of avocado and the freshest crab with lemon mayonnaise, seared scallops and smoked salmon with samphire, a good soup or rabbit, pork and liver terrine all are assured and full of freshness.

Main courses might include seared salmon with roast red peppers, simply grilled sole, chicken breast in bacon with mustard sauce or wonderful rump of local veal with paprika gravy. Vegetarian dishes are challenging, for example in a steamed leek pudding on roast aubergine.

Puddings are simple but good (Bakewell tart, sticky toffee pudding, chocolate mousse tart, for example) and there is a selection of tip-top Welsh cheeses. A compact well-chosen wine list includes some interesting Italians.

MEALS: L 12-2 £3 £9; Sunday L 12-2 £6.95 £10.95; D 7-9 £18 £21
Cards: All major
CHEF: Gareth Johns. PROPRIETOR: Charles Dark
WTB: 2 ★★
Rooms: 23, £45 S, £70 D

Local interest: Centre for Alternative Technology, Celtica, Tabernacle, RSPB nature reserve, Cardigan Bay.

99 Machynlleth

Ynyshir Hall

Fglwysfach
Machynlleth
Powys
SY20 8TA
Tel: 01654 781209
Fax: 01654 781366

e-mail:
info@ynyshir-hall.co.uk
www.ynyshir-hall.co.uk

The image of this lovely white house set off by lawns and magnificent trees stays with you long after you have left. It is one of Wales's very finest country house hotels with a stunning interior of dramatic but restful rooms brilliant with Rob Reen's vibrant paintings. Comfortable sofas, bright rugs and cushions are everywhere. Such is the uniquely warm welcome from Rob and his wife Joan that you feel instantly at home.

The three-course dinner preceded by hot canapés features four options at each stage. The kitchen delights in setting the central ingredient of the dish in a mix of unusual accompaniments, for example, in starters of a crisp delicately smoked ham boudin on a bed of skinned broad beans on onion marmalade gravy, or seared salmon topped with a lobster fishcake on beurre blanc sauce.

The theme continues with main courses such as grilled breast of Gressingham duck sliced on a potato cake with apple fritters, calvados sauce and heavenly celeriac purée or grilled lamb cutlets with a miniature moussaka, a perfect potatoe purée singing with the

fragrance of good olive oil, all on caper gravy!

Puddings get similar treatment in a timbale of strawberies with a little summer pudding topped with sharp lemon ice cream or the famous box of apple crisps filled with apple and sultana compote on rice pudding, all topped with Horlicks ice cream.

This food is very good and presented with a real sense of quiet enjoyment. An evening here is very much amongst friends and pleasurable in every aspect.

MEALS: L 12.30-1.30 £22; Sunday Lunch 12.30-1.30 £22
D 7-8.30 £37
Closed: January 5th-28th
Cards: All
CHEF: Les Rennie. PROPRIETORS: Rob and Joan Reen
WTB: 5 ★★★★★
Rooms: 10, £110-£150 S, £125-£170 D, £180-£205 Suites

LOCAL INTEREST: Centre for Alternative Technology, Powis Castle, Celtica, National Library of Wales, Tywyn railway.

Mid Wales

100 Montgomery

Dragon Hotel

Montgomery
Powys
SY15 6PA
Tel: 01686 668359
Fax: 01686 668287

e-mail:
reception@dragonhotel.com
www.dragonhotel.com

Montgomery is a pretty town and the Dragon Hotel provides the perfect watering-hole for visitors. Mark and Sue Michaels run the hotel with enthusiasm and care, while chef, James Riches, brings his own dedication to the team as he researches local ingredients and cooks them in a classic British style with Mediterranean influence.

Eat in the cosy bar and you will find a fixed-price menu with specials chalked up on the board – for example, cauliflower and Stilton soup or baked goat's cheese with walnut and red wine dressing to start the meal. Main dishes might include grilled whole trout with caper and almond butter or braised beef and sausage casserole with red wine and creamy mash. A higher-priced dinner menu makes exciting reading. Hors d'oeuvre cover breast of duck served with savoy cabbage, goats' cheese and walnuts tossed in Dijon mustard, red wine vinaigrette and walnut oil dressing, and mixed fish ragout.

Five meat main courses might include rack of lamb rolled in paprika and coarse pepper and served with a warm lemon dressing and houmus, medallions of Welsh Black beef with mushrooms, bacon, blue cheese crust and red wine demi-glace and supreme of chicken filled with Welsh brie. There are also fish and vegetarian options.

For pudding, perhaps, banoffi pie topped with dark chocolate curls and vanilla sauce, sticky toffee pudding on a rich dark fudge sauce or a tuile biscuit basket filled with lemon and lime sorbet and surrounded by raspberry coulis.

MEALS: L 12-2 £18.50; Sunday Lunch 12-2 £11.95; D 7-9 approx £25
Cards: All major

Chef: James Riches. Proprietors: Mark and Sue Michaels
WTB: 3 ★★★
Rooms: 20, £45 b&b S, £75 b&b D
LOCAL INTEREST: Montgomery Castle, Old Bell Museum, Robbers Grave, Offa's Dyke, Powis Castle.

101 New Quay

New Quay Honey Farm

Cross Inn
New Quay
Ceredigion
SA44 6NN
Tel: 01545 560822
Fax: 01545 560045
e-mail: nqhf@talk21.com

Ten years ago the Coopers sold their dairy herd to emigrate to Canada. But property prices dropped and so they went into bees instead, and business blossomed. It happened that their son, eight at the time, had been given a hive and interest just grew from there.

Today, they operate an imaginative honey museum with three working bee colonies, lots of advice and a shop selling every possible honey product, from soap and medicinal cures to pots of every kind of honey, honey lemon curd and a fine range of "properly made" mead.

Best of all, visitors can enjoy a cup of tea and fine cake in the tea room, run along the simplest of lines by Mariana. The white painted walls, floor matting and pine furniture set the scene for uncomplicated food, well cooked and presented.

Most of the vegetables and salads used are organic or locally produced. The cakes and scones are all made on the premises and local producers are celebrated with goods from Penbryn cheese in the neighbouring village, Mary's Farmhouse ices and to the excellent Wendy Brandon jams.

Home-made soup is served with a roll and butter. Welsh cheese or locally smoked salmon are offered as salads and the range of sandwiches is freshly made.

For tea there are cream teas or bara brith and butter, scones, toasted tea cakes and cakes of coffee, chocolate, lemon or boiled fruit flavours. There is, naturally, honey ice cream here, too!

MEALS: All day
Closed: November - Easter
Cards: All major
CHEF/PROPRIETOR: Mariana Cooper

Local interest: Dolphins often seen in the sea at New Quay.
Tea room is part of the earliest independent chapel in the area.

102 Newtown

Appearances can be deceptive, and most would not give this very ordinary-looking roadside pub a second glance; but, for once, that sign really does mean what it says.

Having moved to Mid Wales three years ago in search of a new challenge, Colin and Melanie Dawson set to work on revamping the

Talkhouse

Ty Siarad Pontdolgoch
Caersws
Newtown
Powys
SY17 5JE
Tel: 01686 688919
Fax: 01686 689134

interior, creating a beautifully furnished lounge, a relaxing bar and a civilised dining-room; its tables topped with candles, flowers and linen napkins, while a dresser displays some of Melanie's home-made chutneys and marinated olives.

Listed on an ever-changing blackboard menu in the bar is the imaginative range of dishes on offer, all carefully prepared and well presented by Colin. Follow nibbles from the bar – home-made parsnip crisps and olives tossed in oil and herbs – with chicken liver pâté and home-made chutneys and pickles, or Roquefort soufflé with mixed leaves and roasted pine nuts, accompanied by a warmed half loaf of bread with a choice of butters – such as the garlic-and-chilli!

Move on, perhaps, to spiced slow-roasted lamb shank with Bombay potatoes, grilled Cornish rockling with a baked prawn crust, venison and beef casserole with bubble-and-squeak and quince jam, or wild Pembrokshire sea trout with caramelised wilted endive, beans and lemon.

If you have room, round off with Lakeland pudding with hot caramel sauce, or chocolate and orange mousse. There is a well chosen list of wines from Tanners and 10 by the glass, including champagne.

MEALS: L 12-1.30 approx £10; D 6-9 £15-£20
Closed: All day Sunday and Monday lunch
Cards: All major
CHEF: Colin Dawson. PROPRIETORS: Colin and Melanie Dawson

LOCAL INTEREST: Markets at Llanidloes, Machynlleth, Newtown and the forest experience rally school at Carno.

103 Trecastle

Castle Coaching Inn

Trecastle
Powys
LD3 8UH

Tel: 01874 636354
Fax: 01874 636457

e-mail:
hotel.reservation@btinternet.com
www.castle-coaching-inn.co.uk

Traditional Sunday lunch is popular at this 17th-century coaching inn on the A40 just west of Brecon. However, it's probably best known for its three-course à la carte menu (available Friday and Saturday evenings only, with restaurant bookings on other evenings subject to availability). To start, there may be game and venison terrine served with red onion compote or a continental pottage with sautéed mushrooms, continental sausage, garlic and croutons served with walnut and sultana bread. Entrées could include chicken with wild mushrooms or fillet of north Atlantic cod on chargrilled vegetables. Desserts tend to be styled on classic patisserie – clafoutis with blueberry ice cream, chocolate tart with fresh fruit and a sharp raspberry coulis – or try the Welsh farmhouse cheese selection that may contain St Davids, Harlech, Y Fenni and Brecon blue.

Bar meals are available daily, lunchtime and evening. Try lamb chops from the Brecon Beacons with rosemary and redcurrant sauce, steak and mushroom puff pastry pie, home-made chicken Kiev or salmon paupiette filled with smoked salmon mousse with tomato and basil cream sauce.

Their wine list is truly global with at least one wine from almost

every major wine-producing country. On tap in the bar is real ale from a local brewery, alongside guest ale. As well as fresh ground and speciality coffees, you will be offered a range of fine teas including herb and fruit.

MEALS: L 12-2 from £4.95; Sunday L 12.30-2.30 from £4.95; D 6.30-9.30 from £6.50
Closed: Chirstmas Day
Cards: All except Amex and Diners
Chef: Bryn Chamberlain. PROPRIETOR: Lew Chamberlain
WTB: 3 ★★★
Rooms: 10, £45 S, £50 D, £60 Suites

LOCAL INTEREST: Western Brecon Beacons, Black Mountains, Dan yr Ogof Caves, Ystradfellte waterfalls.

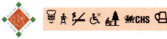

104 Welshpool

National Trust Restaurant

Powis Castle
Welshpool
Powys
SY21 8RF
Tel: 01938 551920
Fax: 01938 554336

Housed in the old stable block, the tea rooms at Powis Castle are worth a visit, even when the magnificent gardens are closed. White-washed walls, great stone flags on the floor and chunky wooden trestle tables lend a simple quality to the place, which is reflected in the food.

Self-effacing Diane Henry runs a small team of excellent cooks and they bow to customer demands with good will. "We'll do anything anyone wants if we can. Today it was straining the juice off baked beans to serve in a jacket potato with cheese!"

Everything is home-made, from soups, pies, casseroles, quiches and cobblers to a wonderful array of cakes.

Lunch, served from noon, offers perhaps apple and cheese soup, Clive's "Petit Pâtés" (sweet lamb pies developed in 1768 by Lord Clive of India during a stay in the French town of Pezenas), Welsh onion cake and Welsh cheese-and-leek flan.

The range of puddings includes, "Powis pond pudding" – a tangy steamed lemon sponge with lemon sauce, and rich chocolate fudge-nut pudding, and Mrs Henry's cabinet pudding-heaven for the sweet-toothed.

The bara brith has to tried to be believed – moist even gingery and full of fruit – served, of course, with Welsh butter, while the shortbread is as crisp and short as it comes.

MEALS: L 11-5 from £5
Closed: Mondays, November - April, July and August
Cards: Visa, Mastercard
CATERING MANAGER: Diane Henry

LOCAL INTEREST: Powis Castle and Welshpool.

South West Wales Entries

105   Broad Haven

Druidstone Hotel

Druidstone Haven
Broadhaven
nr Haverfordwest
Pembrokeshire
SA62 3NE
Tel: 01437 781221
Fax: 01437 781133

The "good ship" Druidstone sits firmly anchored atop its piece of Pembrokeshire cliff, watching the sea nibble at the coast, like life on a liner. If the end of the world rolled in from the west, you could watch it in comfort and still be smiling. For those who secretly yearn for a life where Art is the boss, look no further.

An informal gallery meets one on entering with local artists' work predominating. The bar has the sensation of being underground but its French doors alternately open to splendid ocean sunsets and vigorous ocean gales.

Stepping happily round the world, Caribbean curries rub shoulders with cawl, baked avocado with Camembert and Scottish salmon. Little flowers mark vegetarian choices to the point that carnivores could get the impression that they have been ignored.

If there is any room after the handsome portions of a savoury course, desserts range from the 'oh I couldn't' to the 'how could I not?'.

The wine list is an interesting tour of curious corners of the world where French estates share with earthy Morrocan and Lebanon alternatives.

MEALS: L 12.30-2.30 £6.50; Sunday L 1-2 £15; D 7.30-9.30 £15
Closed: November, January and February – closed mid-week
Cards: All major
CHEFS: Angus Bell and John Lewis. PROPRIETOR: Jane Bell
Rooms: 9 – £35   b&b
LOCAL INTEREST: Beaches, Pembrokeshire coastal path.

106   Carmarthen

Capel Dewi Uchaf Country House

Capel Dewi
Carmarthen
Carmarthenshire
SA32 8AY
Tel: 01267 290799
Fax: 01267 290003
e-mail: uchaffarm@aol.com
www.walescottageholidays.uk.com

Freddie gives excellent directions to her wonderful house tucked away in the Towy Valley. Welcomed as old friends, her visitors are settled into comfortable rooms, in perhaps the same manner as pilgrims were looked after some 500 years ago on their way to St David's.

Dinner, served around one huge table, might include hors d'oeuvre of speciality meats and fish on a bed of fresh salad – served with home-made bread – or home-made broccoli and Stilton soup. To follow, perhaps roasted pork fillet with cranberry and port cream or pan-fried chicken served with Dijon mustard sauce.

A selection of desserts might produce pear and chocolate tart, apple and orange pie, rich chocolate mousse laced with brandy and white chocolate topping or fresh strawberries straight from the garden.

Breakfast is perhaps the main event at Capel Dewi – with half a fresh baby pineapple, a wealth of fruits and fruit juices, croissants, pain-au-chocolat, home-made fruit loaf with honey and an array of home-made jams to accompany a plate of bacon with egg, mushrooms and tomatoes, and freshly brewed coffee.

If you are so minded book a day's fishing on the farm's stretch of river, and who better to cook the catch than Freddie?

MEALS: D 8pm £25 for 5 courses
Cards: Visa and Mastercard
CHEF/PROPRIETOR: Freddie Burns
WTB: 4 ★★★★
Rooms: 3, £40 S, £57 D

LOCAL INTEREST: National Botanical Gardens, Aberglasney Gardens, Gelli Aur, Dinefwr Castle, Paxton Tower, fishing, walking, cycling.

107 Carmarthen

Glasfryn Guest House and Restaurant

Brechfa
Carmarthen
Carmarthenshire
SA32 7QY
Tel/Fax: 01267 202306

Joyce Hart's homely stone-built guest house dates from around 1900 and stands in the centre of Brechfa, tucked away in the rolling Cothi Valley. In addition to three well-appointed en suite bedrooms, Joyce offers simply cooked food in her downstairs conservatory restaurant. Decorated in shades of pink, with local artists' paintings on the wall and a mahogany floor, it has a relaxing, convivial atmosphere.

The menu, served all day in summer, features local ingredients such as home-made cheddar-and-onion quiche, lamb hotpot and a hearty bowl of Welsh cawl, filled to the brim with chunks of vegetables and lamb in a full-flavoured stock, served with warm bread and Cenarth cheese.

An evening carte, though not overly adventurous, will find baked Welsh Brie, local farm lamb noisettes with redcurrant sauce, and seasonal specialities such as Towy sewin served with white wine and butter, or salmon with asparagus sauce. Joyce uses only fresh vegetables in season and prefers to hand-cut the chips that accompany her sirloin steaks. Round off with home-made nursery puddings such as apple pie and bread-and-butter pudding, or opt for a plate of Welsh cheeses.

Cariad wine from Llanerch Vineyard flies the flag for Wales on a short list of wines. Sunday roast lunches are particularly popular.

MEALS: L 12-2; Sunday L 12-2; D 7-9.30
Cards: All major
CHEF/PROPRIETOR: Joyce Hart
WTB: 3 ★★★
Rooms: 3, £25.30 S, £45 D

LOCAL INTEREST: National Botanic Garden, Aberglasney Gardens, walks and cycling in Brechfa forest.

108 Carmarthen

Quayside Brasserie

The Quay
Carmarthen
Carmarthenshire
SA31 3JP
Tel: 01267 223000
Fax: 01267 232444

Ignore the rather uninviting entrance off a busy roundabout for once inside, what a surprise! Wooden floors and a beamed ceiling are softened with winding hop bines and dried flowers and tables are comfortably spaced.

An overhead menu clearly lists the vast menu with fish, fresh from Swansea market, and a good choice of local meat and game to choose from. Director Ian Williams has recently teamed up with one of the original chefs, Lee Edwards, cooking at one end of the restaurant in full view of customers. The staff is charming and well informed.

Starters could be a bowl of rich bouillabaisse, or a well-seasoned seafood salad. To follow, perhaps pheasant with Dijon mustard, crispy Pembrokeshire duck with brandy sauce or baked cod accompanied by creamy garlic potatoes and little nests of al dente shredded swede, carrots, leek and cabbage.

With the cheeseboard, which offers a good selection of Welsh cheeses, come home-baked oatmeal biscuits. Desserts include peach and apricot crumble and hot chocolate torte.

On a sunny day eat outside on the deck overlooking the River Towy.

MEALS: L 12-2.30 from £6; D 6-10
Closed: Sunday L
Cards: All
CHEFS: Ian Williams and Lee Edwards.
PROPRIETOR: Ian and Ruth Williams

LOCAL INTEREST: Carmarthen Market, and farmers market.

109 Cynghordy

Llanerchindda Farm

Cynghordy
Llandovery
Carmarthenshire
SA20 0NB
Tel: 01550 750274
Fax: 01550 750300

e-mail:
nick@cambrianway.com
www.cambrianway.com

Standing high in the southern foothills of the Cambrian Mountains, with far-reaching views across the Towy Valley to the Myddfai Hills and Black Mountains beyond, Nick and Irene Bointon's isolated stone farmhouse is the perfect base from which to explore the heart of Wales and red kite country, especially on foot.

Once here, you will find comfortable bedrooms and the atmosphere friendly, informal and relaxed. Lashings of tea and crumpets are offered on arrival and best enjoyed, especially after a long exhilarating walk, by a roaring log fire in the lounge.

Suppers are simple, hearty and freshly prepared, using local produce, and served "en famille" around a large wooden table in the dining room. Expect a choice of thick, warming soup, perhaps minted lentil, beef and tomato or carrot, ginger and lime, followed by venison in orange casserole, steak-and-ale pie, or a huge satisfying portion of shepherds pie, all served with fresh vegetables. Traditional nursery puddings like spotted dick and farm fruit crumbles with custard should appease the heartiest of walking appetites.

To find Llanerchindda, leave the A483 five miles north of Llandovery,

signed to Cynghordy Station, turn first right, then follow the lane beneath the railway viaduct and keep going onwards and upwards to the end of the road.

MEALS: D 7pm from £12
Closed: seldom
Cards: None
CHEF/PROPRIETOR: Nick Bointon
WTB: 2 ★★
Rooms: 9

LOCAL INTEREST: Spectacular walking, cycling and bird watching.

110 Felingwm Uchaf

Allt-yr-Golau Uchaf

Felingwm Uchaf
Carmarthenshire
SA32 7BB
Tel: 01267 290455
Fax: 01267 290455

www.visit–carmarthenshire.co.uk/alltygolau

This charming house has to be a temple to the goddess of dwellings, or blessed with an industrious fairy godmother. Organic and positively eco-friendly are the underlying themes of the decor. There is nothing like the warm glow of natural wood and the creak of floorboards. Thoughtful ornaments adorn every available space and from the windows can be seen steep valley scenery, hiding behind tall graceful pines.

The rooms are warm and comfortable with beds eminently worthy of sound slumber while the lounge is so well-equipped with games, books and comfort that you almost pray for rain.

Breakfast is rather like a Welsh morning meze. Cereals, neatly labelled preserves, home-made bread and freshly squeezed fruit juices occupy one end of a splendid elm dining table. Tea and coffee appear as often as required. The perfectly poached or rich yellow scrambled eggs, local sausages, bacon, Welsh potato cakes and toast, croissants, rolls, marbles of butter and yet more preserves.

It could be very easy to sit here all day, perusing the papers, setting the world to rights and ignoring the world outside.

MEALS: Breakfast only
Closed: Christmas and New Year
Cards: None
WTB: 4 ★★★★
CHEF/PROPRIETORS: Jacquie and Colin Rouse
Rooms: 3, £20 S, £40-£45 D, bandb

LOCAL INTEREST: National Botanic Gardens, Aberglasney, castles of Tywi Valley.

111 Fishguard

The Manor House

Main Street
Fishguard
Pembrokeshire
SA65 9HG
Tel: 01348 873260
Fax: 01348 873260

This pretty hotel and restaurant also houses a very tempting antiques shop. In fine weather, host Ralph Davies will offer pre-dinner drinks outside in the garden, with its stunning views of Fishguard harbour, whilst his wife Beatrix supervises the kitchen. She just loves to cook and enthuses over the quality and supply of local ingredients she uses throughout.

First course offers a varied choice and plenty for vegetarians; perhaps a smooth terrine of feta cheese, herbs and black olive served with spiced pears, or patties made from fresh crab, spring onions and mayonnaise sautéed and served with salad leaves. Main courses are based on the best local produce, from organic sirloin steak served with sharp salsa verde, rack of lamb, roasted and served with a garlic and aubergine purée, to an escalope of beef wrapped around sun dried tomato tapenade and finished with red wine. A good choice of fish includes perhaps turbot and Dover sole, with interesting vegetables such as cabbage with caraway seeds and new potatoes with fresh herbs.

Delightful puddings include plum and almond tart, gooseberry flan with almond custard and cream of tangy lemon on a delicate rum-and-sponge base.

A selection of local cheese is available too.

Visitors to this warm and friendly hotel are offered a special rate for dinner and also benefit from Beatrix's full Welsh breakfast at whatever time the Rosslare ferry is running!

MEALS: D 7-8 approx £19
Closed: Christmas and annual holidays
Cards: Visa, Mastercard
CHEF/PROPRIETOR: Beatrix Davies
WTB: 3 ★★★
Rooms: 6, £30-£8 S, £54-62 D
LOCAL INTEREST: Pembrokeshire National Park and Coastal Path, Gwaun Valley, Last Invasion Tapestry, West Wales Art Centre.

112 Fishguard

Three Main Street

3 Main Street
Fishguard
Pembrokeshire
SA65 9HG
Tel: 01348 874275
Fax: 01348 874017

An elegant Georgian house in the centre of Fishguard, now a restaurant with rooms that overlook Fishguard docks, where ferries arrive and depart for Ireland that is run by Inez Ford and Marion Evans, her cooking is excellent, with fine pastry skills and ingenious use of the best of local ingredients. Ask whether they have been produced organically and the answer might well be, "Oh, I expect so, most things are around here".

The welcome is warm and stripped-pine furniture creates a casual atmosphere at lunchtime, when menus offer a selection of six to eight

dishes, of which at least three are vegetarian. Confit duck, succulent with mixed leaves, home-cooked ham, layered with melting cheese on mashed potato, and crispy light tartlets of tomato and goats' cheese set the tone.

At dinner, a surprise appetiser of roast red pepper soup, served in a decorative coffee cup with a warm baked roll, might be followed by sea bass, tenderly cooked with crisp skin and served with fennel baked in cream and bacon with French beans – or fillet of Welsh Black beef grilled to pink perfection and full of flavour.

Puddings include excellent hazelnut meringue with fresh raspberry coulis while Welsh cheeses cover a fine range.

The well-chosen wine list reflects the love and care in everything one experiences here: don't even miss a visit to the loo on the first floor for a wonderful view across Fishguard Bay!

MEALS: L 12-2 £3-£10; D 7-9 £23-£28
Closed: Sunday and Monday and February
Cards: None
CHEF: Marion Evans. PROPRIETORS: Inez Ford and Marion Evans
Rooms: 3, £45-£50 S, £70 D

LOCAL INTEREST: Pembrokeshire National Park coastal path, and Last Invasion Tapestry in Fishguard.

113 Fishguard

Tregynon Farmhouse Restaurant

Gwaun Valley
Fishguard
Pembrokeshire
SA65 9TU
Tel: 01239 820531
Fax: 01239 820808

tregynon@online-holidays.net
online-holidays.net/tregynon

A 16th-century beamed stone farmhouse with huge inglenook, this is a true country retreat tucked away deep in the Gwaun Valley, well signposted however, to encourage visitors to take the long track off road.

Run as a hotel-with-restaurant, accommodation is in self-contained units, where guests can relax in the knowledge that someone else will cook dinner.

Starters include the likes of chestnut and sage soup, kidneys in wholemeal pastry and local goats' cheese served warm on a muffin. Main courses might be stuffed mackerel, chicken escalopes and venison in a berry sauce. In addition to the special table d'hôte menus there are alternatives such as rack of Pembrokeshire lamb with a herb crust, served with a rosemary and elderberry sauce and steak Cymraeg, a prime Welsh fillet steak served with a mustard, brandy and cream sauce. Vegetarian options are simply cooked and home-made bread comes with the meal.

Great care is taken with special diets and it is wise to ring through your dinner order the day before to help with the planning. Local produce, including organic ingredients, is much in evidence and used in an imaginative manner. There is an air of self sufficiency too, with home-made marmalade, home-smoked bacon and gammon and local free-range eggs. Friendly, helpful staff are all local too.

MEALS: D 7.30-8.30 £23.50
Closed: Sundays and Thursdays and Wednesdays off season

Cards: All major
CHEFS and PROPRIETORS: Peter and Jane Heard
WTB: 4 ★★★★
Rooms: Three self catering units, Six en-suite bedrooms
LOCAL INTEREST: Bluestone country, Pentre Ifan, Gwaun Valley.

114 Haverfordwest

Gardeners Rest

Hilton Court
Roch
Haverfordwest
Pembrokeshire
SA62 6AE
Tel: 01437 711000
Fax: 01437 711074

Hidden down a long lane, overlooking St Brides Bay, on the road between Haverfordwest and St David's is the ever-changing Hilton Court Tea room. As well as the small tea room which overlooks the lake and gardens, there is now a group of small shops run by Pembrokeshire crafts people and artists. Visitors flock to this oasis and particularly to the tea room which is painted a very welcoming shade of yellow.

Homely food includes specials of the day such as pork and apple casserole, lamb and mint bake and spinach and ricotta cannelloni. There are two or three choices for vegetarians and healthy selections for children. All the desserts and cakes are home-made – perhaps a Pavlova, moist walnut chocolate brownies with fudge sauce, lemon cake, thick pieces of treacle tart and top quality buttery shortbread.

The tearoom is unlicensed but there is a wide choice of fruit cordials, as well as tea and coffee. The adjacent shop in the courtyard also sells jams and chutneys made on the premises and work is continuing to convert further buildings into holiday cottages.

MEALS: L 10.30-4 from £4.50
Closed: January
Cards: None
CHEF: Rachel Morgan. PROPRIETOR: Mrs C. L. Lynch

LOCAL INTEREST: Newgale Beach, Solva, St David's.

115 Haverfordwest

The George's Restaurant

24 Market Street
Haverfordwest
Pembrokeshire
SA61 1NH
Tel: 01437 766683
e-mail: LEWIS6140@aol.com

Situated right in the centre of the town George's is a popular meeting place of great character and there is surely something for everyone here. From a vast all-day menu, starters include hazelnut, fresh sage and cream cheese terrine, hot smoked bacon and cheese salad, George's prawn and pineapple cocktail and mushroom and sunflower seed terrine.

Listed as 'dishes from around the world', Pembrokeshire hot and spicy sausage pie comes first, followed by Scottish smoke-roasted salmon, Cornish fish pie, Thai-style chicken curry, Irish steak and ale Pie, Mexican taco pot, Normandy crab bake and even Cypriot makaronia toufournou.

Vegetarians are very well catered for, with hot and spicy spinach dahl, George's Stilton and leek macaroni cheese, vegan nut stuffed aubergines and wild mushroom pasta.

George's specialities include steaks, Welsh lamb, chicken Kiev, apple chicken, whole duck breast a l'orange, and fish dishes from, baked crab, plaice and halibut to seafood pie and chowder.

Puddings please the sweet-toothed with marmalade bread-and-butter pudding, pavlova and fruit tarts. Initially good and very friendly service has sometimes lapsed towards a certain feeling of neglect later on.

MEALS: L 12-6.30 from £3; D 6.30-9.45 from £5
Closed: Sunday, Bank Holidays
Cards: All except Amex
CHEF: Lesley Lewis. PROPRIETORS: Lesley Lewis and John Glasby

LOCAL INTEREST: Site of old brewery, original brick vaulted cellar.

116 Haverfordwest

Stone Hall

Welsh Hook
Haverfordwest
Pembrokeshire
SA62 5NS
Tel: 01348 840212
Fax: 01348 840815

Stone Hall is a wonderfully rambling house, full of interesting nooks and crannies. On the ground floor, the breakfast room looks out on to a spacious lawn studded with trees and shrubs while the bar of simple, stone flags and ancient timbers makes a good antechamber for the discreet formality of the dining room.

Martine Watson bravely carries on alone since the death of her husband; she is happy here in rural Wales, although her taste and style is firmly rooted in the French countryside. Snails with bacon and cream in flaky pastry, onion tartlets, crevettes with garlic and French goat's cheese with cumin seeds provide a perfect introduction.

Main courses range from a rich and robust cassoulet (it must be a legend by now) and fillet steak with St Agur, to the more delicate Dover sole, served simply with butter and parsley and duck breast or rack of lamb. Vegetarians are encouraged to discuss alternative options.

Desserts are also in the French domain, from tarte tatin to a delicate chilled nougat. For those who prefer, French cheeses are available.

The wine list rambles through the best of French wines, with a fair sprinkling from the New World, all at reasonable prices. House wine is referred to as Reserve de la Maison and they are happy to leave the bottle on the table and charge you accordingly.

MEALS: L; D 7-9.30
Closed: Sunday, Monday/Tuesday
Cards: All
CHEF/PROPRIETOR: Martine Watson
Rooms: 5, £48 S, £76 D
LOCA INTEREST: Pembrokeshire coast.

117 Haverfordwest

The Wolfe

Wolfscastle
Haverfordwest
Pembrokeshire
SA62 5LS
Tel: 01437 741662
Fax: 01437 741676

The entrance to the Wolfe has changed a few times in the last few years and now lends to a well-lit and well-stocked L-shaped bar. Gianni, your dapper Italian host, has a story for every occasion and a waistcoat for every evening!

There are three dining rooms, tucked away out of the bustle – two of stone, with blackened timber joists and an array of Welsh and Italian artefacts on the shelves and the third a conservatory, light and cheerful in summer.

The menu delivers handsomely prime local cuts, robust sauces and conventional marriages – lamb and mint, chicken and tarragon, beef and cracked pepper, duck with berries and port – but tenderly cooked and well-presented; it changes periodically but does not attempt to tread an adventurous path. Vegetarians are welcome, but could be forgiven for thinking that they are largely unexpected!

Predictable starters are described with a dash of the exotic; "naked prawns clothed in marie rose sauce" drew a few laughs at the novel use of language. Desserts are described as 'yumptious', an agreeable sentiment.

Overall, one can expect quality Welsh food, European style, made from mainly local produce, in restrained and neatly rustic surroundings.

MEALS: L 12-2 £5; D 7-9 £20
Closed: Sunday night, Monday in winter
Cards: All except American Express and Diners
CHEF: Mike Lewis. PROPRIETOR: J. L. Di Lorenzo
Rooms: 3, £30 S, £40 D

LOCAL INTEREST: St David's, Preseli Hills for walking, Fishguard Harbour ferry to Ireland.

118 Wolfscastle

Wolfscastle Country Hotel

Wolfscastle
Haverfordwest
Pembrokeshire
SA62 5LZ
Tel: 01437 741225
Fax: 01437 741383
e-mail: andy741225@aol.com

This 150-year-old building still has a quiet grandeur about it, despite offering all the amenities of a modern hotel. The bright, but comfortable bar is a suitable retreat for those who like a cigarette whilst perusing the menu.

Starters are almost mini-meals in themselves; scallops and king prawns are grilled and laid on a seafood paella although a degree in table manners might be required to get them off the skewer.

With several choices of fish and just about every meat graced with a suitable sauce, main courses are modestly eclectic, using Welsh loin of venison with Burgundy and juniper, baked fillet of cod with cabbage and bacon and lemon sole with smoked salmon and a saffron sauce epitomising an exciting medley of flavours.

Desserts without many surprises are designed to cleanse the palate or burst the belt; or choose the cheese with a sculptured apple.

The wine list is studded with Chardonnay and Sauvignon from around the world, with other grapes and estates scattered through it.

MEALS: L 12-2 £4-£12; Sunday L £12;
D 6.45-9 £10-£15; Closed: 24th, 25th and 26th December
Cards: All major
CHEF: Steven Brown. PROPRIETOR: Andrew Stirling
WTB: 3 ★★★
Rooms: 20

LOCAL INTEREST: Llangloffan Cheese Centre, Melin Tregwynt Woollen Mill, Skomer Island, St David's Cathedral, Scolton Manor.

119 Laugharne

Cors Restaurant

Newbridge Road
Laugharne
Carmarthenshire
SA33 4SH
Tel: 01994 427219

The appearance of this enchanting house and gardens could easily transport you to another time, when summers were recognised by the sun and iced tea was taken on the veranda.

The garden takes up much of Nick's time but his care and attention to detail is also prevalent in the kitchen. Flavours of France and Italy mark the territory of the daily menu and there are vegetarian choices in the same vein. The quest for the perfect scallop ends here, seared and served on a sabayon of chives, tender carpaccio of beef fillet is graced with Parmesan shavings and gnocchi may come with a rich Roquefort sauce.

Rack of lamb with a classic crust of rosemary and garlic is cooked to perfection and presented with red onion confit, tournedos of organic Welsh Black are served simply with a red wine jus, allowing the steak to speak for itself and handsome fillets of brill, chargrilled and laid on chicory, are balanced with a sprinkling of salted capers.

Lemon tart or strawberry pavlova refresh the palate and chocolate nut torte has an irresistible charm, served simply, with just whipped cream.

The wine list takes careful steps around French classics, with a flash of Italy and slender homage to the New World while house wines are particularly fair on the wallet.

MEALS: D 7-9.30 approx £25
Only open Thursday, Friday and Saturday evenings
CHEF/PROPRIETOR: Nick Priestland
Rooms: 2, £60 D

LOCAL INTEREST: Laugharne, the estuary, Dylan Thomas's House, the garden at the Cors.

120 Laugharne

The Stable Door

Market Lane
Laugharne
Carmarthenshire
SA33 4SB
Tel: 01994 427777
Fax: 01994 427819

e-mail:
laugharne-restaurant.co.uk

A cheerfully converted stable block houses this cosmopolitan wine bar up a cobbled lane that could play havoc with your stillettos but nevertheless has a particular charm.

Blinis with smoked salmon, chicken satay and Welsh cheese soufflé are among the starters while the mushroom and Madeira soup has a touch of exotic warmth.

Vegetarians are not forgotten, with a mini-meze of spring rolls, samosas and onion bhajis making a refreshing change.

Main courses step conventionally between continents. Chicken Basquaise, moussaka and sirloin with Stilton butter, reasonably priced, come stacked with golden sauté potatoes and crisp salads or steaming vegetables a touch al dente. You might find a Thai curry with rice and chutney, braised lamb on the bone or spare ribs with barbecue sauce. Mediterranean bake of fennel, tomato and Parmesan or perhaps a Mexican croustade with sweet potato, red beans and avocado are further vegetarian options.

Even if you have vowed to abstain on the grounds of girth, crème brulées also include their unique apple and plum variety. Smooth, sweet and sharp marks out the chocolate and apricot tart, and amaretto and almond cheesecake with raspberries.

MEALS: Sunday L 12.30-3 £6.95 for 1 course;
D from 7pm approx £18 inc wine;
Closed: Winter – Monday, Tuesday, Wednesday;
Summer Monday and Tuesday
Cards: All major
CHEF/PROPRIETOR: Wendy Joy
Rooms: 1, £40 D

LOCAL INTEREST: Dylan Thomas's Boathouse, Laugharne Castle, excellent walks.

121 Llanarthne

Golden Grove

Llanarthne
Carmarthenshire
SA32 8JU
Tel: 01558 668551
Fax: 01558 668069

From its imposing exterior enter a rambling central, warm and woody bar, a formal dining room and a variety of other eating areas. All-encompassing menus, with an enormous variety of choices catering for all tastes conspire to fill the place.

Light bites include half-pints of prawns, spicy chicken wings and battered mushrooms; there are also sandwiches, baguettes and a comprehensive children's menu as well.

Main courses feature local produce wherever possible and range from delicate trout fillets with prawns and mushrooms in filo with a creamy dill sauce, to the more robust rack of salt marsh lamb with blueberry and mint sauce and oxtail – back on the menu, in this case with red wine sauce. A bewildering choice of potato dishes and

vegatables accompanies.

The dessert list is as long as your arm – lemon meringue pie, bread-and-butter and sticky toffee puddings hold the traditional flag, while raspberry brulée and almond and pear tart are carefully modern.

There is a predictable range of popular wines, although those looking to improve their cellar can choose from a short connoisseurs list.

MEALS: L 11-3; Sunday L 12-3; D 6-10 from £5
Cards: Visa and Access
CHEF: Colin Thomas. PROPRIETORS: F and J Gamble
WTB: 3 ★★★
Rooms: 6, £35 S, £45 D, £65-£70 Suite

LOCAL INTEREST: Garn Goch Iron age Fort, Goldmines at Pumpsaint, Norman castles at Llanstephan, Kidwelly and Laugharne. Aberglasney Gardens, National Botanical Gardens, Paxton Tower and fishing in the Tywi.

122 Llandeilo

Cawdor Arms Hotel

Rhosmaen Street
Llandeilo
Carmarthenshire
SA19 6EN
Tel: 01558 823500
Fax: 01558 822399

cawdor.arms@btinternet.com
cawdor-arms.co.uk

There is something refreshing about the unruly gaggle of soggy umbrellas rammed in their stand in the porch and sofas, dying to be sprawled on geometrically arranged in the spacious lounges John Silver and his wife Sylvia are, however, very friendly and welcoming, their daughter, Jane, is the chef and the hotel has a well-run genteel feel; someone is always bustling by, starched apron crackling, wheeling a trolley or balancing a tray.

Home-baked loaves, sliced at the table, herald the arrival of starters, served on plates that dwarf their contents. Thai fish cakes with chilli jam, wild mushroom tartlet and delicately flavoured soups such as cauliflower and ginger or courgette and almond could well persuade a vegetarian they have not been forgotten.

On a European menu vegetables are chosen to complement each dish and you might find a tranche of salmon with rocket pesto, partridge with red onion charlotte and lentil salad, or chicken supreme with Serrano ham mousseline. Jane Silver shows a healthy interest in flavours and textures and follows it through with sound technique and beautifully cooked presentation.

Desserts that complete the culinary experience include a plum and custard pie that requires early ordering.

Pierce Brosnan stayed here once and, to bend a phrase from his screen persona, 'Once is not enough.'

MEALS: L 12-2; Sunday Lunch 12-1.30 £14.50; D 7.30-9 £21;
Cards: All major
WTB: 4 ★★★★
CHEF: Jane Silver. PROPRIETORS: John and Sylvia Silver
Rooms: 17, £45 S, £60 D, £75 Suite

LOCAL INTEREST: Historic town of Llandeilo, gardens and castles of the Towy valley, fishing.

123 Llandeilo

Fanny's

3 King Street
Llandeilo
Carmarthenshire
SA19 6AA
Tel: 01558 822908
Suet@fsbdial.co.uk

A light and airy room with a hint of chintz, faded denim-blue trim and cotton tablecloths gives a distinct impression that one is drinking in a tea parlour. The place is caught in an amiable time warp, somewhere between the era of lace curtains, caged canaries and wholefood cafés.

The menu on a row of blackboards is written in that curious café script that only the initiated can interpret, but help is at hand with friendly explanations and post-it stickers that inform us which items are temporarily unavailable.

Several varieties of tea and coffee can accompany your scones or cake, along with other classic afternoon treats such as pecan fudge pie.

Hot dishes, from soup to casseroles of meat or beans, and salads abound, and they are very eco-friendly in all their ingredients. There is an array of quiches to succumb to and pies of bean, vegetable and fish perch on their shelves in the cold display cabinet.

The evening menu steps up a level and makes a feature of Welsh produce and flavours.

MEALS: L 11-4 £5-£10
Closed: Sundays and Mondays
Cards: None
CHEF: Rick Toller. PROPRIETORS: Sue and Rick Toller

LOCAL INTEREST: Carreg Cennen, Dinefwr Park, Aberglasney, National Botanic Gardens, Llanarthne, Glli Aur Country Park, Llynllech Owain.

124 Llandeilo

Y Capel Bach at The Angel Hotel

Angel Hotel
62 Rhosmaen Street
Llandeilo
Carmarthenshire
SA19 6EN
Tel: 01558 822765
Fax: 01558 823073
e-mail: capelbac@aol.com

The peeling yellow ochre paint looks set to join the autumn leaves, but do not be put off by the skin – try the fruit inside. A central bar carries a variety of real ales with wooden chairs and tables to one side whilst the other has a little more padding and there is definitely a wisp of Celt in the atmosphere. Two dining rooms can be found behind the bar, the larger for non-smokers.

An almost bewildering array of menus greets the eye; a bar menu, chargrill menu, main menu and fresh fish options chalked on a board. The choice is wide-ranging, from Mexico to France, and would seem to appeal to all manner of tastes. Where else could you have onion rings with peppered duck breast?

Vegetarians and vegans are well catered for; spinach roulade and vegetable fajitas are well-marked for those who are unsure.

Plump crevettes with garlic butter, moist mushrooms with tarragon

cream, warm salad of chicken and Parmesan are amongst the choices for starters.

The chargrill menu has fillet, sirloin, rump, Welsh lamb chops and something called 'Greedy Pig' – not for the faint-hearted, judging by the list of meats to be stacked up on the plate. Five varieties of fresh fish are on offer and three specials on the board include veal, venison and pork loin.

Adventurous desserts include an aristocratic bread and butter pudding made with croissants, white chocolate and creamy custard and pastry that any chef would be proud of.

House wines are well chosen with some good bottles at reasonable prices.

MEALS: L 11.30-2.30; D 6.45-9.30
Closed: Sunday lunch
Cards: All major
LOCAL INTEREST: Carreg Cennen, Dinefwr Castle, Llandeilo historic market town.

125 Llangadog

Cynyll Farm

Llangadog
Carmarthenshire
SA19 9BR
Tel: 01550 777316

Occupying 77 acres of hillside high above the Towy Valley and overlooking Rhiwiau Hill and the Black Mountains, Cynyll Farm is a working hill farm that Jackie and Terry Dare moved into in 1972. Their friendly greeting is epitomised by a reviving pot of tea served in the lounge-cum-dining-room.

Dinner is freshly prepared by Jackie and only provided by arrangement to guests staying overnight. Using fresh vegetables from the garden, or from a local organic farm, house-produced lamb on the farm and meat from local butchers, her evening meal might feature, lamb chops with Cumberland sauce, beef stew and cheese dumplings, local venison cooked in red wine with bacon, onion and garlic, stuffed pork tenderloin, or smoked haddock pie. The choice of six or seven vegetables, includes the likes of leeks in cheese sauce, cabbage with bacon and roast potatoes.

Vegetarians will not be disappointed with lentil and mushroom haggis or autumn vegetable hotpot with cheese scones.

Among the home-made puddings might be almond and apricot tart, stem ginger and orange trifle with Cointreau and excellent ice cream made from fresh cream straight from the farm's dairy herd.

Next morning, Jackie's full farmhouse breakfast will set you up for the day ahead.

MEALS: D 6.30-8 £9
CHEF/PROPRIETOR: Jackie Dare
WTB: ★★ farm
Rooms: 2, £17 S, £34 D

LOCAL INTEREST: National Botanic Gardens of Wales, Aberglasney Gardens, Carreg Cennen Castle, Dolaucothi gold mines, Brecon Beacons, Llyn Brianne reservoir, Dinefwr Park, salmon and sewin fishing in River Towy.

126 Llanrhidian

Welcome to Town Bistro

Llanrhidian
Gower
Swansea
SA3 1EH
Tel: 01792 390015

e-mail: welcome@welcometotowngower.org.uk
www.welcometotowngower.org.uk

A bona-fide family affair, Welcome to Town is a special place – the sort you would love to have as your local and wish other publicans would emulate.

Within the confines of a village pub lies a bistro, café and bar, dainty with white lace and floral cushions, but with more variety and choice than your average inn.

Robert and Sheila Allen are supported by their sons Philip and Tim, the latter stepping into mum's cooking shoes. The food, with all things that are conjured up by the phrase "home-made", and local produce always featuring strongly, is certainly comforting – perfect on a cold, wet day, or any time you are in need of sustenance.

For Sheila and Tim's full repertoire of dishes, visit on Thursdays to Saturdays, or for simpler blackboard choices, dine earlier in the week; either way, you'll be happy you came. Warm goat's cheese salad might be an ideal way to begin, or perhaps Llanrhidian gratin, with its mix of laverbread, leeks, cockles and bacon under a crumble topping. Move on to Welsh Black beef fillet with red wine and grain mustard sauce, a more exotic chicken with apricots, almonds and coconut milk, or game ragout comprising venison, wild boar and rabbit. Seasonal vegetables are more than generous and lovingly cooked.

To follow, try the coffee marshmallow meringue with Tia Maria cream, mixed nut fudge pie, or a plate of Welsh cheeses. Wines are plentiful on a user-friendly list, with a refreshing alternative non-alcoholic Welsh elderflower spritz.

MEALS: L 12-2 £12-£15; D 7-8.30 £15-£25
Closed: Sunday and Monday
Cards: Visa, Master, Amex
CHEF: Sheila and Tim Allen. PROPRIETOR: Robert Allen

LOCAL INTEREST: Gower Peninsula.

127 Mumbles

Now firmly established as a popular haunt, the High Tide café continues to please with its youthful, upbeat image.

A flexible menu, all-day opening, organic Fair Trade coffee, day-long

High Tide Café

61 Newton Road
Mumbles
Swansea
SA3 4BL
Tel: 01792 363462

snacks, use of local produce and organic beef or veggie burgers have all remained steadfast.

Stop by at any time for Mocha chocacinos, smoothies or pain-au-chocolat; or start off your day with buttery, organic scrambled eggs with Welsh smoked salmon. If you pop by at lunchtime or at night, menu mainstays such as American deluxe burgers, chicken fajitas and lighter side dishes like Greek salad or home-made hummus are popular choices. Sandwiches such as roast veg and pesto cream cheese or triple deck club accompanied by tortilla chips are also available from lunchtime until late in summer. Out of season, opening hours are more limited, so you should check.

Sweeties are as their name implies – the likes of hot chocolate brownies and Canadian waffles with fruit, maple syrup and local Joe's ice cream placate any final tummy rumblings.

Don't forget to peruse the blackboard for the day's specials and wines and beers of the month.

Visitors to the café cannot fail to notice the enticements of Mumbles that make a trip to High Tide doubly attractive.

MEALS: L 12-3 £9; D 6-9 £12
Closed: Winter evenings, Christmas and Boxing Day
Cards: All except Amex
CHEFS: Emily Cosgrove and Sheree Warren.
PROPRIETOR: Emily Cosgrove

LOCAL INTEREST: Gower, Mumbles.

128 Mumbles

L'Amuse

93 Newton Road
Mumbles
Swansea
SA3 4BN
Tel: 01792 366006
Fax. 01792 368090

This delightful restaurant on the busy main road through Mumbles is ebullient and colourful – full of French country style, as one could only expect from its owner, the inimitable Kate Cole. Bright and breezy rods decorate the interior and the atmosphere is Gallic through-and-through.

A two-course set menu offers around six starters and seven main courses. Amuse bouche may comprise a rustic and rich terrine spread over crispbread accompaniments. Perfectly-executed dishes follow in the likes of fricassée of snails with spinach and walnut biscuits or a simple but superb salad of roasted tomatoes with polenta. Main courses continue in the form of a tender supreme of guinea fowl complemented by tarragon and sherry, or plaice with a fricassee of local cockles and mussels with appropriately delicate saffron sauce.

Desserts are adventerous, though there is also the choice of French Alpine cheeses instead. Silky pannacotta with blackberry coulis and intense chocolate fondant are nonetheless too delicious to resist.

Coffee is a must, if there is room, as pretty petits fours are equally accomplished.

MEALS: L 12-2 from £7.95; D 7-9.30 from £18.50
Closed: Sunday and Monday
Cards: All major
CHEF/PROPRIETOR: Kate Cole

LOCAL INTEREST: Close to the Castle, a few minutes from the sea.

129 Mumbles

P.A.'s Wine Bar

95 Newton Road
Mumbles
Swansea
SA3 4BN
Tel: 01792 367723

An intimate, softly lit, wine bar just a stone's throw from the sea, attentive, unobtrusive staff add to its pleasant, friendly atmosphere.

A straightforward bistro menu, supplemented by half-a-dozen daily fish specials, produces robust, no-nonsense cooking.

To begin, choose from a punchy goats' cheese tartlet with Parma ham and sun-dried tomatoes, warm asparagus with poached egg and hollandaise sauce or wild mushroom pâté with home-made plum chutney. To follow are roast breast of Barbary duckling with carrot timbale and Cointreau jus, chargrilled fillet of sea bass with king prawns, spring onion and ginger, or baked hake with basil and smoked salmon. Main dishes are accompanied by boiled potatoes smothered in parsley butter and/or sauté potatoes and vegetables such as mashed swede, crisp broccoli spears and carrots.

Home-made puddings tempt the palate with rich white and milk chocolate mousse cake, oranges in Grand Marnier and tangy lemon souffle.

MEALS: L 12-2.30 £4.95; D 6-9.30 £12.95
Closed: Sunday Evening
Cards: All cards
CHEFS: Liz Richards, Jon Cox and Stuart Phillips.
PROPRIETORS: Steve and Kate Malone

LOCAL INTEREST: Gower Peninsula, Oystermouth Castle, Mumbles.

130 Mumbles

Patrick's

638 Mumbles Road
Mumbles
Swansea
SA3 4EA
Tel: 01792 360199
Fax: 01792 369926

www.patricks-restaurant.co.uk

Along the famous "Mumbles Mile", lies this most pleasant surprise; Patrick's restaurant a favourite with locals in the know, Patrick's can only be described as a place with a real buzz about it. This is also a restaurant with a sense of humour – take a look at the cow-themed toilets and news update on the menu that tells which members of staff "are on tranquilisers"!

All jokes aside, Patrick's takes its food and service seriously. Nothing seems to be a problem for the amiable staff and when plates arrive, you might think you've entered an art gallery, as the presentation is just so.

Start with the likes of bacon, cockle and laverbread sausage with a mustard dressing for a truly local flavour, crispy chicken balls with cheese and sage breadcrumbs, or mussels with leek and coriander.

A specials board offers plenty of fish options such as salmon with goat's cheese crust and precisely timed sea bass. Other dishes, such

as beef with black pudding on buttery mash, aim to comfort, accompanied by plentiful vegetables.

Desserts include Jameson's Irish coffee cream cup with a chocolate cup, and traditional favourites such as apple and mixed fruit pie. For a savoury alternative, try Welsh Rarebit with Patrick's home-made bread.

MEALS: L 12.-2.20 £8; Sunday L 12-2.30 £8; D 6.30-9.45 approx £25
Closed: Sunday evening
Cards: All major
CHEFS: Dean Fuller and Patrick Walsh.
PROPRIETORS: Catherine and Patrick Walsh, Dean and Sally Fuller
LOCAL INTEREST: Mumbles Pier, Langland and Caswell Bays, Clyne Gardens.

131 Nantgaredig

Four Seasons Restaurant

Nantgaredig
Carmarthenshire
SA32 7NY
Tel: 01267 290238
Fax: 01267 290808

This long, low beamed restaurant is warm and friendly with an open kitchen that allows diners to watch the two resident chefs using its four-door Aga to capacity, enough to make Aga users marvel.

Head for the cosy, slightly cramped bar to choose from a remarkably tempting menu.

Starters cover a dozen choices from fresh, creamy tomato soup, Black Mountain smoked salmon with warm cucumber and mint salad to fresh king scallops with roasted hazlenut and coriander butter.

Main course might be tender rack of lamb, sliced with a criss-crossed golden outside and served with broccoli, herby potatoes and a perfect light gravy, breast of free range chicken with Brie wrapped in Carmarthen ham, or fresh salmon and spinach wrapped in pastry comes with chive and cream sauce. Vegetarians might be offered fresh spinach, tomato and Teifi cheese pancakes or a wild mushroom risotto, produced before your very eyes.

Puddings range from fresh strawberries with raspberry sorbet to crisp almond and pear frangipan tart – a lovely light touch here.

The wine list supplied by the restaurant's own Towy Valley wine company offers remarkably good choice and value.

MEALS: D 7.30-9.30 £22.50
Closed: Sundays and Mondays
Cards: All major
CHEFS/PROPRIETORS: Maryann Wright and Charlotte Pasetti
WTB: 3 ★★★
Rooms: 6, £40 S, £56 D, £80 Suite

LOCAL INTEREST: Aberglasney, National Botanic Gardens.

132   Nantgaredig

Y Polyn

Nantgaredig
Carmarthenshire
SA32 7LH
Tel: 01267 290000

Well-signposted and standing at a junction of rural roads above the Towy Valley south of Nantgaredig, Y Polyn (or The Pole) is one of the former toll houses raided during the famous Rebecca Riots by locals dressed up as women rebelling against toll charges. It was rescued from closure and neatly refurbished two years ago by enterprising young owners Tim and Sue Horton, who could see its potential as a pub and restaurant.

In addition to visitors, discerning locals swell the numbers in search of good food. Those just wanting a snack can choose from sandwiches, baguettes and traditional favourites such as chilli, spaghetti Bolognese or Provencale vegetable tart in the small bar. The culinary skills and ambitions of the chef are evident on the regularly-changing restaurant menu, which is more imaginative and features produce sourced from local suppliers.

Begin, perhaps, with Welsh goats' cheese salad with olives and red peppers, locally smoked salmon served with blinis and a lemon and dill dressing, or pan-fried cockles, bacon and laverbread with croutons. Move then to freshly-made salmon and laverbread fishcakes with chive and lemon sauce, leg of salt marsh lamb roasted with rosemary and garlic, or chicken wrapped in Carmarthen ham with a creamy Stilton sauce. On the specials board, you might find locally-shot pheasant with red wine and bacon and fish such as sea bass with oriental vegetables or Towy salmon with lemon butter sauce.

Puddings might include white chocolate and amaretto tart and Bailey's crème brulée. There is a short list of wines from Towy Valley Wines, and Brain's real ale on handpump.

MEALS: L 12-3 approx £10; D 6-11 approx £20
Closed: Mondays (October to April)
Cards: Visa, Mastercard, Amex
CHEF: Tim Horton. PROPRIETOR: Tim and Sue Horton

LOCAL INTEREST: National Botanic Gardens, Aberglasney Gardens.

133   Narbeth

Winnies

Noble Court
Redstone Road
Narbeth
Pembrokeshire
SA67 7ES
Tel: 01834 860213
Fax: 01834 861484

Once the family home of the Evans-Pritchards, who own the caravan site and leisure centre, this building has been converted into a very pretty bistro. Decorated a soft shade of green with simple pine tables and chairs, it has a warm and welcoming atmosphere. Chef Andrew Cody has moved to Narbeth from Bristol and is starting to make a name for himself with a menu of five or six choices at each stage.

Starters might include goats' cheese tart with a rich, buttery pastry, cream of local vegetable soup and prawn terrine with lemon and dill dressing.

Fish lovers will find roasted cod topped with mushroom spring onion crust, finished with a red pepper sauce or darne of salmon poached in lime butter and encased in filo pastry. Vegetarian choices may well be a roast vegetable strudel or roast aubergine and mozzarella cutlets. Game in season could be pigeon or roast pheasant with a game and blackberry jus, all served with a selection of fresh vegetables.

Apart from a selection of cheeses and ice creams, desserts might include rich chocolate liqueur terrine, almond sponge pudding with crème anglaise or lemon and mixed berry gratin garnished with a white rum and kumquat coulis. Service is efficient and charming and the wine list offers a selection of Old and New World wines at reasonable prices.

MEALS: D 7-9.30 approx £20
Closed: Tuesday
Cards: All major
CHEF: Andrew Cody. PROPRIETOR: Joanna Rowland

LOCAL INTEREST: Narbeth village, Oakwood leisure park, Tenby, Saunderfoot.

134 Newport

Café Fleur

Dolphin House
Market Street
Newport
Pembrokeshire
SA42 0PH
Tel: 01239 820131
Fax: 01239 820958

This Belgian style café in the centre of Newport, with tiled floor and wooden tables, is the setting for Alan and Diane's charming eatery. Recently returned from abroad, they have brought some sparkling new ideas to this very special Pembrokeshire village.

The main item on the menu is galettes – large light pancakes traditional to Brittany – filled with chicken and Mediterranean sauce or the classic ham and egg Bretonne, for instance served straight from the stove onto huge china plates and accompanied by dressed leaves.

Salads with local crab or prawns, home-made soups and croque monsieur, all served with home-made soda bread, are popular alternatives.

Sweet Belgain waffles and crepes, freshly cooked in front of customers are filled with lemon and sugar, maple syrup and banana or hot chocolate sauce and ice cream; otherwise, plump for a slice of tarte au citron, impossibly lemony, with a crisp pastry crust.

Excellent Belgian coffee is served with little chocolate flowers – the perfect place for a cup of coffee (newspapers provided), a quick snack or, better still, a long, lazy lunch. During the summer months, families head here for a treat when the weather is not good enough for a picnic on the beach.

MEALS: L 10.30-6 approx £7.50; D 7.30 approx £15
Closed: Sunday, Monday and Tuesday lunch.
All evenings except Saturday
Cards: Switch, Visa and Mastercard

CHEF: Diane Griffiths. PROPRIETOR: Alan Griffiths

LOCAL INTEREST: Seaside town, harbour and beach. Walking, golf, riding, cycling.

135 Newport

Cnapan

East Street
Newport
Pembrokeshire
SA42 0SY
Tel: 01239 820575
Fax: 01239 820878

e-mail:
cnapan@online-holidays.net
www.
online-holidays.net/cnapan/

One of Pembrokeshire's unspoilt coastal jewels, Newport boasts one of the most satisfying restaurants-with-rooms in the area. This pink-washed, comfortable, listed townhouse is the home of a two-generation Welsh-speaking family. Lace cloths cover pink napery, vases have posies of fresh flowers, baroque music plays discreetly in the background and service is friendly and professional.

Lunches tend to be light yet wholesome affairs, with flans, soups, baked ham and salmon. The evening menu homes in on local fish, game and meat dishes: duck breast with soured cherry sauce, roasted guinea fowl with celery and fennel, grilled fillet of cod with crusted pesto top. Vegetarians are in their element, with herby crepes and roasted filled peppers for starters and three choices of main-course, including hot avocado and Glamorgan sausages. The home-made bread such as cheesy savoury buttery slice, served with fennel and fresh coriander soup, is divine.

Speciality puddings range from the irresistible Piggy's Delight – chocolate sponge soaked in boozy orange sauce, black cherry filling and cream – to a wonderful light brioche-based bread-and-butter pudding with custard. Welsh cheeses include Llyn, Llanboidy, Rosebush and the Irish Cashel, Wadworth 6X ale is offered warm or cold, water is organic Llanllyr and there is a wide choice of good value wines, including organic and Welsh. Don't pass without stopping – but you'll need to book in season.

MEALS: L 12-2 £11; Sunday L 12-2 £10.75; D 6.45-8.45 £23
Closed: Tuesday, Christmas, Januray and February
Cards: Visa, Mastercard, Switch Delta
CHEF/PROPRIETOR: Judy Cooper
WTB: 4 ★★★★
Rooms: 5, £58 D

LOCAL INTEREST: Pembrokeshire Coatsal Path, Newport Golf Course, the seaside.

136 Newport

Right beside the boathouse, adjacent to the Pembrokeshire coastal path, this small café has picture – book views of families messing

Morawelon

Parrog
Newport
Pembrokeshire
SA42 0RW
Tel: 01239 820565
Fax: 01239 820565

Welsh produce at its best

about with boats in the river. Campers and holidaymakers make good use of the small shop and, although the dining area is quite small, it extends into the garden on fine days.

Mother and son supervise a team of smiling competent 'young' to look after you. Five or six dishes-of-the-day might include Welsh lamb chops, cooked pink in the middle, and braised beef with crisp puff pastry served with ample bowls of fresh Pembrokeshire potatoes, broccoli, carrots and beans.

Lighter meals include club sandwiches, easily enough for two, of real bread groaning with fillings of salad and bacon or smoked salmon and cream cheese. Three or four vegetarian dishes and salads are varied and original, with local crab a specially popular choice.

A favourite pudding has to be waffles, hot and freshly-made with ice cream and fruit or delectable Belgian chocolate sauce. There are wines, beers and a selection of soft drinks including elderflower cordial and good, strong coffee.

Morawelon provides good value for all the family with its plentiful portions of well-flavoured food that include half portions for children.

MEALS: L 12-3 from £3
Closed: November and December
Cards: All major
CHEF: Richard Watts. PROPRIETORS: Brian and Christine Watts

LOCAL INTEREST: Castell Henllys Iron Age Fort, Pentre Ifan burial chamber, walking in Bluestone country, Newport golf club.

137 Neyland

The Bar at Neyland Yacht Haven

Brunel Quay
Neyland
Pembrokeshire
SA73 1PY
Tel: 01646 602550
Fax: 01834 813578

Welsh produce at its best

The cheerful, modern ambience of this bistro-style establishment is most welcoming; perched above the marina, looking out over a forest of expensive masts. The furniture is bright and breezy and arty photos on the walls are for sale, clean and tidy, slightly cluttered and certainly relaxed.

The menu complements the marina's clientele, with portions to reflect the healthy effect of all things nautical, seafood that is fresh and tasty – salmon fishcakes and monkfish with stir-fried vegetables underpin a small, select choice. Some starters may also be served as main courses – prawns that are worth peeling because they actually have a taste, mussels with attitude, or perhaps a plate of cold sliced sausages. For main course rump of lamb or baked chicken breast, while vegetarians are restricted to a choice of soup or pasta

Desserts are few in number and vary from helpings of home-made rice pudding with preserves and almonds, either wrapped in filo with apricots or nestling up to fresh figs. The menu changes twice a month and side dishes come as extras.

House wines are robust, good value and well chosen. The wine list

has some gems waiting to be drunk if you are prepared to pay the higher restaurant prices.

MEALS: Bar open 11-11. Meals from £8
Closed: December 25th, 26th
Cards: Visa, M/C
CHEF/PROPRIETOR: Guy Morris

LOCAL INTEREST: Milford Haven Museum, Kaleidoscope Discovery Centre, Pembroke Castle, Lamphey Bishop's Palace, Upton Castle Grounds.

138 Pembroke

The Left Bank

63 Main Street
Pembroke
Pembrokeshire
SA71 4DA
Tel/Fax: 01646 622333
e-mail: emmagriffith@leftbankrestaurant.co.uk
www.leftbankrestaurant.co.uk

It's hard to imagine the last manager of this erstwhile bank approving of the colourful and artistic decor that greets the visitor now. Whether for coffee, light lunch, a browse in the top floor gallery or an evening meal, a warm and friendly welcome is assured.

The daily-changing menu, an inspiring choice of dishes, awakens the appetite. Andrew Griffith is obviously in love with the culinary arts of France but with some extra twists that appeal. Salad of confit duck with black pudding, bacon and poached egg has the flavour of an exotic breakfast not to be taken before eleven.

Amongst the main dishes, non meat-eaters are informed, almost as an afterthought, that there is an option available for them. Welsh lamb, beef, chicken and fish take pride of place with imaginative accompaniments and their presentation is more artistic than some of the paintings. It's refreshing to see chump and ribeye steaks receive the attention they deserve, all too often neglected in favour of safer cuts, though tenderly-cooked vegetables can be a curious let down in comparison to the dishes they accompany.

Desserts are another artistic treat, colourful and cleansing with well balanced combinations of sweet and sharp. Sorbets and ice creams marry well with shortcake and flavoured creme fraiche while chocolate addicts will easily satisfy their cravings.

MEALS: L 12-2.30 £4.95; Sunday L 12-3 £12.95; D 7-9.30 £19.95 and £24.95;
Closed: 3 weeks January, 1 week October
Cards: All
CHEF: Andrew Griffith. PROPRIETORS: Andrew and Emma Griffith

LOCAL INTEREST: Pembroke and surroundings.

139 Penally

A Gothic-style mansion surrounded by six acres of garden and woodland stands on the site of a former 6th Century abbey. Carefully

Penally Abbey

Penally
Nr Tenby
Pembrokeshire
SA70 7PY
Tel: 01834 843033
Fax: 01834 844714

e-mail:
penallyabbey@bt.internet.com
www.penally-abbey.com

restored by Steve and Elleen over 14 years, the hotel is decorated throughout perfectly in keeping with its character. Some of the bedrooms boast four-poster beds and in one, hidden by a mirror, a little staircase lends down to a quirky but luxurious bathroom. Draw back the curtains in the morning to enjoy a view of Carmarthen Bay and Caldey Island.

A cosy bar and drawing room set off the elegant dining room, complete with chandelier, to create a splendid setting for dinner. Amongst the starters are crab cakes and vegetable samosas with chilli relish, banana-wrapped ham in a grilled cheese sauce, Mediterranean vegetable terrine and avocado with marinated salmon in honey, mustard and dill.

Main-courses include tangy pigeon with orange and Tabasco, fillet of beef filled with Stilton wrapped in bacon and finished in red wine, breast of duck with whisky and onion marmalade, and grilled Dover sole with lime and ginger.

Pudding choices include crème caramel, blackcurrant cheesecake, luxury bread-and-butter pudding and dark chocolate torte with Bailey's Cream. The cheeseboard includes a good Welsh selection.

MEALS: L 12noon £16; D 7.30 £28
Cards: All major
CHEF: Eleen Warren. PROPRIETORS: Steve and Elleen Warren
WTB: 4 ★★★★
Rooms: 12, £98 S, £108-£132 D

LOCAL INTEREST: Tenby's walled town, Pembroke Castle, Pembrokeshire coastal park.

140 Pen-y-Cwm

Whitehouse

Pen-y-Cwm
Nr Solva
Pembrokeshire
SA62 6LA
Tel: 01437 720959

bandb@whitehouse.prestel.co.uk

Follow the brown youth hostel signs leading off the coast road between Newgale and St David's and you will come to Whitehouse, tucked in beside the hostel at Pen-y-Cwm. Patricia and Ken Cross run both the hostel and their serene bed and breakfast with boundless energy.

The best deal is to stay for a couple of nights and not only enjoy the lovely Pembrokeshire scenery but indulge thoroughly in Pat's magnificent cooking.

Pat has a passion for local produce and, harnessed with her ability to cook like a dream, this raises the only complaint from visitors – to be allowed a greater length of time between courses to enjoy them more fully!

The set menu might include a laverbread gratin, made with lardons of smoked bacon, laverbread, white wine and topped with cream and grated cheese before being toasted under the grill. For a main course, perhaps a fish Wellington made from layers of salmon and cod with spinach and ricotta cheese, all wrapped in puff pastry and served with a lemon and dill hollandaise. Vegetables are a feast in themselves, perhaps country-baked potatoes cooked in their skins, then sliced and baked with olive oil dribbled over to give that extra crunch.

Pudding might reflect a recent trip to Provence, with layers of meringue and puréed chestnuts topped with cream and grated chocolate.

Ken and Pat do take time off from the business several times a year and return full of enthusiasm to tackle the next adventure in her excellent kitchen.

MEALS: D 7.30 £11.50
Closed: Please ring
Cards: None
CHEF/PROPRIETOR: Patricia Cross
WTB: 4 ★★★★
Rooms: 3, S, £36 p person for 2 nights or more

LOCAL INTEREST: St David's Cathedral and Bishop's Palace, the RSPB reserve on Ramsey Island, Llangloffan Farm Cheese Centre, Cwm Deri vineyard at Martletwy.

141 Saundersfoot

Swallow Tree Gardens

Saundersfoot
Pembrokeshire
SA69 9DZ
Tel: 01834 812398
Fax: 01834 812558

e-mail: goodfood@swallowtree.com
www.swallowtree.com

Overlooking Carmarthen Bay, just on the outskirts of Saundersfoot, housed within a leisure complex, this venue is becoming increasingly popular with locals.

Well-cooked and nicely presented, the food is exciting. At lunchtime and in the early evening light bites encompass chargrilled fillet of salmon topped with a toasted cashew nut, sun-dried tomato and coriander, mayonnaise and strips of chicken sautéed in butter with garlic, chilli, tamarind and honey finished with sesame oil and served on a chargrilled croute with melted Mozzarella.

The evening menu offers first courses of spinach and mascarpone roulade, gravadlax of salmon, chicken live pâté, fresh scallops seared with diced onion, smoked bacon and fresh thyme served on an olive oil croute with puy lentil and chilli vinaigrette.

Main courses might be loin of lamb griddled and served on a pea and mint mash with redcurrant and port jus, oven baked duck breast seasoned with Chinese spices, roasted and sliced on to a bed of stir-fried vegetables with soy, garlic, balsamic and honey sauce, or pork tenderloin coated in cracked pepper, grilled and served with cider, apple and thyme sauce accompanied by parsnip crisps.

Home-made puddings include perhaps ginger pudding or apple and raspberry tart.

MEALS: L 12-2; D 6-9.30
Closed: Opening times vary, please ring first
CHEFS: Debbie Weak and Melanie Fairman.
PROPRIETOR: John Hancock
WTB: 5 ★★★★★, holiday park

LOCAL INTEREST: Tenby Museum and Art Gallery, Tudor Merchant's

House, Manor House Wildlife and Leisure Park at St Florence, Colby Woodland Garden.

142   Solva

The Old Pharmacy Restaurant

Solva
Haverfordwest
Pembrokeshire
SA62 6UU
Tel: 01437 720005
Fax: 01437 721106

e-mail:oldpharmacy@aol.com
www.solvanet

The relaxed ambience and warming decor would not be out of place in a busy town street, but here it creates a pleasant diversion from the uniform identity of many establishments. Stephen holds sway in the kitchen and his brother Martin Lawton discreetly patrols the dining rooms, rather like an indulgent headmaster.

Fresh fish and crab are prominent and there is also plenty of imaginative choice for vegetarians. Stephen seems to favour the delicate spicy flavours of Thailand but is just as happy to serve cuttlefish with Mediterranean herbs or chicken breast with asparagus and tarragon. Marinaded duck breast sounds a British note but with a Chinese cadence and everything arrives like a picture on the plate. Classic desserts continue this culinary adventure with white chocolate crème brulée and Stephen's unique interpretation of Tiramisu. Wines live up to the menu a concise tour of the world with a few well chosen and fairly priced surprises.

MEALS: L 11-3 £3.25-£12; D 6.30-9 approx £20-£25
Closed: Tuesdays
Cards: All major
CHEF: S J Lawton. PROPRIETORS: M P and S J Lawton

LOCAL INTEREST: Solva harbour, village, St David's Cathedral, coastal path, scenery, beaches, walking, riding.

143   Stackpole

The Boathouse

Stackpole Quay
Stackpole
Pembroke
Pembrokeshire
SA71 5DE
Tel: 01646 672058

On the slipway leading down to Stackpole Quay, this pretty tearoom is a clever conversion of the old boathouse that Penny Jackson has leased from the National Trust. She serves up high quality home cooking, using the best and freshest produce of the area.

Visitors to the area return year after year to enjoy the setting as much as Penny's wonderful baking. Tea, coffee and home-made cakes are served all day, as well as a simple list of savoury dishes such as Mediterranean salad with tuna, prawns and olives, dippy prawns shell-on with garlic mayonnaise and granary bread. The Farmers Lunch of locally made sausages with a spicy relish, Rambler's Lunch of ham and Welsh cheese and traditional Welsh rarebit abound in fresh local ingredients.

Cakes include shortbread, treacle tart with clotted cream, coffee and walnut cake and a moist orange and almond cake. Upton dairy ice cream is served during the summer.

Lunchtime specials might be a large bowl of freshly-made broccoli and Stilton soup, pasta carbonara or succulent pork sausage and fresh vegetables.

Service is efficient and friendly; no matter how busy this is an ideal resting place for walkers and families spending a day on this beautiful part of the National Park.

MEALS: L 12-3.30 £3.85-£6.25
Closed: November - February
Cards: None
CHEF/PROPRIETOR: Penny Jackson

LOCAL INTEREST: Stackpole Quay, Pembrokeshire coastal path, Bosherton lily ponds.

144 St David's

Morgan's Brasserie

20 Nun Street
St Davids
Haverfordwest
Pembs
SA62 6NT
Tel: 01437 720508

morgans@stdavids.co.uk
morgans-in-stdavids.co.uk

The two dining rooms and tiny reception area give the impression of a well-ordered doll's house. The tables are laid with pristine precision and Stan Rosenthal paintings neatly adorn the walls.

Fresh fish figures widely in each evening's choice, Dover sole with citrus butter, baked turbot with mussel and saffron sauce, or parcels of salmon and monkfish. Lamb, fillet steak, roast duckling and partridge, all with conventional sauces, defer to European influences.

Starters cover an assiette of pickled and marinated fish has echoes of fiords, while tiger prawns with basil in filo and sweet and sour sauce echoes the flavours of Thailand and homage to France is paid with confit of duck.

Desserts have a definite conventional flavour; oranges marinaded in Grand Marnier, chocolate framboise and Bailey's crème brulée.

The wine list holds plenty of interest; prices are fair for quality wines and house wines good value. Prices reflect the class of visitor this food can expect – and book for early in the evening; as they only have 10 tables, the choice of dishes can rapidly diminish.

MEALS: D 7-9 £20-£25
Closed: January, February – other times during season
Cards: Visa, Mastercard, Amex
CHEF/PROPRIETOR: Ceri Morgan

LOCAL INTEREST: Pembrokeshire coastal path, St David's Cathedral, beaches etc.

145 St David's

Warpool Court

St David's
Pembrokeshire
SA62 6BN
Tel: 01437 720300
Fax: 01437 720676

e-mail: warpool@enterprise.net
www.stdavids.co.uk/warpoolcourt

An elegant drive leads up to this imposing Victorian hotel, which looks like a cross between the convent it once was and an ornamental castle. Inside it has a comfy feel, and magnificent coastal views; the staff extend a universally warm welcome.

The menu changes daily, and makes good reading.

Local fresh crab is neatly parcelled in pasta and presented on spinach with tomato coulis; home-smoked salmon features with lightly battered tiger prawns, and there could be wild mushrooms in a delicate risotto or partridge terrine with fig chutney.

Sorbet is served between courses, refreshing the palate before many main courses of roast monkfish with wild mushroom sauce, steamed chicken breast on tomato and coriander with couscous and new potatoes or honey-roast duck with red cabbage and rosti potato.

From the dessert menu, steamed treacle sponge with proper custard nestles beside poached fruits with ginger; amongst other favourites, crème brulée, and surely something for those who cannot move without chocolate.

The wine list reads like a history of quality estates, so be prepared to spend your inheritance on some of the bottles! House wines are nonetheless good value and reflect the quality that is shown elsewhere.

MEALS: L 12-2; D 7-9.15
Closed: January
Cards: All
CHEF: John Daniels. GENERAL MANAGER: Rupert Duffin
WTB: 4 ★★★★
Rooms: 25, from £73 S, from £122 D

LOCAL INTEREST: Pembrokeshire coastal path and beaches, St David's Cathedral and Bishop's Palace.

146 St Florence

Bramleys Tea Room

Plough Penny Field
St Florence
Pembrokeshire
SA70 8LP
Tel: 01834 871778
Fax: 01834 871430

www.bramleystearoom.co.uk

It is hard to find fault with Bramleys, a charming little tea room tucked away behind the garden centre in St Florence, run by Liz Hainsworth. The atmosphere is welcoming, the staff competent and friendly and the food as home-made as it gets.

Locals and visitors flock here regularly for the daily menu, special evenings, the ever-popular Sunday lunch or just a cup of tea and slice of home-made cake. The tea room is unlicensed but customers may bring their own wine, although tea, coffee and elderflower cordial is available.

At lunch, home-made soup may be lentil, vegetable or tomato. The ploughman's lunch includes local Pembrokeshire cheese, perhaps from the local cheesemaker just across the road. Main courses include

home-made steak pie with vegetables and potatoes, home cooked ham with parsley sauce, chicken, leek and mushroom pie, peppered pork casserole, Glamorgan sausages with mushroom and sherry sauce, tuna and tomato bake, sewin fishcakes with tartare sauce and a range of jacket potatoes, sandwiches and rolls.

Puddings are first class and benefit from Liz's light pastry touch. There are fruit tarts and a faultless moist orange, brandy and chocolate sponge terrine. Local ice creams are always available.

MEALS: L 12-3 from £2.50
Closed: Monday, Tuesday and Wednesday during winter
Cards: All major
CHEF/PROPRIETOR: Liz Hawsworth

LOCAL INTEREST: Situated in country nursery, scenic rural village.

147 Swansea

Chelsea Café

Ty Castell House
17 Saint Mary's Street
Swansea
SA1 3LH
Tel: 01792 464068

Down a side road between Wind Street and the bustle of the old market, there stands this refurbished three-storey building, with an ivory-washed, tongue-and-grooved-lined dining room. If this is going to give him room to expand, Nick Bevan's made a wise move when he came here to start out on his own. There's a happy buzz from diners as they tuck into his exuberant fare, and from staff who don't keep you waiting.

Nick takes time and care in sourcing his ingredients from fishermen in the harbour and a farmer on Gower who grows herbs organically nor does he drown them in complex sauces. An astonishing range of meat and fish one Monday lunchtime included starters of lamb cawl, soused trout, deep-fried brie, and a wild mushroom, basil and tomato tart. Shark, monkfish, black bream or sea bass, or turkey, rump steak, pork, pheasant, partridge, guinea fowl, wild boar, lamb shank, duck breast, or Welsh Black beef fillet, each put in an appearance with appropriate jus, salsa, pesto, cream or relish.

Desserts on this occasion ran to bread-and-butter pudding served with sherry, and ice cream, and apple fritters with vanilla cream. Alternatively there is always a full Welsh cheeseboard on offer.

MEALS: L 12-2.30 £8.95; D 7-9.30 £20-£22
Closed: Sunday and Monday evening
Cards: All major
CHEF: Nick Bevan. PROPRIETORS: Nick Bevan and Lisa Recke

LOCAL INTEREST: Swansea city centre.

148 Swansea

Dermott's Restaurant

219 High Street
Swansea
SA1 1NN
Tel: 01792 459050
Fax: 01792 459050

Without doubt Dermott's is hot stuff – the cooking is very good and as much love and care goes into the presentation as the preparation. Inter-course treats like the small cup of Stilton and cauliflower soup before the starter and a dainty dish of lemon posset prior to the pudding demonstrate the chef's desire to go the extra mile.

Dermott and Wendy have the ambience right, too. Pre-dinner drinks and canapés are taken on a comfy sofa and anyone waiting for a tardy dinner date can flick through the pile of magazines and newspapers.

Decor is bright, airy and modern; the atmosphere is easy-going and staff make guests feel comfortable and welcome.

To start, enjoy roasted breast of wild woodland pigeon with tatties and neeps, Highland haggis with light tarragon sauce or pan-seared scallops topped with flash-fried baby squid with creamed butternut squash and light squid ink.

To follow, are roasted fillet of pink sea bream served on crushed lemon grass-scented potatoes, candied onion relish and a flat parsley and bacon cream and loin of Welsh lamb on creamed celeriac and mint with chargrilled vegetables and black olive and thyme jus. These dishes come with fresh vegetables, many of which are grown by Dermott's father-in-law.

Anyone with a hearty appetite can slot in cheeses with home-made walnut bread before iced nougatine glacé on a summer berry and sambncca compote with crisp tuiles, warm bread-and-butter pudding with home-made honey ice cream and rum-and-raisin custard or milk chocolate and Cointreau torte with burnt oranges and marshmallow ice cream.

MEALS: D 7.30-9.30 £23.50
Closed: Two weeks at Christmas, Two weeks in July
Cards: All major
CHEF. Dermott Slade. PROPRIETORS: Dermott and Wendy Slade

---

149 Swansea

Didier and Stephanie

56 St Helen's Road
Swansea
SA14 DE
Tel: 01792 655603

e-mail:
sdanvel@hotmail.com

A long-time fixture of Swansea's St Helen's Road, fans of the former "Annie's" will be pleased that the new owners have kept true to its French theme. Background music has a Gallic voice while the familiar stripped pine tables, church pews-chairs and an overall warm glow ensure diners feel thoroughly cossetted.

The monthly changing menus are a delight; it is classically French, revealing a penchant for buttery sauces and local produce. Begin, perhaps, with a creamy snail lasagne with marsh samphire, pigeon salad and fine beans, or salad of pigs' trotters with red port dressing. Among the main courses, expect pleasingly gamey saddle of wild

rabbit with mustard sauce, monkfish stuffed with tapenade, or fine sewin with sound but rather rich beurre blanc.

The assumption that desserts and petit fours are where the French excel holds true here. Gratin au caramel is a soufflé delight with perfect toffee sauce, while instead of French farm cheeses, try a refreshing alternative of fromage frais with cleansing herbs and a flick of sugar. The petits fours – physalis dipped in chocolate and chocolate with coconut – are rare treats to accompany after-dinner coffee.

MEALS: L 12-2.30 £8.90; D 7-9.30 approx £25
Closed: Sunday and Monday
Cards: All major
CHEFS/PROPRIETORS: Didier and Stephanie

150 Reynoldston

Fairyhill

Reynoldston
Swansea
SA3 1BS
Tel: 01792 390139
Fax: 01792 391358
e-mail: postbox@fairyhill.net
www.fairyhill.net -1

Victorians headed to the spas for rejuvenation; the modern aesthete should surrender, instead, to the likes of Fairyhill. No artifice here – the Fairyhill crew might be emissaries of the good life, but thankfully without pomposity. Relaxation is the name of the game at this country house on the Gower Peninsula that was once a private Georgian residence. Much of Fairyhill's character indeed is down to partners Andrew Hetherington, Paul Davies and Jane and Peter Camm, who come up with amusing quips with pleasing regularity.

All said, spotlight still rests on its acclaimed food and laudable wine list – which seems continually to expand to more than 400 bins from 13 countries. Paul's menus take in both classical and modern ideas and consistently champion Welsh produce.

Canapés in the lounge include deep-fried cockles, a must on the Gower, whilst these also feature in a gratin starter with leeks and laverbread. Other starters include a distinctive seafood sausage surrounded by vivid saffron sauce. Main courses come with seasonal, home-grown vegetables and include tender, pink loin of Brecon venison with venison sausage, apple and coriander; grilled Welsh Black fillet with horseradish soufflé and whisky sauce, and potato, nut and vegetable galette with chilli and coconut cream.

Paul's culinary prowess extends to desserts, such as an accomplished white-and-dark chocolate terrine with Mocha sauce and cinnamon ice cream. An up-dated Welsh rarebit or predominently Welsh cheeseboard offer an alternative end to the Fairyhill experience.

MEALS: L 12.30-2 £17.50 for 3 courses; Sunday L 12.30-2 £19.50;
D 7.30-9 £35 for 3 courses
Cards: Visa, Mastercard, Amex
CHEF: Paul Davies.

PROPRIETORS: Paul Davies, Andrew Hetherupton,
Jane and Peter Camm
WTB: 5 ★★★★★

Rooms: 8, from £110 S, from £125 D

LOCAL INTEREST: Walking on Gower, watersports, Dylan Thomas trail, Swansea market festival.

151 Swansea

La Brasseria

28 Wind Street
Swansea
SA1 1DZ
Tel: 01792 469683
Fax: 01792 470816
www.labraseria.com

Fall into the Mediterranean trance invoked by flamenco rock, wine casks and clay pots, sawdust-strewn wooden floor and woven basket lamp shades which surround one at this ever-popular eatery to understand why La Brasseria steadily attracts the crowds year in, year out.

What makes this Spanish Bodega-style restaurant a winner with so many Swansea folks is dependability, with food that does not aspire to haute cuisine, but remains immensely satisfying in its simplicity.

'La Bras', has a formula that works, primarily; fish, meat, poultry and game chargrilled, pan-fried, sautéed or baked in the open kitchen. Diners order at the bar, behind which some 200 wines and Armagnacs beckon. Most begin with salad before moving on to choose from the blackboard. Starters include gambas in garlic butter, fish soup and calamari, followed by main courses of sea bass in rock salt, steak, suckling pig and all manner of fish from swordfish with wine and garlic to turbot, monkfish and wild sewin. Although the main bar is downstairs, don't order before viewing the seafood on display upstairs. For vegetarians there are fewer options, listed in small script, as this eatery is primarily a place for fish-and-meat lovers, so be warned!

MEALS: L 12-2.30 £6.95; D 7-11.30
Closed: Sundays
Cards: All major
CHEFS: Ian Wing and Paul Vaughan. PROPRIETOR: Manuel Tercero

LOCAL INTEREST: Swansea City Centre and Waterfront.

152 Swansea

How comforting to find a friendly family-run hotel in a city centre, without the slightest touch of corporate hospitality. Pam and Ron Rumble, who have run this elegant Georgian hotel for 30 years, offer a very personal service to their guests and their staff could not be more

Windsor Lodge Hotel

Mount Pleasant
Swansea
SA1 6EG
Tel: 01792 642158
Fax: 01792 648996

friendly. Furnishings are comfortable and the atmosphere relaxed.

Menus reflect the best of local produce, sought from good suppliers including the nearby Swansea market. Start, perhaps, with roast duck breast on a celeriac, apple and sultana salad with hazelnut dressing or tiger prawns with fresh rocket and mango.

Main courses might be rump of lamb niçoise, or a trio of smoked haddock, salmon and fresh scallops on spinach and tagliatelle with a creamy vermouth sauce. Follow then with orange and lemon tart, raspberry and white chocolate fromage frais cheesecake or chocolate and raspberry gateau.

Late for breakfast? Well, this is one place where it really doesn't matter and you will have a fresh pot of coffee, too, whenever you want.

MEALS: L 12.30-2.30 from £15; D 7-9.30 from £22
Closed: Christmas Day/Boxing Day
Cards: All major
CHEF: Tina Stewart.
PROPRIETOR: Mrs Pam Rumble
WTB: 2 ★★
Rooms: 19, £55 S, £65 D

LOCAL INTEREST: Glynn Vivian Art Gallery, walking distance to the shops, Dylan Thomas Centre, Swansea Beach, Mumbles and Gower.

153 Swansea Marina

Hanson's

Pilot House Wharf
Trawler Road
Swansea Marina
SA1 1UN
Tel: 01792 466200
Fax: 01792 201774

Situated at the very edge of Swansea Marina, Hanson's restaurant is housed in a distinctive building next to the fishing boats. Climb up a spiral staircase to a small dining-room with tiny windows that scarcely take in panoramic views over the water. However, Hanson's does take its fishy neighbours seriously.

A blackboard near the bar highlights the daily specials, such as hake with prawns, or sea bass with fettuccini on a flavourful tomato coulis. But before jumping too far ahead, local produce shines in appetisers like deep-fried cockles, laverbread and Llanboidy cheese parcels on tomato and basil sauce, whilst a king prawn brochette with saffron rice and spicy salsa is delicious, more suited to a Thai green curry! More staid options appear in the form of ubiquitous prawns and melon with marie rose sauce.

Aside from the blackboard full of aquatic temptations, the menu features main courses such as tender medallions of venison on a puff pastry case with creamed leeks, honey-and-peppercorn glazed duck breast on stir-fried vermicelli with light orange sauce, and various steaks with "au poivre" or port and blue cheese sauces. For afters, try a fluffy yet wickedly good lemon meringue pie.

MEALS: L 12-2 £12.95; D 6.30-9.30 £22

Closed: Sunday evening, Christmas evening, Christmas day and Boxing Day
Cards: All major
CHEF: Andrew Hanson.
PROPRIETORS: Andrew Hanson and Helen Tennant

LOCAL INTEREST: Marina, Swansea market.

154 Tenby

The Mews

Upper Frog Street
Tenby
Pembrokshire
SA70 7JD
Tel: 01834 844068

Welsh produce at its best

If it's fish you want, then head for the Mews, situated near the centre of Tenby – a lively, buzzing place, popular with both locals and tourists, that offers locally-sourced ingredients, particularly fish and other seafood.

Daily specials might include fresh monkfish, gently steamed and served on a julienne of Welsh leeks in creamy Dijonnaise sauce. Skate au poivre, salmon hollandaise, slip sole grilled in herb butter and fillet of Caldy Island sea bass might also feature.

Mackerel mania – a selection of dishes using the catch of the day – could be butterfly fillets with herbs and grilled in sea salt and peppercorn crust, or boneless fillets deep-fried in a mild spiced beer batter and served with lemon and herb mayonnaise on new-potato wedges.

Starters include filo parcels of fresh fish and seafood, sweet potatoes with creole stuffing, warm goats' cheese parcels served with salad and home-made soup of the day. Welsh Black beef is on the main-course menu, served either in a brandy and peppercorn sauce or Wellington-style, encased in puff pastry.

Desserts include perhaps chocolate profiteroles, lemon cheesecake, local ice creams and a plate of quality Welsh cheeses available as an alternative.

MEALS: L; D from 6.30 £17-£19
Closed: Sunday and Monday in winter
Cards: All except Amex
CHEFS: Mike Evans and Andy Swales. PROPRIETOR: Mike Evans

LOCAL INTEREST: Walled town of Tenby.

155 Tenby

A clever conversion of the stable block attached to this popular pub and hotel, access is through an alley packed with tables which are

Paxtons

Tenby House Hotel
Tenby
Pembrokeshire
SA70 7AJ
Tel: 01834 842000

e-mail: tenby.house@virgin.net
www.tenbyhousehotel.com

nearly always occupied by families in summer. Helpful staff offer smoking or non-smoking areas in the relaxed long room which is decorated with reclaimed slate and tiled floors.

Pub food features old favourites such as prawn cocktail marie rose more adventurous Celtic mussels marinière, chilled melon and Carmarthen ham and grilled sardines with Parmesan.

Alongside a good selection of Welsh black beef steaks, lamb chops and chicken, fish dishes of the day stand out, as in grilled halibut with lemon butter, fresh dressed Tenby crab, grilled whole plaice, baked Tenby bass with basil, lime and lemon, grilled hake, half a fresh local lobster (when available) and grilled Dover sole.

Home-made curries and steak-and-ale pie are on offer as well as a limited range of vegetarian and pasta dishes.

Nursery puddings arouse schoolboy sentiments, with spotted dick and custard, rum-and-raisin pudding with chocolate sauce and deep filled apple pie and cream.

MEALS: L 12-3; D 5.30-10 from £5
Closed: Sunday evening and Monday even during winter –
call to check
Cards: All major
CHEF: Steve Rossi. PROPRIETORS: Lesley and Griff Fisher
WTB: 3 ★★★
Rooms: 18, £50 b&b S, £80 D

LOCAL INTEREST: Paxtons is Sir William Paxton's town house –
historically important.

156 Tenby

Plantagenet House

Quay Hill
Temby
Pembrokeshire
SA70 7BX
Tel: 01834 842350
Fax: 01834 834915

Be sure to take a peep at the cavernous 12th-century Flemish chimney: proprietor Barney Stone is immensely proud of his flue and with good reason, for not only is it one of the oldest in Britain, it is so enormous that a couple of beefy prop forwards could dine in there in comfort.

The restaurant is slotted away in one of Tenby's higgledy-piggledy back streets, next to the Tudor Merchant's House. Open for coffee and lunch as well as dinner, it is a handy watering hole for lunches of sausages (both meat and vegetarian), made to Plantagenet's own recipe and an inventive sandwich selection served on various home-made breads.

At dinner, local produce features strongly. Starters include carpaccio of Welsh Black fillet marinated with olives, olive oil and shaved garlic and Tenby crab bisque with Cognac. Main courses offer a choice for everyone; rack of organic lamb grilled with a lavender, juniper and oatmeal crust or St David's cheese, red onion and smoked pepper frittata with orange and thyme marmalade.

Home-made puddings include chocolate and amaretto torte and fruit Pavlova, as well as daily specials.

Parents will be glad to know that children are welcome, with good junior fodder such as all cod fish fingers, bangers, home-made vegetarian burgers and, of course, loads of chips.

MEALS: L 12-3; Sunday L 12-4; D 6-11
Closed: Times vary during the year – please call to check
Cards: Visa, Matsercard
PROPRIETOR: Barney Stone

LOCAL INTEREST: Tenby Museum, Art Gallery and Tudor Merchant's House, Hean Castle at Saundersfoot, Caldey Island and Abbey.

157 Tenby

The Reef Café

St Julian Street
Tenby
Pembrokeshire
SA70 7A5
Tel: 01834 845258
www.reefcafe.com

You'll find the Reef right in the middle of Tenby as you make your way down to the harbour. This new bistro, decorated in Mediterranean style, occupies what used to be a tea-room and the food has a similar feel.

Ian Hunt is a local chef who came back to the area after working in Cheltenham. A range of starters such as fresh mussels in a light, Parmesan and garlic cream, smoked salmon and avocado timbales with soured cream, potato rosti with roast Mediterranean vegetables, Mozzarella and basil oil and chargrilled prawns with lime and coriander seeds sets out his stall.

The menu changes regularly to include Thai-spiced green chicken curry, venison steak cooked in stout, mushroom and cream, lamb fajitas with soured cream, chives and green sauce and chargrilled sardines with sea salt, lemon, green salad and home-made bread. There is a good selection of reasonably priced wines.

Desserts feature lime-and-lemon cheese, chocolate mousse, lemon and almond roulade, sticky toffee pudding and Mississippi mud pie.

Lunchtime fare is more informal, with filled rolls, baguettes and ciabiatta for hungry holiday-makers.

MEALS: L 11-4.30 £3-£6; D 6.30 £15
Closed: Sunday and Monday evening during the winter
Cards: All major
CHEFS: Christa Cook and Tom Hunt.
PROPRIETOR: Matthew Thomas

LOCAL INTEREST: Tenby town and harbour and Caldy Island.

South East Wales Entries

158　　　Abergavenny

The Walnut Tree

Llandewi Skirred
Abergavenny
NP7 8AW
Tel: 01873 852797
Fax: 01873 859026

www.walnuttree.co.uk

Franco and Anne Taruschio have sold the Walnut Tree and as The Red Book goes to press, this most famous of all restaurants in Wales is under new management.

In the 35 years that Franco and Anne led Wales in gastronomic excellence, there was never anything stuffy about this famous inn, and although pilgrims would make the journey from afar, local people also popped in regularly for a quick bite. They always found fresh paint on every sill, flowers bursting with glory in the bar, tantalising smells wafting out of the kitchen, and a menu that could compete with any in Britain. The fact that some of the staff stayed the course of time bears testament to the kind of leadership that Anne and Franco Taruschio gave.

This spring Stephen Terry takes over in the kitchen. He has impeccable credentials having started work at 18 for Marco Pierre White at Harvey's in Wandsworth, followed by a stint of La Gavroche, Breaval Old Mill in Aberfoyle with Nick Nairn and back to London to open the Canteen for Marco and Michael Caine in Chelsea Harbour in 1992. After cooking in France and USA, Stephen set up Coast in Mayfair, London and his own restaurant in Frith Street. As international as his culinary skills are, though, Stephen's in-laws come from Brecon!

Business partner Francesco Mattioli will front the restaurant maintaining the Italian/Welsh theme with the menu offering the Franco classics of Vincisgrassi, Llanover Salt Duck, Bresaola and a full range of fish and game, in season.

Changes may come slowly to the menu, but the restaurant has already been converted into a larger bistro. Reservations can be made throughout, Sunday lunch is available and major credit cards are now accepted.

MEALS: D and Sunday L from £35
Closed: Mondays
Cards: Visa, Mastercard
CHEF: Stephen Terry. PROPRIETOR: Francesco Mattioli.

LOCAL INTEREST: Abergavenny, Hay, Monmouth.

159　　　Bettws Newydd

Here is a pretty inn and restaurant that is tucked away in a village just off the B4598 between Abergavenny and Usk. A canopy above the entrance announces 'Cooking by Molyneux', referring not to a faceless restaurant chain but to the surname of the chef proprietor. Inside are a cosy bar and two restaurants, all decorated with horse brasses and National Hunt racing memorabilia. The bar offers real ales and

The Black Bear

Bettws Newydd
Nr Usk
Monmouthshire
NP15 IJN
Tel/Fax: 01873 880701

excellent draught ciders, while the wine list focuses on France and includes a good-quality Fleurie.

Ever found it difficult to choose from a menu, or do you like surprises? If so, "whatever comes out of the kitchen" is great fun and usually good value, too. Once the customer has decided whether to have meat or fish as a main course, Stephen chooses the rest. The price is inclusive of three courses.

Meanwhile, the daily-changing blackboard lists starters such as smoked salmon terrine, melon with cherry liqueur, terrine of chicken and herbs, and avocado served with hot seafood.

Main dishes come in generous portions and range from monkfish with peppercorn cream sauce, salmon with lemon butter and chicken supreme with sweet sherry sauce, to fillet of Black beef with Madeira sauce.

Desserts might include glazed lemon tart, lime and coconut ice cream and chocolate and orange mousse tart.

The list of main dishes might sometimes seem limited (and, indeed, vegetarians might find little to choose from), but this is usually due to careful buying of the best local produce on the day. The result is simple, delicious food that is sensitively cooked.

MEALS: L 12-2 from £5.50 Sunday L 12-2 from £11.95 for 3-courses; D 6-9.30 from £10
Closed: Monday lunch except Bank Holidays
CHEF/PROPRIETOR: Stephen Molyneux

LOCAL INTEREST: Salmon fishing on the Usk, local pheasant shoots, walks.

Caerleon

The Priory Caerleon

High Street
Caerleon
Newport
Gwent
NP18 1AG
Tel: 01633 421241
Fax: 01633 421271

A wonder that such a small town as Caerleon is positively brimming with history – the Priory is a towel's throw from the Roman Baths in the centre of this one-time capital of Wales. Approach by night and its twinkling stained-glass windows suggest this is where country hotel meets Mediterranean taverna. Ancient flagstones, sconce-like lighting and framed hunting scenes mix with an unfussy, Latin ambience.

As befits feasts of old, the emphasis here is on fresh meat and fish displayed raw on shaved ice, the very food that will be cooked for you to order. The waiting staff will help the uninitated and if you just cannot wait, help yourself to a bowl of salad, and start with succulent crevettes, melt-in-the-mouth seared scallops, or hearty fish soup.

Follow with sea bass baked in a crust of sea salt and filleted at the table, simple firm white monkfish, or a seasonal special such as a juicy pheasant or partridge in a light citrusy sauce.

Chips, boiled potatoes and bread are available, but you might want to save some room for sticky toffee pudding or crème brulée.

The wine list offers some unusual wines, such as a Galician Albario, at reasonable prices.

MEALS: L 12-2.30 from £5.95; D 7-11.30 from £15
Closed: Christmas Day
Cards: All
PROPRIETOR: Miguel Santiago
WTB: 3 ★★★
Rooms: 22, £55 S, £75 D, £130 Suite

LOCAL INTEREST: Roman Ruins.

161 Cardiff

Armless Dragon

97-99 Wyverne Road
Cathays
Cardiff
S Glamorgan
CF24 4BG
Tel: 029 2038 2357
Fax: 029 2038 2055

e-mail:
paul@armlessdragon.uk

It has not been an easy first year for Paul Lane, since he took this restaurant over from David Richards in the autumn of 1999. However, with new decor, front-of-house staff, and Paul still rooted in the kitchen, things are coming together well.

The overgrown greenhouse effect has gone from the front windows and a cleaner cream and terracotta/dark red colour scheme has replaced it. The interior is still pretty much the same, although feeling warmer, with some interesting art on the walls. The menu has developed slowly over the year and some old favourites from before are still there, such as laverballs for starters, lots of fish dishes, a mash of root vegetables and good use of game.

Starters might include Thai almond and mushroom toast and fish platter of oyster, herring, crab and small sesame prawns.

For main courses, amongst the fish options there could be halibut with crab. Steak with bubble-and-leek cake, vegetable platter which is a mix of small vegetarian dishes including parsnip crisps and a savoury bread pudding with mushroom ragout are other options.

Vegetables are crisp, apart from the root vegetable mash – perhaps too crisp for some.

Puddings can be excellent, as in the yogurt bavarois, delicious, smooth and tangy, the coconut crème brulée, or sharp lemon tart. Cheeses are British and the wine list is well priced with good house wines.

MEALS: L 12-2; D 7-10
Closed: Sunday, Saturday and Monday lunch
Cards: All major
CHEF/PROPRIETOR: Paul Lane

LOCAL INTEREST: Cardiff city centre, museum and theatre.

162   Cardiff

Bosphorus Turkish Restaurant

31 Mermaid Quay
Cardiff Bay
CF10 5BZ
Tel: 029 2048 7477
Fax: 029 2045 2977

Cardiff Bay may not be Istanbul, but there is certainly an element of Eastern Promise as you sit in this restaurant on its stilts over the water. Waiters of Turkish origin give you a quality of service that might have been offered to the Sultan at the Tekke Palace.

It is possible to dine on soup of the day, grilled salmon fillet and crème brulée but then you would be missing the main event. The cooking here is authentically Turkish and exciting, the meze is particularly recommended. Start with a mixture of rich creamy hummus, tarama and cacik, a yoghurt-base dip with cucumber and fresh mint.

Also served on this platter of good tastes are yaprak sarma or stuffed vine leaves, peynir salata, feta cheese mashed with chilli peppers, sesame seeds and olive oil, patlican salada, roasted and mashed aubergines and peppers with yoghurt, olive oil, and garlic and kisir, which is crushed wheat mixed with mint, spring onions, parsley, tomatoes, walnuts, chillies, lemon juice and olive oil.

Leave room for the beautifully spiced lamb and chicken kebabs that follow. Other main courses from the grill could be, adana kofte – minced lamb prepared with chillies, onions and herbs or chicken sarma – minced chicken wrapped in thin flat bread and topped with yoghurt and melted butter. There are main courses cooked in sauces too.

Puddings range from fresh figs, stuffed apricots, quince topped with nuts and, of course, those pastries dripping in syrup, such as baklava and kadayif – such Turkish delights.

MEALS: L 12-3.30 Set menu, Sunday L; 1-4; D 5.30-11 £25
Cards: All major
CHEF: Mr Aziz. CONTACT: Mr Adnan
LOCAL INTEREST. Cardiff Bay.

163   Cardiff

Brava

71 Pontcanna Street
Cardiff
South Glamorgan
CF5 1ET
Tel: 029 2037 1929
Fax: 029 2038 4525
e-mail: sez.daf@virgin.net
www.bwyd.com

On a warm summer's day you can sit outside at the pavement tables or out in the garden with a glass of wine, or in winter – steep yourself in Brava's chatty atmosphere as you flick through the daily papers over an espresso.

This is a café in true European style, where customers are encouraged to linger and be sociable rather than drink up and push off, and emphasis is placed on using the freshest produce, organic and local where possible. Regulars on the menu include Welsh rib-eye steak with fries, salad and aioli; salad Nicoise; grilled goat's cheese

with stir-fried vegetables and harissa vinaigrette; free-range egg omelette with ham, cheese, mushroom, herb and leek, which you can try with side dishes like hot green bean vinaigrette or a leafy salad.

Daily specials on the blackboard feature smoked haddock fishcakes with roast tomatoes and chilli sauce, the chef's special chowder, or for vegetarians tasty chickpea patties with salad and relish.

Baguettes and sandwiches can be eaten in or taken out, with inspired fillings like roast red pepper and feta cheese, BLT with dressing and fresh basil or blue cheese, walnut, apple and chicory.

The pudding menu is not extensive – there's generally a simple choice of sticky toffee pud or citrus cheesecake.

MEALS: B 9-12 £4.25; L 12-5 £4-5
CHEF: Dafydd Lloyd. PROPRIETOR: Dafydd and Sarah Lloyd

LOCAL INTEREST: Cardiff City centre.

164 Cardiff

Buffs Restaurant and Wine Bar

8 Mount Stuart Square
Cardiff Bay
Cardiff
CF10 5EE
Tel: 029 2046 4628
Fax: 029 2048 0715
e-mail: helen@mgy.co.uk

Something of an institution in Cardiff Bay's commercial quarter, alongside such prestige addresses as the former Corn Exchange, Helen Young's venue continues to thrive into its 15th year, its success firmly based on a fiercely loyal business clientele.

The ground-floor wine bar is always abuzz and selections on offer range from generously garnished sandwiches, such as smoked salmon with yoghurt and dill and salads, perhaps of smoked duck with pears and walnuts. Hot alternatives include gratin of laverbread and bacon and the ever-popular venison sausages with mash and redcurrant gravy. Up to a dozen wines are served by the glass.

An upper-level restaurant features high-backed settles and polished mahogany tables, from the best of which diners may look down across the square. Seasonal menu choices vary little from a tried-and-tested formula – in decidedly man-sized portions. Start with grilled chèvre on a bed of leaves or crab cakes with tomato and chilli dressing, following with market-fresh cod baked under a herb crust or generously thick slices of calves' liver on a bed of leeks with Madeira sauce. While vegetables "of the moment" are tossed into large round bowls, new midi-potatoes come modishly unskinned and unsalted sauté potatoes from the fryer.

Tangy lemon tart with a lemon sorbet is as good as it gets in these parts, whilst a wodge of bread-and-butter pudding is not for the faint-hearted. Bread comes to every table commendably fresh and service from Helen's team of girls is informal yet unfailingly charming and attentive.

MEALS: L 12-3; D
Closed: Saturday and Sunday
Cards: All except Diners

LOCAL INTEREST: The Coal Exchange, Mount Stuart Square, the newly developed Cardiff Bay.

165 Cardiff

Champers
Le Monde
The Brasserie

60-62 St Mary Street
Cardiff
CF10 1FE

Tel: 029 2038 7576
Fax: 029 2066 8092

e-mail:
mail@le-monde.co.uk
www.le-monde.co.uk

The longstanding formula introduced to Cardiff by Benigno Martinez and now extended to a number of outlying villages is still amazingly popular. Champers, the Brasserie and Le Monde, cheek by jowl at the end of St Mary Street, are now under the new management of Simon Howard, they are places to go if you are looking for an excellent steak and chips or baked potato washed down with any number of good French or Spanish wines.

The Brasserie is more French in emphasis (crepes and gateaux for dessert) and le Monde is stronger on fish. Champers focuses on things Spanish – tapas at lunchtime and lively Iberian background music. It has dark wooden beams, bare tables, white-washed walls and sawdust on the floor.

There is no booking for groups of less than eight. You are allocated a table and then jostle chaotically with other diners to make your choice from the overflowing chilled cabinets stacked high with steaks and fish – whole and filleted seafood, kebabs, suckling pig and duck – all on a bed of ice. Starters could include whitebait, asparagus, shrimps in garlic sauce and mussels. Salads are a help-yourself affair running to very basic potato, lettuce, sliced tomato, pepper and onion. These are good quality ingredients simply prepared and served without embellishment.

Desserts are limited in Champers to bought-in mousses in different flavours. San Miguel is on tap and served in a jug at your table. Service is brisk and impersonal, unless you are a recognised regular.

MEALS: L 12-2.30 from £5; D 7-12 from £12
Closed: Sunday lunchtime
Cards: All cards
CHEF: David Legge. PROPRIETOR: Simon Howard

LOCAL INTEREST: City centre, local amenities, National Museum and Gallery of Wales, Millennium Stadium.

166 Cardiff Bay

With three champagnes, 13 wines, and one dessert wine all sold by the glass, Cutting Edge is a serious wine bar, boasting one of the finest wine lists in the area. It provides an excellent watering hole for the local business community and members of the National Assembly housed nearby.

Cutting Edge

Discovery House
Scott Harbour
Cardiff Bay
CF10 4PJ
Tel: 029 2047 0780
Fax: 029 2044 0876

This narrow slither of a restaurant, tucked neatly into the sharp end of an office block in Cardiff Bay, has large glass windows along the north side and stylish minimalistic decor.

Chef Peter Farrow prepares simple dishes based on local ingredients cooked with flair to fit the situation.

Daily specials might be grilled scallops, rocket and sweet chilli dressing, Welsh rarebit on ciabatta with tomato and chive salad, or curried tiger prawns with Thai spices all designed to stimulate the palate as they should. The grilled sea bass with sweet peppers and basil dressing can be a main course too, to join sausage, mash and onion gravy, salmon fishcake with lemon and coriander butter sauce or mushroom and spinach tagliatelle with Parmesan.

"Desserts by Maria" are never quite as they read on the menu but appear as a modern and usually more delicious adaptation. Try the cherry Bakewell and custard, warm chocolate brownie with vanilla ice cream or pineapple tarte tatin for a real surprise. For cheese lovers, the trio of Welsh cheeses is well balanced and, of course, the wine list must be taken seriously.

MEALS: B £5; L 12-3 £15; D 7-9.30 £25
Closed: Saturday lunch and Sunday
Cards: All except Amex and Diners
CHEF: Peter Farrow. MANAGER: Tony Gilmore.

167 Cardiff

De Courcey's

Tyla Morris Avenue
Pentyrch
Cardiff
South Glamorgan
CF15 9QN
Tel: 029 2089 2232
Fax: 029 2089 1949

e-mail:
dinedecourceys@aol.com

This dignified neo-country house restaurant lies just outside Cardiff's urban perimeter. Rebuilt after a large scale fire nine years ago by the Theilmans, who have recently retired, the new owner, Jan Meek, continues with the same grand style, courteous service and an atmosphere of hushed formality.

The food is as orthodox as the surroundings, with hospitable touches like canapés, served with your pre-dinner drinks to make you feel nurtured.

There is a choice of a house or gourmet menu. House options include smoked fish boudin with chive fish sauce and chicken liver parfait, salad leaves and a shallot and cassis dressing, followed by lamb cutlets with dauphinoise potatoes and Mediterranean vegetables and medaillons of pork with a grain mustard mousse on red cabbage and a cider jus.

The gourmet menu kicks off with crab and tomato mille-feuille with chilled cucumber, tomato and pepper sauce and warm asparagus and leeks with herb butter and poached egg, while mains feature loin of lamb with leek mousse and red wine and thyme sauce and peppered beef fillet with horseradish mash and mushroom sauce.

Puddings are selected from a single menu and include an inspired

goats' cheese and almond cheesecake with orange caramel sauce, hot apricot soufflé with caraway ice cream and shortbread biscuits, dark chocolate parfait with caramelised banana and white chocolate sorbet.

Coffee brewed at your table and home-made chocolates finish things off in the grand manner you would expect.

MEALS: D 7-9 £24.95; Sunday L 12-2.30 £15.95
Closed: Sunday and Monday night
Cards: All major
CHEF: David Leeworthy. PROPRIETOR: Jan Meek

LOCAL INTEREST: Cardiff City centre.

168 Cardiff

Earl's of Llandaff

48 High Street
Llandaff
Cardiff
CF5 2DZ
Tel: 029 2056 7711
Fax: 029 2056 7711

This lively eating house has developed a popular following and at the weekend it is bursting at the seams. Despite the pressure of numbers the staff remain competent, friendly and cheerful.

The exterior is unassuming, but inside, simple wooden tables and chairs and unfussy decor appear tastefully uncluttered. The basic menu is democratically priced (as is the ample wine list) and is supplemented by a range of daily specials. Although perfectly acceptable and enjoyable, do not expect wonders from the cooking – this is a jolly bistro, not a serious foodie experience.

Starters include very good chunky fish broth full of monkfish, squid, mussels and prawns and flavoured with lemon grass, spare ribs marinated in garlic, rice wine, plum sauce and five spices and tossed green salad with duck, served both crispy and confit.

Diners can then choose from medallions of Welsh lamb on creamed leeks with crispy laverballs as a main dish, pork fillet with stir-fried vegetables and oyster sauce, or roast duck with a honey glaze. Dishes come with vegetables such as cauliflower cheese and carrots.

A blackboard featuring the pudding list is brought to your table. Choices range from a very creamy mille-feuille to fresh fruit Pavlova and a citrusy chocolate and orange torte.

Round off the evening with cappuccino, expresso, latte or filter coffee and a port or brandy.

MEALS: L 12-2.30; D 6.30-10.30
Closed: Dayime Saturday, Sunday evening
Cards: All
CHEF: Earl Smikle. PROPRIETOR: Jan Mitchell and Earl Smikle

LOCAL INTEREST: Cathedral, craft shops.

169 Cardiff

Gilby's

Old Port Road
Culverhouse Cross
Cardiff
CF5 6DN
Tel: 029 2067 0800
Fax: 029 2059 4437

Tucked behind the TV studios at Culverhouse Cross, where Cardiff's outskirts meet the Vale of Glamorgan, the barn-like interior is the only obvious clue to this building's past. The decor is durable, corporate neo-traditional, with Italian veneer tables and pictures by the metre, and stands up well to the day's demands.

Special lunch and early-evening flier menus offer good value, though bread and vegetables are extra: smoked haddock kedgeree with oyster mushrooms, followed by hot honey and marmalade glazed gammon with colcannon, and a pudding.

The same menu offers prawn cocktail, fish and chips, and bangers and mash, and if they claim to be a fish restaurant, that does not mean that meat-eaters or vegetarians are short-changed, and real alternatives are given.

From the à la carte menu, starters of Tokyo-style monkfish tempura, carpaccio, or risotto of preserved lemon and fennel jam, could be followed by pan-fried turbot, sticky glazed lamb shank or sesame asparagus hollandaise with grilled polenta. There's a good choice of grilled fish, oysters and lobster and well-hung beefsteaks.

Wines have obviously been chosen by someone who likes the work, and include an organic duo from Italy. There are plenty of alternatives suggested, with or without alcohol.

The staff are well trained – when asked about a sauce they will give a well-informed reply.

MEALS: L 12-2.30 from £8.95; Sunday L £14.95;
D 5.45-10.30 from £12.95
Closed: Sunday evening and Mondays
Cards: Visa, Amex
CHEF: Martin Cornock. PROPRIETOR: Anthony Armelin

LOCAL INTEREST: Cardiff Castle, Cardiff Bay, National Museum and Art Galleries, Museum of Welsh Life, Dyffryn Gardens.

170 Cardiff

Greenhouse

38 Woodville Road
Cathays
Cardiff
CF24 4EB
Tel: 029 2023 5731
e-mail: greenhouse.cardiff@
www.ntlworld.com

Deep in the student quarter of Cardiff, this diminutive restaurant is cosy both in space and light wood decor. Be prepared to squeeze in and enjoy a relaxed atmosphere with friendly, informed service.

The small menu is chalked on the board daily and three items for each course are likely to change during the evening as ingredients run out. The cooking of Ian Young is vibrant and sensitive to his ingredients. For non-vegetarians, the choice of fish is always tempting, and starters and pudding choices cover a variety of styles.

To start, the choice might include butternut squash soup with red

chilli and mint, fresh Greek salad or a bowl of steaming Cornish mussels cooked with tomatoes, basil and white wine.

For main courses, cannelloni comes filled with organic greens, Pecorino cheese and walnuts and is served with sun-dried tomato-bread. The fillet of hake and parsley has the lightest garlic crust with a tomato and fennel sauce and wild mushrooms are cooked in a coulibiac with onion, thyme and port gravy.

Desserts might be Italian orange and apple sponge, banoffi pie or mango and poached apricot salad with ice cream or vegan cream.

MEALS: D from 7pm approx £15
Closed: Sunday and Monday
Cards: Not Amex and Diners
CHEF/PROPRIETOR: Ian Young

171 Cardiff

Gwalia Tearooms

Museum of Welsh Life
St Fagans
Cardiff
South Glamorgan
CF5 6XB
Tel: 029 2056 6985
Fax: 029 2056 6985

e-mail:
enquiries@applecatering.co.uk
www.applecatering.co.uk

The open-air Museum of Welsh Life, with its impressive collection of reconstructed buildings from all over Wales, is the ideal location for the recreation of a 1920s tea room that could be both an educational and a gastronomic experience.

The Gwalia Tea Rooms are almost there – the brown and green paint, the old Oxo posters, and the aspidistra in the corner, but the tableware lacks the expected gentility – where are the doilies, the sugar tongs and bone china?

The afternoon tea menu, which for a change is bilingual, offers a wide range of Welsh cakes as well as sandwiches. The bara brith and the Anglesey fruit cake are dark and spicy, the Welsh cakes light and the warm, freshly baked scones are a real treat. Unfortunately the teisen lap ("moist cake") does not always live up its name.

Considering that the Turog Bakery is just over the road and the Gwalia Stores – selling quality Welsh products – downstairs, the sandwiches could be made with better ingredients and these different outlets could thereby advertise each other.

There is an impressive list of teas, both traditional pots of good strong tea like Auntie makes and the herbal variety, soft drinks and Welsh wine. The service is cheerful and efficient.

MEALS: L 10-5 from £3.50
Closed: Christmas Day and Boxing Day
Cards: Visa and Access
CHEF: Jason Humphries. PROPRIETOR: Mike Morton

LOCAL INTEREST: Largest open air folk museum in Europe.

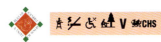

172 Cardiff

Hanover International Hotel – Cardiff Bay

Schooner Way
Atlantic Wharf
Cardiff
CF10 4RT
Tel: 029 2047 5000
Fax: 029 2048 1491

The nautically themed Halyards Restaurant finds itself in one of the of new hotels catering mainly for business people that are popping up at what is Europe's most exciting new waterfront at Cardiff Bay.

If the menu is anything to go by summer seems to reign forever here. In the depth of mid-autumn, one may choose a summer salad as a starter or summer pudding as a dessert, and even the local asparagus is eternal.

Other starters include classic Caesar salad or Mediterranean salad, Loch Fyne salmon mousse, spicy crab cakes and various pasta and noodle dishes.

For the main event one may choose from a tender braised shank of lamb with garlic mash, roasted vegetables and a rosemary jus, caramelised breast of duck with braised cabbage, fondant potatoes and a delicately perfumed five spice sauce, or a simple grilled fillet of beef, with the usual trimmings. The seasonal theme does mean that some components of the dishes might be unexpectedly cold.

The flourish comes with the desserts. The aforementioned summer pudding is fine, but might sometimes arrive with a variety a Cornish clotted cream than can be miraculously squirted from an aerosol can. The vanilla and amaretto crème brulée is sublime and the assiette of chocolate contains an exquisite, rich, dark squidgy concoction which is pure manna for chocoholics.

A good choice of wines, many also in half-bottles, is available from the regular list and there is also a fine wine selection. The waiting staff are friendly enough but sometimes lacking the polish one might expect from a four-star hotel.

MEALS: L 12-2.30 from £8.45; D 7-9 from £18.95 for 3 courses
Cards: All
CHEF: Sean Armitage. MANAGER: Paul Evans
WTB: 4 ★★★★
Rooms: 156, £100 S, £120 D

LOCAL INTEREST: Cardiff Bay.

173 Cardiff

Izakaya may be Japanese for pub, but an evening here is hardly a night out at the local. You know you are entering a different world when you see the bold Chinese characters on the sign and the simple raked gardens in the window. The diner is greeted with a hearty "Irrashaimase!" and shown either to a Western-style table and chairs

Izakaya Japanese Tavern

Mermaid Quay
Cardiff Bay
Cardiff
CF10 5BW
Tel: 029 2049 2939
Fax: 029 2049 2939

or a place at the bar, or to some Japanese-style low seating. The typical rustic style is created by wooden beams, bamboo fittings and paper lanterns.

Helpfully, the menu has pictures of the dishes and it may come as a surprise to those who think sushi and sashimi are the sum of Japanese cuisine. They are both there – the sushi is of the DIY variety but Izakaya is an excellent place to sample all the different styles of Japanese cuisine, such as skewered meats (chicken and leek, chicken meat balls, chicken liver, and chicken wings), tempura (deep-fried vegetables and/or seafood in light batter), fish dishes, such as mackerel marinated in ginger and miso, omelettes, tofu steak (which is surprisingly good), noodle dishes – udon (wheat) with vegetables and seafood, soba (buckwheat) with pork and vegetables and simple dishes like soya beans in their pods, grilled rice-balls, or pickles and a deeply-flavoured miso soup.

Eat Japanese style. Order a drink – perhaps some sake (there are plenty to choose from), a Japanese beer or some green tea – and a few dishes to go with it, and then perhaps another drink and a few more dishes. While a wine list is available, your waiter will be happy to help you if in doubt. Many of the dishes are meant for sharing, and if you are not so proficient with your chopsticks it's even greater fun.

"Domo arigato gozaimashita" is the farewell chorus from the staff as you leave. You might like to reply "Gochisosama deshita" – that was a feast.

MEALS: L 12 -2.30; D 6-10.30
Closed: December 24th – January 2nd
Cards: All major
CHEF: Peter Mansbridge. PROPRIETOR: Iestyn and Yoshiko Evans

LOCAL INTEREST: Cardiff Bay.

174 Cardiff

Le Cassoulet

5 Romilly Crescent
Cardiff
CF11 9NP
Tel: 029 2022 1905
Fax: 029 2022 1905
e-mail:
lecassoulet@ukonline.co.uk

This is not just French style - you could almost be in a small smart French country restaurant with pictures of the Toulouse rugby club rubbing shoulders with Toulouse Lautrec, simple white-clothed tables, oil-filled candles, walls bordered with impressive Chateaux labels, and youthful French service in halting English.

In an urban suburb of Cardiff, Gilbert Viader, continues to offer a high-quality classic provincial French menu, starting with a delicate amuse-bouche of smoked salmon mousse, tomato, and herbed crème fraiche.

Five starters include truly superb eggs Benedict on a muffin with creamed spinach and hollandaise sauce, salade de chevre chaud or foie gras de canard.

For main course, you might choose the cassoulet – a large, robust and deeply flavoured dish of beans, duck, sausage and pork. Lighter options include a single vegetarian dish on request, filet d'agneau or boeuf au Roquefort with savoy cabbage, confit shallots and dauphinoise potatoes and risotto de volaille.

Desserts run to jasmine-flavoured crème brulée, a light pudding of brioche with mixed fruit and crème anglaise or an extensive cheeseboard imported from Fromagerie Xavier in Toulouse. The confident imaginative touches and overall attention to detail are supported by technical skill and excellent ingredients.

The classically French wine list ranges from house wine at £11.50 to a rare 1990 Ch Petrus at £950. It is the nearest you will get to a genuine French eating experience in Cardiff.

MEALS: L 12-2 £13.50 for 3 courses; D 6-10 £25
Closed: Sun and Monday
Cards: All major
CHEF/PROPRIETOR: Gilbert Viader

LOCAL INTEREST: Cardiff City centre.

175 Cardiff

Le Gallois

6-10 Romilly Crescent
Canton
Cardiff
CF11 9NR
Tel: 029 2034 1264
Fax: 029 2023 7911

e-mail:
le.gallois@virgin.net

Definitely one of the most fashionable restaurants in Cardiff, the two tier extended and made-over Gallois looks for all the world like a page out of a Sunday modern living supplement – and this extends to the presentation of the food itself. Aegean blue and sunflower-yellow walls, etched-glass windows, mirrors, metal art nouveau balustrades, MDF cupboards, pale wooden floors and some extremely unusual glassware and cutlery – every element has been chosen with great care.

Padrig Jones's menu is light modern French/European. His complex dishes are prepared with imagination and confidence and presented with style. The complimentary appetiser – usually an intense soup – is served in a doll's house tureen. Starters could include a "breakfast" of soft duck eggs and caviar served with buttery soldiers, or rich roasted foie gras with mushroom risotto and langoustine – much like a Picasso still life.

Main courses come multi-layered – sea bass on a slice of aubergine, on top of a pasta gallette – all sitting on a thick tomato and chilli salsa. Or pink and meltingly tender milk-soaked pigeon breast served on a bed of savoy cabbage and bacon with a separate roundel of Pommes Anna. There is plenty of fish and many dishes come with mash or puy lentils.

For dessert you might be offered an assiette of crème brulées in different flavours, a decadent hot chocolate fondant with pistachio ice cream or apple tarte tatin. Different home-made breads star and the two-course lunches are superb value. An extensive wine list covers the globe, with a French emphasis.

MEALS: L from 12 noon £12-20; D from 6.30 £40
Closed: Christmas to New Year and 3 weeks in August
Cards: All except Diners
CHEF: Padrig Jones. PROPRIETOR: Anne Wynn Jones

176 Cardiff

Madhav

Lower Cathedral Rd
Cardiff
CF11 6LW
Tel: 029 2037 2947

This is probably one of our more unusual entries, in that Madhav is a shop which also sells freshly cooked food rather than a restaurant. Describing it as special, however, is rather understating this unique little place tucked away in Riverside.

Serving fellow subcontinent émigrés as well as locals in the know, the capable Pushpa Gaikwad stocks all manner of Indian goods. Sift through heaps of spices, nuts, flours, pulses, bottled pastes, paneer, naan breads, sweets and fresh produce like fenugreek leaves and strangely shaped gourds. While shopping, regulars know to ask for a few hot snacks like batat wadas – spicy potato balls in gram flour batter – the best you'll find outside Bombay, and that's coming from an Indian!

Given one day's advance notice, Pushpa can create a takeaway meal that is the essence of Indian home cooking. No ubiquitous curry house could come close to this kind of food and indeed, it is almost sad to let this best-kept secret out. Never mind that the food is purely vegetarian, you'll perhaps try bhendi bajia (okra with tomatoes and onions), wadai subji (spinach with small gram dumplings), mattar paneer (northern cheese and pea dish) and dal with curry leaves and ginger, along with rice and flatbreads like wheat chapatis or jowhar (sorghum) rotis. Pushpa errs on the spicy side, so if you'd rather have your food mild, let her know.

As this book was going to press, Pushpa was in the process of expanding into a little café next door. Pretty soon, you should be able to eat in or out at Madhav.

MEALS: 10.30-8 from £3
CHEF/PROPRIETOR: Pushpa Gaikwad

177 Cardiff

For about 10 years now, Charles Street in Cardiff has felt as if it is about to take off. Metropolis is part of that. It's new, it's smart, it's central, and it's trying hard.

Run the gauntlet of the sound system in the ground floor bar and go upstairs, where you dine. It is calm, airy and comfortably subdued – stylish chairs and lights, pale walls, blue carpet and pictures by Welsh

Metropolis

60 Charles Street
Cardiff
CF10 2GG
Tel: 029 2034 4300
Fax: 029 2066 6602
e-mail: innactive@aol.com

artists Neil Canning and Harry Holland.

The menu gives eight or nine choices of starters and main courses, with a couple of vegetarian options in each, and reads like a roll-call of the chef's top 20 of the 90s. The mashes are flavoured, the jus scented but chorizo and cherry tomato tartlet works well, and it is always good to see Welsh Black beef.

Vegetarians are not sidelined but have choices such as buffalo Mozzarella salad, with smoked beef tomato, basil and rocket, or a red pepper stuffed with couscous, and dressed with a roasted ratatouille. Wisely, they keep the fish to two choices in both courses, balancing a new-traditional fish and chips with mushy peas and lemon oil, and a lemon-grass and ginger-scented salmon, served with a spring roll, noodles and soy jus.

There is a choice of five or six puddings; Worcester apple crumble comes with vanilla pod ice-cream, and a mille feuille of forest berries with a nutmeg cream.

Snacks are served all day in the downstairs bar.

MEALS: L 12-3 £6-£16; D 6-11 £8-£16
Closed: Sundays
Cards: All major
CHEF: Steve Brookes. Proprietor: David Williams

LOCAL INTEREST: Cardiff City centre.

178 Cardiff

New House Country Hotel

Thornhill Road
Thornhill
Cardiff
CF14 9UB
Tel: 029 2052 0280
Fax: 029 2052 0324
e-mail: enquiries@newhousehotel.com
www.newhousehotel.com

The drive to New House offers sweeping views of Cardiff on the left, perhaps the reason one goes to a country hotel is to live out the fantasy that one is a member of the minor aristocracy spending the weekend with a lot of other frightfully nice people. Everything should be "just so", but in a confidently comfortable way. Large G and T in hand, one warms oneself by the roaring fire in the lounge, idly contemplating the handsome lady in the oil painting.

A little plate of dainty amuse-boucles arrives, to interrupt one's musings. On the à la carte or the menu of the day, warm duck confit, black pudding and crisp speck ham on chilli dressed leaves is an excellent way to begin as is the hearty smoked haddock rarebit with poached egg and a honey dressed endive, cooked to perfection. The same, alas, cannot always be said of the roast pheasant breast stuffed with a game faggot. The truffled wild mushrooms with leeks and cream in a courgette and Parmesan roulade is perfectly nice but the truffled wild mushroom element might still be hiding in the forest.

Some excellent wines adorn a somewhat hourglass-figured list.

To follow is a selection of mature Welsh cheeses but the pudding to plump for is that combination reputed to have melted the heart of the Iron Lady – bananas and caramel, served here with a delicate shortbread. In true country-house style, one may retire to the lounge

Welsh produce at its best

for coffee, petits fours and a little brandy.

The New House is grand without being stuffy, the service professional and friendly, good use is made of fine Welsh foods and with a tighter marriage between the dishes and their description, it would be "just so".

MEALS: L 12-2 £15; D 7-9.30 £18.50
Cards: All major
PROPRIETOR: Stephen Banks
WTB: 3 ★★★
Rooms: 36, from £60 S, from £80 D, from £100 Suite

LOCAL INTEREST: Views of the city, Caerphilly Castle, Caerphilly Castle, Cardiff city centre.

179 Cardiff

Razzi

The Hilton Hotel
Kingsway
Cardiff
CF10 3HH
Tel: 029 2064 6400
Fax: 029 2064 6401

The goldfish bowl, glass-encased restaurant imposed on the front of the Cardiff Hilton offers a surprisingly intimate experience, combined with a view of Cardiff Castle and passing metropolitan life. This is a contemporary experience – blond wood, etched glass, chrome, tiles. The excellent value, set-price menu based on the number of courses consumed, matches fashionable modern fusion cooking, dramatically arranged in small domestic sculptures.

Warm herby bread rolls come with olive oil and Mozzarella; hot and cold starters include a "torta" of wild mushrooms and pancake with truffle broth and Parmesan crackling and charlotte of asparagus with curried mussel ragout – the latter a circular fence of upstanding asparagus spears surrounding a fishy mousse decorated with mussels in their shells.

Main courses cover the range of fish, lamb, beef and chicken appearing on the menu as wood stone, oven-roasted canon of lamb with ratatouille and polenta with a hint of garlic – all presented on the giant white plates in elaborately designed formations. But wonderfully, the quality of the food on the plate more than matches the descriptions — the combination is chosen with care to complement and contrast and the technical execution is superb.

Divine desserts star – intense strawberry and balsamic sorbet and dense creamy elderflower-infused pannacotta with apple and ginger compote.

The wine list is well illustrated and informative, with a reasonable range. The team behind the scenes is certainly working magic, although front of house is not quite up to the same standard.

MEALS: L 12-3 £14.95; Sunday L 12.30-4.30 £15.95;
D 6.30-10.30 £21.50
Cards: All major
CHEF: Michel Gehrig. CONTACT: Patrick Lemaigre
WTB: 5 ★★★★★
Rooms: 197

LOCAL INTEREST: Cardiff Castle and city centre.

180 Cardiff Bay

St. David's Hotel and Tides Restaurant

Havannah Street
Cardiff Bay
CF10 5SD
Tel: 029 2045 4045
Fax: 029 2048 7056

e-mail: reservations@thest.davidshotel.com
www.rfhotels.com

Sir Rocco Forte's purpose-built flagship hotel stands strikingly on the lip of a lagoon formed by Cardiff Bay's new barrage. Balconied bedrooms, angled to the water, are afforded views across the estuary to Penarth or back past the old docks towards a regenerated business quarter that is scheduled to house the new Welsh Assembly. As befits such a flagship, Tides Restaurant and its attendant Son et Lumiere bar – with similar waterside views and a promenade of grooved wooden decking – has a muted ocean liner appeal, though sadly its minimalist interior decor, no less than the informal attire of the stewards, falls short of reflecting any such sense of occasion.

In similar vein, an unevenness in much of the cooking here seems to indicate that it too might have missed the boat. Deceptively simple menu descriptions – quail eggs Florentine and jambonette of chicken with crab beignets from the market menu, scallop and herb risotto and vegetable tart with basil and rosemary dressing from the carte – conceal a variety of complex creations which can be strangely out of trim. Therein lies a profusion of culinary twists and turns in the modern idiom, with subtle adornments such as herb veloute, sauce café au lait and vinegared onion marmalade that, if experimental, do not always succeed.

Anchors aweigh to follow for some extraordinary leek and caraway seed ice cream or an exemplary roast apple with apple sorbet and a sturdy sabayon as proof positive that Tides is far from all-at-sea.

MEALS: L 12.30-2.30 £14-£19; Sunday L £23;
D 6.30-8.30 £30 approx
Cards: All
WTB: 5 ★★★★★
CHEF: Martin Green. MANAGER: Ingo Hell
Rooms: £140 S, £170 D, £355 Suite

LOCAL INTEREST: Cardiff Bay.

181 Cardiff Bay

Woods Bar and Brasserie

Pilotage Building
Stuart Street
Cardiff Bay
CF10 5BW
Tel: 029 2049 2400
Fax: 029 2048 1998

Blending the old with the new, Woods Bar and Brasserie sits in the historic pilotage building in Cardiff Bay with a sleek and urbane interior. Chef Martyn Peters is known for his passion and careful sourcing of prime ingredients, while his wife Debs makes a most amicable hostess.

From the outset, all augured well for Woods – with its globally influenced, modern British cuisine. Recent changes include a fishy inclination – with emphasis on catch of the day, but long-time favourites like Caesar salad still hold their own.

Treat yourself to delights such as giant seared scallops, full of nuttiness with a lickable pea and mint puree. Thai fishcakes with dipping sauce are equally good to start off with, but it is best to avoid a prawn salad that reveals nothing of the culinary wizardry of which Martyn is undoubtedly capable. Fast forward to risotto of butternut squash with vanilla oil, pan-fried calves' liver and bacon with mash and lime jus or an exceptional chargrilled squid with Italian bacon and chilli salsa with just the right bite. Fish such as sea bass, John Dory, sea bream and more comes with your choice of sauce, from hollandaise to pesto.

Puddings include the ever-popular chocolate nemesis and selection of ice creams to a rather disappointing Eton mess with strawberries. A selection of unpasteurised French cheeses ought to restore the faith, and perhaps a latte or macchiato to end the meal.

MEALS: L 12-2; D 7-10 £16.50-£23.50
Closed: Sundays, 25th, 26th, 31st December
Cards: All major
CHEF: Martyn Peters. PROPRIETOR: Deborah Peters

LOCAL INTEREST: Cardiff Bay.

182 Clytha

Clytha Arms

Clytha
Nr Abergavenny
Monmouthshire
NP7 9BW
Tel: 01873 840206
Fax: 01873 840209

If Clytha were a village it would be envied for its pub, the kind whose passing is everywhere lamented, where they still play shove ha'penny and bar skittles, with six real ales on tap, and home-made bar snacks like faggots and peas, wild boar sausages with potato pancakes, or leek and laverbread rissoles; and whose landlord and his lady do not need prompting twice when there's an excuse for a party in the offering.

But that is not the half of it, Bev and Andrew Canning, with daughter Sarah, also find time to run the best restaurant for miles around. In an age when every hotel coffee shop in the country claims to send the

chef to market at dawn (where all he finds is Kenya beans, baby corn and courgettes), it is good to eat somewhere where they really do buy Welsh produce, and make the most of it, as in monkfish beefed up with Carmarthen ham and leeks. This is knowledgeable cooking, with contrasting choices: a plateful of queen scallops on their shells, just cooked, under crisp, savoury breadcrumbs, or wild boar rillettes, or pheasant boudin blanc in wild mushroom sauce, or crab and avocado Salad, could precede steamed game pudding, roast lamb or duck, wild mushroom soufflé, calves' liver, sea bass with Thai herbs, Caribbean fruit curry, or a T-bone steak.

There are 14 vouched-for puddings to decide from, and well-kept cheeses; enthusiasm and generosity nor do flag when it comes to the wine list.

A converted dower house, the Clytha is on the old road (B4598) between Abergavenny and Monmouth. Set among lawns and gardens, it is well worth a detour.

MEALS: L 12.30-2.30 approx £9.50; D 7.30-9.30 approx £25; Sunday L 12.30-3 £14.95
Closed: Monday lunch
Cards: All major
CHEF/PROPRIETOR: Andrew Canning
Rooms: 4, £45-65 S, £60-£80 D

183   Cowbridge

Basil's

2 Eastgate
Cowbridge
Vale of Glamorgan
CF71 7OG
Tel: 01446 773738
Fax: 01446 775292

An easy place to eat, the relaxed, smooth running of Basil's makes it a good choice for quiet dinners, larger gatherings of friends or family outings. It has pine floors, simple decorations and a changing menu chalked up on the board above the bar, supplemented by a seasonal, monthly set menu.

Choose from the board and, again, the emphasis is on seasonal ingredients, with choice of hot and cold starters, a wide selection of fish, meat, poultry and game, with chargrilled dishes too.

The garlic bread is a great temptation to accompany perhaps a cold salad of avocado, bacon and spinach or a warm salad of sauteed chicken livers.

Main courses might be duck breast, chargrilled butterfly lamb chops, venison and pheasant pie with mushrooms and Madeira sauce, potato, courgette and tomato pie, panpiette of lemon sole with salmon and basil mousseline.

A panaché of fish might include as many as six varieties, for example, salmon, monkfish, prawn, hake, sea bass and tuna, in a creamy parsley sauce. Vegetarian choices are good, with a filo parcel of spinach and feta. Vegetables are served separately, perhaps root mash, crisp beans, baby new potatoes and very good chips.

Puds can be excellent as in a soft and creamy crème brulée.

MEALS: L 12-2.30 from £5; D 7-10 from £13
Cards: All major
CHEF/PROPRIETOR: Alain Dubois

LOCAL INTEREST: Historic market town with good shops.

184 Cowbridge

Farthings Wine Bar

54 High Street
Cowbridge
Vale of Glamorgan
CF71 7AH
Tel: 01446 772990
Fax: 01446 775091

Welsh produce at its best

Farthings might have changed hands in the summer of 2000 but you would never know. "Why change something that works?" asks Natalie Dobson, the new owner, recently returned from London. This lovely, quaint old building, with its relaxed atmosphere and friendly staff has everything going for it.

At lunch enjoy the same wonderful comforting food, as you like it, with close friends, young children, difficult relatives or for a business lunch. Call in just for coffee and cake, two starters or a three-course meal.

Perhaps start with Farthings moneybags of smoked chicken, fresh mango and apple wrapped in filo pastry or smoked salmon crostini with cucumber and horseradish salsa.

Light lunches offer chicken livers with fresh marjoram, Penclawdd cockles sautéed with crispy bacon and laverbread, glazed with mature Welsh cheese and main courses of perhaps fish pie or chargrilled balsamic chicken.

The dinner menu has changed and booking is advised. It offers dishes of carpaccio of beef or warm chicken liver, oyster mushroom and smoked bacon salad, followed by duck cassoulet, baked cod with crab and spring onion crust and one of the marvellous home-made puddings such as the raspberry and hazelnut meringue.

There is definitely a flavour of Wales to the menu. Not only are ingredients sourced locally but a real effort has been made to produce and celebrate Welsh dishes.

MEALS: L 11.45-3 from £8; Sunday L 12-3 £7.95; D 7-10 from £12
CHEF: Damian Jones. PROPRIETOR: Natalie Dobson
Closed: Sunday and Monday nights
Cards: All except Amex Diners

LOCAL INTEREST: Takeaway service.

185 Cowbridge

Impeccable service, immaculate white table line, comfortable chairs, hushed chatter and soft music, Huddarts offers a special setting for a special evening. Neatly tucked into the busy high street of

Huddarts Restaurant

69 High Street
Cowbridge
Vale of Glamorgan
CF71 7AF
Tel: 01446 774645

Cowbridge, a black board on the pavement tempts passers-by with the specials of the day.

While Julie runs front of house, husband Andrew cooks, creating a picture out of any ingredient, with modern touches of drizzled dressings, crispy deep fried garnishes and two-colour sauces.

On the mid-week menu, four choices at each course might include home-made soup or salmon and tiger-prawn tails, with main courses of chicken Caribbean, fillet of salmon or sirloin steak Madeira, followed by a choice of desserts, coffee and mints.

The à la carte menu covers a selection of six starters such as seared fish platter (tuna, monkfish and salmon, drizzled with lime and spinach dressing, garnished with crispy seaweed) or goat's cheese salad of Pant ys Gawn cheese served on a salad of roasted walnuts, asparagus, orange and mixed leaves.

Main courses cover duck, pork, veal, turbot, Welsh Black beef, salmon and king prawn tails and lamb, described as best end of Welsh, rolled with herbs and seasoned, lightly roasted and sliced, with a fresh minted pea purée, served with a rich red wine and lamb jus reduction, topped with crispy fried leeks.

Puddings again stunning to look at, cover rich chocolate tart, the softest or Pavlova and a good variety of ice-creams.

Coffee is good, the wine list extensive and well chosen. House wines are excellent.

MEALS: L 12-2 £10; Sunday L 12-2 £14.95; D 7-9.30 £20
Closed: Sunday night and all Monday
Cards: All except Diners
CHEF/PROPRIETOR: Andrew Huddart

LOCAL INTEREST: Ancient market town of Cowbridge.

186 Creigiau

Caesar's Arms

Creigiau
Nr Cardiff
South Glamorgan
CF15 9NN
Tel: 029 2089 0486
Fax: 029 2089 2176

Miles down a dark and winding country lane, well beyond Creigiau, is the illuminated oasis of Caesar's Arms – a large whitewashed well-heeled stone pub with extensive conservatory restaurant extension and tarmacked car park. You walk straight into the heavily furnished and upholstered pub lounge bar with restaurant, open-plan kitchen, dark wooden tables, ornate picture frames and plenty of foliage. Service is friendly and helpful as you are guided to your table and then instructed in the routine of choosing your meal from the displayed produce.

Well-lit food counters, verging on the supermarket, hold quantities of chilled uncooked fish, meat and poultry – a carnivore's delight (vegetarian dishes are available on request, but not advertised).

An excellent choice of more than 100 wines from around the globe is

racked to the ceiling, with a good selection by the glass.

The menu is chalked up with regular starters and main courses, plus daily specials. These might include a tasty fish soup Provencale, a succulent wild mushroom risotto with Parmesan shavings, asparagus, spicy Bajan fishcakes or chicken winglets. You can get almost any variety of fresh fish, shellfish or meat cut, fried, grilled or baked, with a choice of sauces – garlic, Provencale, Barbados. To this, add french fries, baked or boiled potatoes and serve yourself from a choice of very basic salads from another chilled cabinet.

Desserts include a range of standard gateaux, Pavlova, mille feuille, summer pudding and fresh fruits in season.

Caesar's Arms will not win prizes for originality but provides a predictable but reliable formula.

MEALS: L 12-2.30 from £5; Sunday L 12-3.30 from £7.95;
D 7-9.30 from £7
Closed: Sunday evening
Cards: All
CHEF: Debbie Coleman. PROPRIETOR: Mark Sharples

187 Cwmavon

Mill Farm

Cwmavon
Pontypool
Gwent
NP4 8XJ
Tel/Fax: 01495 774588

The valley Afon Llwyd, between Blaenavon and Pontypool, was one of the busy cradles of the industrial revolution, the river, for most of this century, a discoloured stream of industrial pollution. Most signs of this are hidden now as grass and trees grow back, and Mill Farm Bed and Breakfast's buildings look over a stream which sparkles again as it did when the stone for them was quarried from the hillside above.

If the standardised anonymity of hotel chains is not to your taste, Mill Farm might be. Nowhere else could be like it, for nowhere else can have the same past, but it has now become a superbly comfortable and relaxing haven where you would not expect to find one. Winding stairs, rooms out of rooms, low doorways and huge fireplaces, and then you find the pool, with a lounge built round it – and you get to choose the music!

Breakfast is served until noon. The Jaynes like a guest with a good appetite but the dogs don't, they say, as they'll get anything that's left. There's plenty for everybody, an incitement to gluttony. Dry-cured bacon, free-range eggs, sausages from the local butcher and so many cereals, preserves, and fruit and juice that it seems rude not to try some. You can always work it off with a clamber round the fields and woods.

MEALS: L packed; D by arrangement from £15
Closed: 15.12-2.1
CHEF/PROPRIETOR: Caroline Jayne
WTB: 3 ★★★
Rooms: 6, £25 S b&b, £50 D b&b

LOCAL INTEREST: World Heritage area and the farmhouse and swimming pool on site.

188 Dinas Powys

Huntsman

The Square
Station Road
Dinas Powis
Vale of Glamorgan
CF64 4DE
Tel: 029 2051 4900
Fax: 029 2051 4900

Peter and Hilary Rice run their small, friendly restaurant with charm and competence. Situated in the car park of the Star Inn in the centre of Dinas Powys, this is the ideal place for a casual supper or large family celebration. Peter's relaxed manner front-of-house belies a highly organised undercurrent of skill. Hilary cooks single-handed, with local help brought in for busy nights. Even then, both Hilary and Peter find time to chat with customers at the end of the evening.

Starters include a memorable apple, blue cheese and red onion tart, served warm with rhubarb chutney, crab and tuna mousse with crisp salad and wholemeal toast, smoked chicken, beef tomato and black olive salad and a fresh soup of the day.

Vegetarians are well served with a main course such as parsnip and pine nut pancake with melted cheddar cheese, – while carnivores choose between six main courses, perhaps a Welsh Black fillet steak, roast breast of duck with Cumberland sauce or noisettes of Welsh lamb with asparagus and béarnaise sauce. At least one fish course is available and vegetables are served separately, fresh and crisp.

Puddings are available to suit all manner of apetites, a small crème brulée or a much larger home-made apple pie.

MEALS: L 12-2; D 7-9.30 approx £25
Closed: Sunday night, Monday, Tuesday and Wednesday lunch
Cards: Access, Visa, Mastercard, Delta Switch
CHEF: Hilary Rice. PROPRIETORS: Peter and Hilary Rice

LOCAL INTEREST: 10 minutes from Cardiff city centre and the bay.

189 Llantrisant

Brookes

79-81 Talbot Road
Talbot Green
Llantrisant
Mid Glamorgan
CF72 8AE
Tel: 01443 239600
Fax: 01443 239600

A lively hyacynth-blue has replaced the sober exterior green paint of this restaurant, which used to be Woods. True to its colour, this vibrant blue shows an artistic flair evident throughout the restaurant and on to the plates, which are huge and varying in shape. Crisp white linen and experienced table service set a high standard.

The lunchtime menu offers many old favourites such as Caesar salad, pâté and soup of the day. Again, the display is artistic, with drizzled balsamic dressing making circles around a triangular plate.

Main courses cover safe options of salmon fishcake with a butter sauce, stuffed chicken breast and well-cooked tagliatelle served on a bed of red onions with a good selection of roast vegetables.

Puddings are rich and filling, – delice of chocolate, or warm sponge with marmalade sauce.

The dinner menu is extensive with twelve starters and twelve main courses with almost as many desserts. Choose perhaps, seared diver-caught king scallops, watercress and pancetta salad, sweet chilli jam followed by rib-eye of Welsh beef on bubble-and-squeak with classic sauce Diane, and finish with a basket of home-made ice creams and sorbets.

MEALS: L 12-2.30 approx £10; D 7-10.30 approx £25
Closed: Sunday evening and Monday
Cards: All except Diners
CHEF: Craig Brookes. PROPRIETOR: Craig and Kevin Brookes

LOCAL INTEREST: Quaint old stone village of Llantrisant with arts and crafts centre.

190 Llantrisant

La Trattoria

11 Talbot Road
Talbot Green
Llantrisant
Mid Glamorgan
CF72 8AF
Tel: 01443 223399
Fax: 01443 226143

La Trattoria looks every bit the Tuscan oasis, with its iron-grilled windows and patio. Everything from the bare brick walls, flagstones and wooden beams inside, down to crocheted doilies on the plates, accentuates an authentic rustic feel.

Begin with mussels in white wine or calamari rings in a light batter, or venture to chef Massimo Berzolla's home region, Parma for 'the best part' of its ham served with baby artichokes or a house salad with flakes of Parmesan cheese, walnuts and eggs. Pasta dishes such as home-made tortelloni filled with rocket and ricotta, penne al pesto or a pan-tossed lasagne can be ordered as starters or main dishes.

Fish lovers can feast on sea bass baked in paper with prawns, mussels and tomato, while the carnivorous can enjoy a veal chop coated in mustard and served in a white wine, cream and green pepper sauce, chargrilled Welsh lamb cutlets marinated in sage and rosemary or a pork dish, for which Tuscany is so renowned, such as roast loin stuffed with prunes and cooked in brandy.

Finish with a sublime pannacotta with raspberry coulis, a grappa-flavoured semifreddo, or comforting pears baked in red wine.

The wine list is sensibly priced and offers an interesting selection of Italian wines.

The waiting staff are attentive without being obtrusive and will answer any questions you may have.

La Trattoria is an ideal venue for a relaxed evening of good home Tuscan cooking, all at excellent value.

MEALS: L 12-2.30; D 7-9.30
Closed: Sunday evening
Cards: Visa, Amex, Switch
PROPRIETORS: Massimo and Daniela Berzolla
CHEF: Massimo Berzolla

LOCAL INTEREST: Quaint old stone village of Llantrisant with arts and crafts centre.

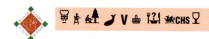

191   Llanvihangel Gobion

Llansantfraed Court

Llanvihangel Gobion
Nr Abergavenny
Monmouthshire
NP7 9BA
Tel: 01873 840678
Fax: 01873 840674
e-mail:
reception@llch.co.uk
www.llch.co.uk

Approaching from the B4598, mid-way between Abergavenny and Raglan, a long driveway passes under the A40 dual carriageway, and climbs to a large expanse of parkland. Fronted by an ornamental trout lake, the building claims 12th-century origins though the present house, a hotel for some eighty years, is built in the style of William and Mary, looking west towards the Black Mountains with Clytha Castle just visible to the south. The bar and lounge are warmed by open fires, the former with a gentlemens' clubby air while the latter is archetypal country house.

The restaurant, housed in former cattle byres, has a welcoming ambience and the daily changing, fixed price table d'hote menus make best use of locally available produce. Seared scallops, with aubergine caviar, come from the Gower, carpaccio of beef, with mustard and sage leaves, is Welsh Black, and the rack of lamb on a tian of peppered spinach may well be from Clytha Hill.

Lunch represents particularly good value with alternative starters such as asparagus and Brie soup with garlic croutons or venison terrine with cranberry and shallot relish, followed by fillet of kingfish on pesto mash or red pepper and artichoke risotto topped with deep-fried leeks.

To follow, an autumn berry pudding with mango purée is topped with spun sugar, while a selection of Welsh cheeses comes with wheat wafers, celery and grapes.

A stylish dinner menu adds the likes of loin of Old Spot pork on an apple and prune compote and whole roast quail stuffed with foie gras.

There is a firm and confident hand in the kitchen here, complemented by service that is warmly welcoming, unstuffy and relaxed – in the tradition of the best country houses.

MEALS: L 12-2 from £10; D 7-9 from £25
Cards: All
WTB: 3 ★★★
Rooms: 21, £70 S, £88 D, £125 Suite
CHEF: Kurt Fleming. PROPRIETOR: Mike Morgan

LOCAL INTEREST: Big Pit mining museum, National Cycle Route, World Heritage site, National Birds of Prey centre, Chepstow Castle.

192 Lower Machen

Hollybush Inn

Draethen
Lower Machen
Nr Newport
Gwent
NP10 8GB
Tel: 01633 441326

The Hollybush Inn serves assiduously executed food in very congenial surroundings. Situated above the pub, the restaurant is buoyant and hums with chat. Although affable enough, the service seems a little haphazard, but this may just be teething troubles in these early days.

The menu is designed to cater for the tastes of a broad church in terms of clientele and that goes for the rather overly generous portions, too. The quality of the cooking is not in question, however.

To start, there is venison terrine with port, orange and redcurrant sauce, field mushrooms in rosemary and garlic butter and egg Benedict on a toasted muffin with smoked bacon.

To follow, diners choose from pan fried lamb's liver with bacon on a bed of creamed potatoes topped with bacon and onions; roast breast of wild duck on a parsnip potato cake with red wine, crème de Cassis and shallot sauce, grilled lemon sole with tartare sauce and home cut chips. Side orders include potatoes (sauté and boiled), mixed salad and bruschetta.

Puddings are beautifully presented, options ranging through an exceptionally good tarte au citron with fruit coulis and orange sorbet, sticky toffee pudding with butterscotch sauce and vanilla ice-cream, and crème caramel with rum-soaked raisins to fresh fruit salad laced with Grand Marnier.

Dinner closes with coffee and petits fours.

MEALS: L 12-2.30 £5.95; Sunday L 12-2.30 £10.95
D 5.30-10 £10.95
Closed: Sunday evening
Cards: All major
CHEFS: Robert Harris and Paul Verallo
PROPRIETORS: Tanya and Paul Verallo

LOCAL INTEREST: Ruperra Castles, good walking countryside.

193 Newport

Junction 28

Station Approach
Bassaleg
Newport
NP1 9LD
Tel: 01633 891891
Fax: 01633 895978

Junction 28 is spacious, seating around 150, but it is cleverly divided into different sections so that diners do not feel as if they are eating in an aircraft hangar. Popular with families, the early evening "flyer men" served between 5.30-7.30 is good value @ £11.95 for 3 courses.

The menu is extensive and one wonders if such a huge range of dishes can be produced without shortcuts. However, our veal sausage, black pudding and foie gras starter was excellent, although the bread selection is not very exciting

Alternatively there are tartlet of Parma ham, olives, peppers and Mozzarella, smoked haddock chowder with coriander and poached egg,

pork and paprika meatballs with tomato and peppers and white crab and horseradish mousse with gooseberry coulis.

And for main dish, perhaps breast of pheasant with wild mushrooms, pâté and smoked bacon, monkfish topped with an olive crust and red pesto dressing or confit duck with crispy noodles and rich orange sauce. Vegetables are priced separately and guests can choose from honey-roasted parsnips, sauté potatoes, mixed vegetables and salad.

For pudding, try baked chocolate pear and almond tart with whipped cream, iced parfait of caramelised hazelnuts with passion fruit coulis or baked lemon curd Alaska flamed in brandy.

MEALS: L 12-2 £10.45; D 5.30-9.30 approx £23
Closed: Sunday evening – last week July, first week August
Cards: All major
CHEF: J West. PROPRIETORS: R C Wallace, J West

LOCAL INTEREST: Cardiff city centre, historic castles.

194 Newport

The Olive Tree

Celtic Manor Resort
Coldra Woods
Newport
Gwent
NP18 1HQ
Tel: 01633 413000
Fax: 01633 412910

e-mail: celtic-manor.com

You can't miss Celtic Manor. It stands high over the M4 approaches to Newport like a Marcher Castle. The way in is not so unmissable, over its own flyover from the A48. No-one, you imagine, ever comes here on foot. From the breeze-block caverns of the underground car parks, you ascend by stages, to the full soaring glory of the glass, mock-marble and cement stone atrium, where be dragons in many forms. Along one long wing is the Olive Tree restaurant, with trompe l'oeil balcony and lofty windows looking out over the peaceful golf course.

It is difficult for a space that needs at times to seat hundreds not to seem daunting when customers are few and for a kitchen which does not blink at banquets but can stumble over a potato. However, the waiting team are reassuringly friendly, and you can start with solid bankers from the Mediterranean buffet, like smoked salmon, liver parfait, and chicken galantine with a red chard salad, or soup of the day. Then perhaps try a Spanish-style mixed grill with chorizo sausage, and smooth, bland tomato sauce, or an asparagus and wild mushroom risotto, or seared tuna, still pinkish, on a bed of herb mash.

Puddings are perfectly presented, and at lunch you help yourself from an admirably presented buffet.

The wine list is many pages long, with a helpful page of recommendations. Under the Welsh heading is Cwm Deri Elderflower, though a price of £15.50 for half-a-litre might make auntie flinch.

There is another, more ambitious and expensive restaurant, Owens which opens in the evening. Starters include Llanover salt duck 'East Meets Wales' and Gower scallops, with main courses of Usk Vale rabbit, roasted pavé of sea bass and Irish breast of duckling.

MEALS: L 12.30-2 £18 ; D £21
Cards: All
CHEF: Peter Fuchs
WTB: 5 ★★★★★
Rooms: 400

LOCAL INTEREST: Golf School of Excellence.

195 Newport

The Woodland Restaurant and Bar

Llanvair Discoed
Penhow
Newport
NP6 6LX
Tel: 01633 400313

Welsh produce at its best

Considerable transformation has taken place at this commendable local, formerly the King's Arms, in a tiny village that stands at the foot of the vast Wentwood Forest. The kitchen has been extended and serves a purpose-built restaurant that has extended the scope of its menus under the supervision of Rob James and Keith Gibbs, both of them highly experienced caterers.

The village bar, however, remains no less of a pub and also serves up quality bar food that encompasses chicken stir-fry, cod in beer batter with mushy peas and tagliatelli marinara at generous prices. Fairly simple-sounding restaurant dishes, revised daily on large chalk boards, leave plenty of room for surprise, for the cooking is accomplished and there is a fine balance both of flavours and accompaniments that demonstrate first-class kitchen skills.

For starters, try the moules mariniers, a warm salad of smoked salmon with goats' cheese or garlic mushrooms in a creamy home-made sauce, accompanied by oven-fresh warm bread rolls.

To follow might be fresh salmon served with creamed leeks, sea bass roast with lemon and rock-salt, and a classic grilled steak bordelaise all tastily balanced with generous portions of vegetables.

No less care goes into the preparation of desserts that might include butterscotch brulée, a glazed lemon tart or traditional bread-and-butter pudding. Sunday lunch is a big family hit with suitably informal and low-key service.

MEALS: L 12-2 from £5.95; D 6.30-9 approx £20
Closed: Sunday evening
Cards: All major
CHEF: Rob James. PROPRIETOR: Rob James and Keith Gibbs

LOCAL INTEREST: Wye Valley, Wentwood forest.

196 Penarth

Local vegetarians will already know Tomlins. The dining room is comfortably sized and fittingly relaxed, the walls pastel orange and yellow, and hung with pleasingly undemanding paintings, the floor-

Tomlins

46 Plassey Street
Penarth
Vale of Glamorgan
CF64 1EL
Tel: 029 2070 6644

www.
tomlinsvegetarianrestaurant.co.uk

polished boards, and large, uncrowded tables laid with white linen. A husband and wife are team in control.

The four-choice, three-course menu ranges from comforting, almost familiar, friends with a new spin, to imported novelties. The cooking is self-confident: stuffed marrow on a bed of creamy turnip gratin making you rethink this under-valued pair. Other successful combinations are grilled red pepper with feta, stuffed aubergine rolls, red kidney-bean stew with peanut sauce, plantain and corn soup, and napoleon of vegetables with goulash sauce. The fruit served with a coconut pudding turned out to be mango and papaya!

In an inspired transformation, at lunchtime, oilcloth replaces linen, and the themed menu simply lists the dishes available that day; you choose as many as you wish, dim-sum fashion. This makes an ideal introduction to meatless dining; no-one finds themselves with a plate of food they wish they had not ordered but all can pick and mix. As befits an exclusively vegetarian restaurant, all the wines and beers on an adequate and very reasonable wine list are organic, and suitable for vegetarians; many are also suitable for vegans.

Tomlins is ethically but not stuffily run, and the pleasure in a good meal is not lessened by knowing we have harmed ourselves, and the world, as little as possible.

MEALS: L 12-3 £7.95; Sunday L 12-2.30 £8.95; D 7-10 £17
Closed: Please ring for details of opening
Cards: All major
CHEF/PROPRIETOR: D. L. Tomlinson

LOCAL INTEREST: Penarth Victorian Seafront.

197 Pontyclun

Miskin Manor Hotel

Pendoylan Road
Groesfaen
Pontyclun
Vale of Glamorgan
CF72 8ND
Tel: 01443 224204
Fax: 01443 237606

e-mail:
info@miskin-manor.co.uk
www.miskin-manor.co.uk

If you would like to enjoy a weekend or meal in baronial splendour in an ancient Grade II listed family seat, this is the place to go. High-ceilinged rooms, baroque gilded mirrors, heads of stuffed horned animals protruding from heavily wood-panelled walls, log fires flickering in large hearths and well-trained waistcoated staff all contribute to a civilised and relaxed experience.

The à la carte menu of complex dishes and the extensive wine list, with plenty of half-bottles, is brought while you take your aperitif on deep leather sofas in the lounge before being led to the elegant, silver service, strictly non-smoking dining room.

Elaborate descriptions of the creative dishes turn into short poems – "Spicy lentil and scallop timbale with sesame seed croute and small salad with vinaigrette" or "Salt marsh lamb stuffed with leeks and apricots, sliced dauphinoise potatoes and caper and mint sauce."

More succinctly, other starters include confit of tuna and crispy bacon, baked cabbage and goat's cheese parcel, while main courses include casserole of pigeon, honey and ginger duckling, venison fillet,

Welsh produce at its best

maize-fed chicken and leek and wild-mushroom risotto. Welsh Black beef in various cuts and monkfish tail appear on a small grill menu and there is a choice of vegetarian dishes. Welsh ingredients are used wherever possible, including the cheese selection.

Desserts run from sticky toffee pudding to an after-eight parfait and pear poached in saffron liqueur on a bed of creamed Arborio rice and lime syrup.

MEALS: L 12-2; D 7-9.45 approximately £25
Cards: All major
CHEF: Tony Kocker. PROPRIETORS: Leah and Colin Rosenburg.
WTB: 4 ★★★★
Rooms: 43, £94 S, £126 D, £152.50 Suite

LOCAL INTEREST: Castles, Cardiff Bay, Cardiff City centre, Brecon Beacons, Swansea and Gower.

198 Southerndown

Frolics

Beach Road
Southerndown
Nr Bridgend
Vale of Glamorgan
CF32 ORP
Tel/Fax: 01656 880127

Welsh produce at its best

Frolics sits in a neat little nook on the aptly named Beach Road, which leads directly to cliffs elaborately carved by the sea. Nothing would be nicer than to have a casual stroll towards the water on a fine summer's evening – perhaps before or after your meal.

Inside the petite restaurant, which also houses a small bistro downstairs during the summer months, the dainty decor is fresh and inviting. Classical technique and an emphasis on prime ingredients comprise many of the dishes from both the à la carte and cheaper table d'hôte menus.

First courses include the likes of crisp hake tempura with a sprightly lime mayonnaise, baked avocado with spicy red onions, tomato, basil and two cheeses, and garlic mushrooms with smoked bacon in a dunkable (though swimmingly so) cream sauce.

Main-course choices show off the chef's prowess with fish, including delicate steamed salmon with saffron sauce and nest of lemon sole with queen scallops, prawns and ginger chilli and lime sauce. A moist roast duck "cooked until crispy and served off the carcass" with caramelised orange sauce delights, while pork tenderloin is a flavourful alternative. Vegetable accompaniments are as good as they get, with plenty to go round; gratin dauphinoise is supremely tasty.

Desserts include raspberry and lemon sorbet, a throwback to the 60s with crêpe suzette and baked Alaska, and winter fruit parfait.

The wine list offers a good range, with desirable house wines.

MEALS: Sunday L 12-3 £13.50, D 7-9.30
Closed: All day Monday and Sunday evening
Cards: Visa, Mastercard, Amex

CHEF: Martin Dobson. PROPRIETORS: Sandra Brown and Martin Say

LOCAL INTEREST: Dunraven Bay and Glamorgan Heritage coastline.

199 Tredunnock

The Newbridge

Tredunnock
Monmouthshire
NP15 1RH
Tel: 01633 451000
Fax: 01633 451001
www.the-newbridge.com

Is it a country pub, a wine bar or a restaurant? The Newbridge, just outside the village of Tredunnock, is all of these and offers something for everyone. Careful planning is evident in the design, which is an agreeable combination of old and contemporary, including art by Irish painter Graham Nuttel. On the ground floor and on a first-floor gallery, table arrangements provide plenty of space for diners. There is also a private dining room-cum-wine cellar available at no extra cost.

The bar offers a good selection of Welsh beers and an impressive choice of wines, many of which are served by the glass, including champagne.

An enthusiastic welcome and confident cooking awaits visitors. The lunch menu offers a range of dishes from soup, club sandwich and fish pie to crispy spicy chicken wings, Mediterranean risotto and chargrilled rib-eye steak.

Of an evening, sink into a squashy sofa (or perch on a stool at the bar) to study the menu and an inventive list of daily specials. On the latter, starters might include mille-feuille of tomato and spicy white crab meat with pearls of vegetables and tomato vinaigrette, or pan-fried scallops, black pudding, mashed potato and herb butter sauce. Main courses might contain a duo of Gressingham duck with red cabbage, soufflé potatoes and red wine and lentil jus, or roast fillet of cod topped with Welsh rarebit with spring onion mash and creamy tomato sauce. From the desserts, choose bittersweet chocolate tart with pistachio ice cream, lemon posset, or raspberry crème brulée.

MEALS: L 12-2.30; Sunday L 12-3; D 7-9.30 £25
Closed: Sunday night and Mondays in January and February
Cards: All
CHEF: Andrew Reagan. PROPRIETORS: Kevin and Sue Farthing

LOCAL INTEREST: Riverside location – watch the salmon jump, heart of Usk Valley.

200 Usk

Jaunty Toulouse-Lautrec posters grace the walls of this easy-going bistro on Usk's main street and there is a bar where guests can perch

Bush House

15 Bridge Street
Usk
Monmouthshire
NP15 1BQ
Tel: 01291 672929
Fax: 01291 671215

on tall stools and have a drink if they don't fancy sitting down straight away. Despite the cosy surroundings, though, the ambience can feel a touch muted.

Nevertheless, little touches steer the food and presentation away from the predictable: orange aioli with the home-smoked duck, for instance, and lime and pink peppercorns embellishing cold smoked salmon. The hearty oven-warm bread is home-made and the pats of butter that melt on to it are served on pretty flat pottery dishes.

Starters include seared scallops and gambas with puy lentils and sauce Armoricaine, laverbread, cockle and bacon fritters on garlic crostini with spiced apricot marmalade or tomato and Parmesan risotto with wild roquette dressing and oven roast tomatoes.

For a main course, there is line-caught native sea bass with vanilla butter and truffle mash, roast tenderloin of Gloucester Old Spot with celeriac and apple purée and a port wine and juniper berry jus, and for vegetarians aubergine and basil parcels with two cheeses and a herbed tomato dressing.

Three different puds are chalked up on the blackboard, choose the chocolate sponge with a tangy berry sauce (a highly successful partnership), lemon tart with Jersey cream or sticky toffee pudding.

MEALS: L 12-2.30 approx £10; D 7-9 approx £20
Closed: Monday-Friday lunch and Sunday evening
Cards: All major
CHEF/PROPRIETOR: Steven Rogers

LOCAL INTEREST: Usk Town and Valley.

201 Walterstone

Allt-Yr-Ynys Hotel

Walterstone
Herefordshire
HR2 0DU
Tel: 01873 890307
Fax: 01873 890539
e-mail:
allthotel@compuserve.com
www.allthotel.co.uk

This beautifully preserved 16th-century building, with its moulded ceilings and oak panelling, was formerly a manor house (and, for a brief time, a farmhouse) before becoming a country hotel with its own clay-pigeon shooting range. It sits on the Monmouthshire-Herefordshire border in 16 acres of ground and is popular with visitors escaping city life, eager to enjoy the tranquillity of this lovely countryside.

On arrival, relax and order a drink. The wines are well chosen, originating from most wine-producing countries, with an allegiance to France. There is a good selection of bordeaux and burgundys as well as two dessert wines.

Lunch might include braised hock of local ham on sun-dried tomato mash with borlotti bean sauce, or Gower cockles and pancetta salad on crispy leaves with honey and sweet chilli dressing. Or how about a "mini-breakfast" salad of chopped bacon, herb and pork sausage, black pudding and warm poached egg?

Of an evening, starters could be roasted fennel and smoked paprika soup with honey sippets, honey-glazed duck confit on caramelised orange and sesame salad, or seared marinated Cornish scallops on sweetcorn relish with sauce vierge.

For main dishes perhaps roasted lemon sole fillet on saffron and rouille potato confit with dill beurre blanc, Welsh Black beef fillet baked with wild mushroom and cheese herb crust with claret cep sauce, or pan-fried breast of local pheasant on an English casserole and laced with a mead and honey sauce.

To finish, choose from caramelised St Clements tart with strawberry coulis, hazelnut meringue praline with guanaja chocolate cream, or local Welsh and French cheeses with fine biscuits, nuts, figs and sweet grapes.

MEALS: L 12.30-2 approx £10; D 7-10 approx £25
Cards: Amex, Visa, Access, Switch
CHEF: Nicholas Walton. CONTACT: Howard Williams
WTB: 4 ★★★★
Rooms: 19, from £65 S, from £95 D, from £130 Suite

LOCAL INTEREST: Abergavenny, Hay-on-Wye, Raglan Castle.

202 Walterstone

Carpenters Arms

Walterstone
Nr. Abergavenny
Herefordshire
HR2 0DX
Tel: 01873 890353

Entering this old traditional country pub is like stepping back in time. Its small rooms, low ceilings, stone walls and traditional furniture all add to the warm welcome from the landlady, who delights in confiding that she was born here. There are a couple of real ales on top but the undeniable attraction is the cider – at least eight varieties, including oak-aged and organic. Wines include an Australian selection in convenient 187ml bottles.

An evolving blackboard menu offers starters such as marinated pork hock with wholegrain mustard sauce, breadcrumbed fishcakes and smoked salmon with free-range scrambled eggs. From the main dishes, try roast breast of local duck with orange sauce, or faggots with mash, onion gravy and mushy peas. The standard menu offers typical pub fare such as Herefordshire steaks, thick lamb chops, chicken supremes and home-made pies (beef and Guinness or cod and prawn). Desserts are home-made and traditional – sticky toffee pudding, apple crumble, bread-and-butter pudding, treacle tart and old-fashioned chocolate steamed pudding.

Sunday lunch is particularly popular and must be booked.

Find the Carpenters Arms next to Walterstone Church, with lovely views over the surrounding countryside, up a country lane about 1 1/2 miles from Pandy on the A465 Abergavenny-to-Hereford road.

MEALS: L 12-2 £12-£20; D 7-9.30 £12-£20
Cards: None
CHEF: Sharon Smith. PROPRIETOR: Vera Watkins

LOCAL INTEREST: Abergavenny, Hay-on-Wye, Raglan Castle.

203 Whitebrook

Crown at Whitebrook

Whitebrook
Nr Monmouth
Monmouthshire
NP 4TX
Tel: 01600 860254
Fax: 01600 860607

e-mail:
crown@whitebrook.demon.co.uk
www.crownatwhitebrook.com

Welsh produce at its best

Nestling in a heavily wooded cleft some two miles above the Wye Valley road (A466), the Crown is very much a destination for the discerning diner. Under new ownership since our last edition it has nonetheless retained its air of warm hospitality. There is a bright new look to the lounge, where diners can choose at leisure from the menu while enjoying aperitifs and freshly produced canapes.

In the kitchen Mark Turton has put his former tutelage to good use, his dishes remaining in a modern British idiom, with more than a nod to French influences and careful thought given to balance of flavours. Good local ingredients play their fair share, with Wye salmon, Monmouthshire-reared venison and Welsh spring lamb featured according to the seasons.

Lunch can be quite a light affair, featuring perhaps a tart of wild mushrooms with Parmesan and mixed leaves and salmon and leek fish cakes with mussel and cream sauce. From a more elaborate dinner menu choose from starters such as duck and foie gras terrine, followed by combination main courses that marry tender Welsh lamb with thyme crust and a roast red pepper tartlet, and chargrilled fillet of beef with mustard sauce and a garlic and chive mash.

Accompaniments are generous to a fault, with good fresh breads and assorted fresh vegetables delicately arranged on a side plate. Home-made clove ice cream accompanies an apple tatin with caramel sauce, and a feast of grapes, celery and biscuits is served alongside an exemplary plate of assorted Welsh cheeses.

Those staying overnight can enjoy a fine selection of malt whiskies or rare brandies, in anticipation of a hearty Welsh breakfast at leisure in the morning.

MEALS: L 12-2 approx £14; Sunday L 12-2 £15.95; D 7-9 approx £30
Closed: Monday lunch
Cards: All major
CHEF: Mark Turton. PROPRIETORS: Angela and Elizabeth Barbara
WTB: 3 ★★★
Rooms: 11, S, £68 D, £95 Suite

LOCAL INTEREST: Walking, golf, fishing, castles.

The Youth Hostels of Wales

Youth Hostels are no longer just for youth. Today they offer good accommodation, perhaps with en-suite facilities, and are definitely family friendly. Often sited in the most wonderful locations in Wales they offer some of the most spectacular views, and what is more, they can provide very good food too. Whether you are walking, climbing, cycling or pottering around in a car, youth hostels can add a gastronomic edge to your trip.

Whilst all hostels provide a good hot meal in the evening it is possible to find an a la carte menu here and there where the best of local produce is cooked with care and the best of home cooking skills.

Much depends on the guardian. Take Alison Crawshaw at Capel y Ffin youth hostel for example.

She has worked hard to create a cosy cottage feel at this old farmhouse with its old beams and open fires. Situated in a remote spot in the Brecon Beacons National Park, the majority of visitors are cyclists and walkers. 'They are very hungry and need a lot of carbohydrate in their diet, so I make up extra dishes for them using potatoes, pasta and rice, as well as the usual 3 course meals'.

Buzzoni macaroni is a particular favourite of local organic spinach with pasta and thick bechamel sauce, served with garlic bread, or the new creation of layers of cooked rice, thick bechamel sauce, sliced hard boiled egg, parsley and tuna.

Alison makes all her own bread, four types are on offer each evening, perhaps walnut loaves, soda bread and a spicy chilli, parsley and chive to go with the soup.

The evening meal would usually consist of a homemade soup or fruit juice followed by a choice of either a meat, fish or vegetarian dish and to finish, a traditional rib-sticking pudding of apple crumble, bread and butter pudding, or fudge sticky toffee, all served with oodles of custard.

It takes a certain amount of enthusiasm and energy to run a hostel like this, with 38 beds in high season, and for Alison, it's a job she really enjoys.

Youth Hostels recommended for their good food

CAPEL Y FFIN   Llanthony, Nr Abergavenny NP7 7NP   Tel: 01873 890650
Guardian – Alison Crawshaw

MANORBIER	Manorbier, Nr. Tenby SA70 7TT	Tel: 01834 871803 Fax: 01834 871101
	Email: manorbier@yha.org.uk Web: www.yha.org.uk *Guardians – Deb and Matt Roberts*	
SNOWDON RANGER	Rhyd Ddu, Caernarfon, Gwynedd LL54 7YS	Tel: 01286 650391 Fax: 01286 650093
	Guardians – Dave and Kath Woods	
LLANGOLLEN	Tyndwr Rd, Llangollen, Denbighshire LL20 8AR	Tel: 01978 860330 Fax: 01978 861709
	Email: Llangollen@yha.org.uk Web: www.yha.org.uk *Guardian – Stan Martin*	
BROADHAVEN	Haverfordwest, Pembrokeshire SA62 3JH	Tel: 01437 781688 Fax: 01437 781100
	Email: broadhaven@yha.org.uk *Guardians – Gary and Susan Jervis*	
CONWY	Larkhill, Sychnant Pass Road, Conwy LL32 8AJ	Tel: 01492 593571 Fax: 01492 593580
	Guardians – Eric Soutter and Jane Carter	
PEN-Y-CWM	Nr Solva, Haverfordwest, Pembrokeshire SA62 6LA	Tel: 01437 721940 Fax: 01437 720959
Email: pen-y-cwm@yha.org.uk		
	Guardian – Kenneth Cross	
BORTH	Morlais, Borth, Ceredigion SY24 5JS	Tel: 01970 871498 Fax: 01970 871827
	Email: Borth@yha.org.uk *Guardian – Keith Bradshaw*	
LLANBERIS	Llwyn Celyn, Llanberis, Caernarfon, Gwynedd LL55 4SR	Tel: 01286 870280 Fax: 01286 870936
	Email: Llanberis@yha.org.uk *Guardian – Paul Semple*	

Chicken with rarebit topping and warm potato, spinach and beetroot salad

A deliciously light cheesy topping to tender chicken. Delicious served on a bed of tangy beetroot, mixed herb and potato salad.

- Serves: 6
- Overall preparation time: 45 minutes
- Per serving: 489 Calories, 23g Fat

What You Need

For the rarebit chicken

6 skinless chicken breast fillets
300g Cheddar cheese, grated
6 x 15ml spoons milk
25g plain flour
25g white breadcrumbs
1/2 x 15ml spoon English mustard powder
5ml spoon Worcestershire sauce
1 medium egg
salt and freshly ground black pepper

For the salad

15ml spoon oil
500g punnet new potatoes, cooked and halved
250g pack cooked beetroot, diced
100g bag spinach leaves
Juice 1/2 lemon

What To Do

For the rarebit chicken: preheat the oven to 190°C, 375°F, Gas Mark 5. Place the chicken on a baking sheet in the preheated oven for 25-30 minutes until cooked through.

Meanwhile place the cheese, milk, flour and breadcrumbs in a saucepan and stir over a moderate heat until the cheese has melted. Allow to cool slightly. Preheat the grill. Transfer the mixture to a blender or food processor and add the mustard, Worcestershire sauce, egg and seasoning. Blend until glossy and smooth, then spoon into a bowl and chill for 20 minutes.

For the salad base: heat the oil and add the potatoes, beetroot, spinach, lemon juice and seasoning to taste.

When the chicken is cooked, place a spoonful of the 'rarebit mixture' on top of each chicken breast to cover. Immediately place under a preheated hot grill for 2-3 minutes until golden and bubbling. Serve straight away on the warm salad.

Griddled chump steaks with balsamic and redcurrant glaze with celeriac mash and green beans

Tender sweet glazed Welsh lamb served on a bed of creamy celeriac mash with fine green beans.

- Serves: 4-6
- Overall preparation time: 40 minutes
- Per serving: 460 Calories, 28g Fat

What You Need

For the chump steaks

6 lamb chump steaks or chops

6 x 15ml spoon balsamic vinegar

15ml spoon finely chopped rosemary

15ml spoon olive oil

2 x 15ml spoon redcurrant jelly, melted

For the celeriac mash

500g celeriac, peeled, diced and cooked in boiling water until tender

500g old potatoes, peeled, diced and cooked in boiling until tender

2 x 15ml spoons milk

small knob butter

salt and freshly ground black pepper

500g green beans

What To Do

For the chump steaks: place the lamb in a non-metallic bowl along with the balsamic vinegar, rosemary, oil and redcurrant jelly. Mix well and leave for 10 minutes.

Heat a frying or griddle pan and cooked the steaks or chops for 5 minutes on each side.

For the celeriac mash: mash together the cooked celeriac and potatoes with the milk, butter and seasoning to taste.

Cook the beans in lightly salted water until just tender and then drain well.

Serve the lamb on a bed of mash and green beans, drizzled with a little extra balsamic if liked.

Sainsbury's
making life taste better

Experience the true taste of fresh bread

With the hustle and bustle of life today, very few of us have time to bake, but that doesn't mean we miss out on the true taste of freshly baked breads and pastries. Flavours that cannot be matched, in this pre packed world.
At Fedwen Bakery we are busy six days a week from 7.30am to 5pm baking a wide range of delicious breads and pastries.

For the health conscious we have a selection of brown, rye, granary and wholemeal breads. For those who like to indulge themselves our selection of pastries taste every bit as good as they look. Daily deliveries to the catering industry.

49 King Street,
Carmarthen
Tel & Fax:
01267 236578

Fedwen Bakery
Proprietor
Mr Kevin Thomas

SWANSEA MARKET

Wales's premier retail market offering you a unique shopping experience

Over 100 separate stalls plus areas allocated to 'casual' traders for the sale of local and specialised produce such as Gower grown vegetables, cockles, laverbread, etc.

Unrivalled variety all under one roof and right in the heart of the City Centre.

LOCAL SPECIALITIES

You must try cockles and laverbread at Swansea Market, the largest covered market in Wales.

CITY AND COUNTY OF SWANSEA
DINAS A SIR ABERTAWE

Telephone:
01656 646333
Fax:
07070 600478

W.W. WESGATE CATERING BUTCHERS

Unit 2,
Pen-y-Bont Ind Est.
Coity Road,
Bridgend,
CF31 1NW

Our family run firm, would like to introduce you to a unique way of business, it is headed by a superb master butcher, who presonally buys all our prime meat himself. This care is carried through to our preparation area, where our team of butchers cut to order.

Our General Price Offers
* All meat cut to order
* Vacuum packed
* Portion controlled
* All meat packed in quantities of five for your convenience

Our á La Carte
* All cuts expertly trimmed to perfection
* Includes Barbary duck breast, veal, barnsley chops, rack of lamb

We specialise in catering for hotels, restaurants and nursing homes, where we can offer very competitive price lists. For nursing and residential homes, we offer a wide range of produce on our general price list. The public is also welcome to visit our cash and carry store, where you can take time to browse while your order is prepared in front of you.

* 24hr Order Line * 24hr Fax Line * Free refrigerated delivery service for business premises, 6 days a week

Gwledd i'r
Llygad liw dydd.
Liw nos
Gwleddwch.

Haul y bore bach yn taenu dros donnau o fryniau a chymoedd tywod yn pelydru wrth i'r traethau ymestyn draw i'r pellter. Yr haul yn machlud tu draw i donnau llyn mynyddig. Yna wrth iddi nosi, medrwch setlo lawr i fwyd a bwyd da mewn bwyty clud. Darganfod cig eidion lleol, llysiau organig, cawsiau blasus o Gymru a rhestri gwin cynhwysfawr.

Mae gwledd yn eich aros yng Nghymru, felly anfonwch am lyfryn Cymru neu ymweld ân gwefan i weld y wledd sydd o'ch blaenau.

I gael eich llyfryn di-dâl
Rhadffon 080 80 1000 000
www.visitwales.com

**Tregroes Waffles,
for a tasty world!**

Unit 2,
Pencader Road,
Llandysul,
Ceredigion, SA44 4AE
Tel: 01559 363468

Free Ranging
Barn Reared on Barley Straw

~ Grain Fed ~
~ Deliciously Original ~

Home-made turkey burgers and sausages a speciality in our Farm Box by Post service!

DAFYDD RAW REES
Tel: 01970 828375
www.farmbox.co.uk

Clam's hand made cakes
"Great Taste Award Winners"

Manufacturers of highest quality traditional type cake / fresh cream truffles

Award Winning Cakes and Truffles

TRY CLAM'S CAKES on your customers and see the effect that these *naughty but nice* individually made products have on your TURNOVER!

11 Station Enterprises, Station Road, Abergavenny,
Monmouthshire NP7 5HY. Tel: 01873 854496 Fax: 01873 854005
E-mail: clamscakes@virgin.net

"Fresh Food - Great Taste"

The Organic Farm Shop

The Organic Farm Shop is the culmination for Romeo and Tania Sarra of organic farming for the last 10 years.

A vast range of potatoes and vegetables are grown throughout the year to ensure the Shop is always stocked with freshly packed and competitively priced produce which undercut the major organic competitors.

Fruit and vegetables not grown in this country are imported but emphasis is on quality and sourcing produce as local as possible.

Dairy produce, butter, eggs, cheeses and poultry are all local or Welsh. The Shop has a full range of groceries, whole foods, sauces, pulses, grains, rice and soups. Everything one needs for cooking delicious meals including wines and beers.

Box Delivery Scheme
A box delivery scheme is being established for Pembrokeshire, where all the produce stocked in the shop and grown on the Farm will be available.

Food you can trust - Check our prices

Delivery on a weekly basis: make enquiries to the Shop:
186 Prendergast, Haverfordwest Tel: 01437 765040 or 762323

FFYNNON LAS VINEYARD

LAMPETER ROAD • ABERAERON

Enjoy a stroll through a Welsh Vineyard

ADMISSION FREE

- Wine Tasting • Picnic Area
- Vine Yard Walks • Self Guided Tours
- Group Guided Tours • Retail Shop
- Some Disabled • Free Parking • Access

OPEN Easter to October 2pm to 5pm

Other times/Coach parties by appointment please

Tel: 01545 570234

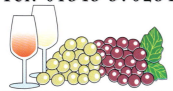

GRAIG FARM ORGANICS

AWARD-WINNING ORGANIC MEAT & OTHER PRODUCE FROM THE HEART OF WALES

RANGE INCLUDES:

BEEF, LAMB, WELSH MOUNTAIN MUTTON, PORK, BACON, SAUSAGES, PIES, FISH, GROCERIES, DAIRY, GREENGROCERY, SKIN CARE, OFF-LICENCE, ETC.

 AVAILABLE FROM OUR FARM SHOP, RETAIL OUTLETS, INTERNET AND MAIL ORDER

Details from:
GRAIG FARM ORGANICS
Dolau, Llandrindod Wells,
Powys LD1 5TL

Tel: 01597 851655

Visit our Website at:
www.graigfarm.co.uk

SNOWDEN & CO.
(CARDIFF) LIMITED

Wholesale Fish Merchants

Suppliers of all types of the highest quality fresh & frozen fish. Providing a daily delivery service to catering establishments throughout South Wales.

Registered Office:
East Bay Close, off Tyndal Street, Cardiff. CF10 4BA.
Telephone: 029 2048 9948 or 029 2048 9998 Fax: 029 2048 0474

The South Wales Borderers and Monmouthshire Regimental Museum of the Royal Regiment of Wales

The Barracks, Brecon, Powys LD3 7EB

Zulu War Room;

Guns, Uniforms, Equipment, Paintings and War Mementoes spanning 300 years of service; Large Medal Collection with 16 Victoria Crosses won by officers and soldiers of the Regiment. Gift counter. Facilities for the disabled.

Opening Times:
9am to 1pm and 2pm to 5pm
1st April to 30th September every day;
1st October to 31st March week days only.

Rorke's Drift 1879

Tel: 01874 613310
Website: www.rrw.org.uk

Hand made preserves, curds, chutneys, marmalade, mustards, jellies & condiments.

A tasty treat from Wales

Own label and recipe development are our speciality

Contact Dio Jones, Marion Jones

Email: welsh.lady@bun.com
Tel: 01766 810496 or Fax: 01766 810067
at Bryn, Y Ffôr, PWLLHELI,
Gwynedd, LL53 6RL.

John Tudor & Son
Contract & Catering Butcher

Suppliers of fresh, frozen and cooked meats to education, health authorities and major catering organisations throughout East, South and West Wales.

A member of the Federation of Fresh Meat Wholesalers.

  Tel 01656 665127
Fax 01656 652780

15 Ogmore Crescent Industrial Estate, Bridgend, CF31 3TE

Don't miss...

Colin Pressdee's restaurant reviews

pick of the bunch wine guide
plus exclusive offers from
The Western Mail Wine Club

recipes from top Welsh chefs

every Saturday in

The Western Mail
magazine

What are your comments?

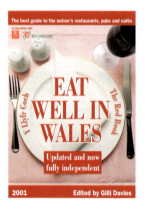

Comments on establishments listed and your recommendations for new entries for the next edition of 'Eat Well In Wales', are welcomed.

Please send them to:
Gilli Davies, Perch Buildings, 9 Mount Stuart Square, Cardiff Bay, CF10 6EE

Name of Establishment(s) ....

Comments/Recommendations ....

....

....

....

....

....

....

....

....

Please Complete

Name: ....

Address: ....

....

....Postcode: ....

Date: ....Signature: ....

North Wales Establishments

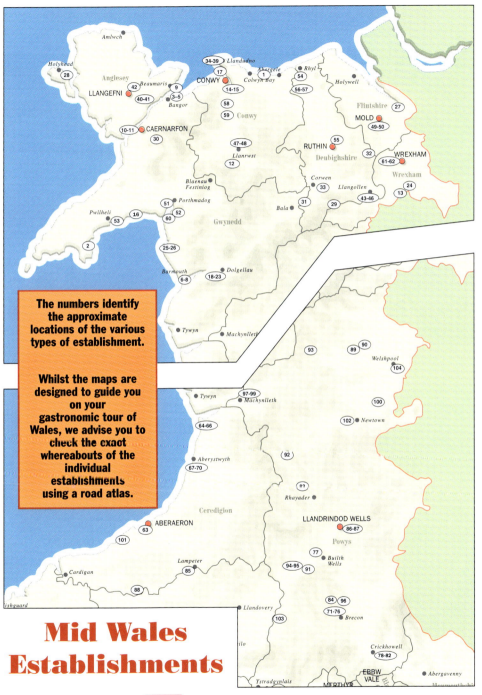

Mid Wales Establishments

South West Wales Establishments

South East Wales Establishments

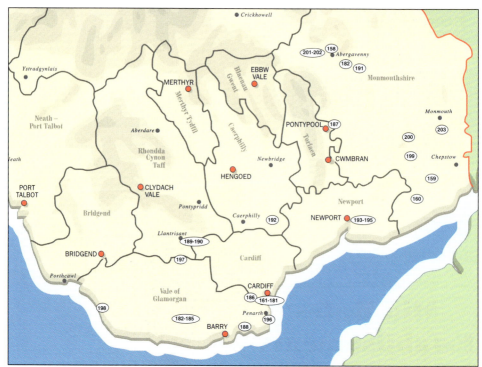

Index of Establishments

	Listing Number
Allt-yr-Ynys Hotel	201
Allt-yr-Golau Uchaf	110
Amser Da	48
L'Amuse	128
Anglesey Sea Zoo	40
Armless Dragon	161
Bae Abermaw	6
The Bar at Neyland Yacht Haven	137
Barratts Restaurant	54
Basil's Brasserie	183
The Bear of Amsterdam	64
The Bear Hotel	78
La Barrica	47
Belvedere	49
Y Bistro	30
The Black Bear	159
The Boat	24
Boathouse	143
Bodysgallen Hall	34
Bodidris Hall	32
Bontddu Hall Hotel	18
Bosphorus Turkish Resturant	162
Bramleys Tea Room	146
The Brasserie	27
La Braseria	151
Brava Café	163
Brecon Beacons Mountain Centre	71
Brookes Restaurant	189
Bryn Howel Hotel	43
Buffs Restaurant and Wine Bar	164
Bush House	200
Café Fleur	134
Café Niccolo	14
Cantre Selyf	72
Capel Dewi Uchaf Country Hotel	106
Carlton House Hotel	94
Carpenters Arms	202
Le Cassoulet	174
Castle Coaching Inn	103
Castle Cottage Restaurant	25
Cawdor Arms Hotel	122
Ceasar's Arms	186
Centre for Alternative Technology	97
Champers	165
Chelsea Café	147
Clytha Arms	182
Cnapan	135
Conrah Country House Hotel	67
Cornmill	44
Cors Restaurant	119
Courtenay's Bistro	10
Crown at Whitebrook	203
Cutting Edge Wine Bar	166
Cyfie Farm	89
Cynyll Farm	125
Da Vincis Restaurant	55
De Courcey's Restaurant	167
Dermotts Restaurant	148
Didier and Stephanie	149
Drapers Café, Tweedmill	56
Dragon Hotel	100
Dremddu Fawr	85
Drovers Restaurant	95
Druidstone Hotel	105
Dylanwad Da	19
Earl's of Llandaff	168
Elan Valley Hotel	83
Empire Hotel	35
Fairyhill Country House Hotel	150
The Farmer's Arms	79
Farthings Wine Bar	184
Fanny's Restaurant	123
Four Seasons Restaurant	131
Frolics Restaurant	198
Gales of Llangollen	45
Le Gallois	175
Gardeners Rest	114
George III Hotel	20
Georges Restaurant	115
Gilby's Restaurant	169
Glasfryn Guest House and Restaurant	107
Gliffaes Country House Hotel	80
Goetre Isaf Farmhouse	3
The Golden Fleece Inn	60
Golden Grove	121
Greenhouse	170
The Griffin, Felin Fach	84
Griffin Inn, Llyswen	96
Guidfa House	86
Gwalia Tearooms, Museum of Welsh Life	171
Hanover International Cardiff Bay Hotel	172
Hanson's Restaurant	153
Harry's @ Swn-y-Don	68
Herbs	4
The Herb Garden	87
High Tide Café	127
Hive on the Quay	63

The Hollybush Inn	192
Huddarts Restaurant	185
The Huntsman	188
Indian Clipper Balti House	7
Izakaya Japanese Tavern	173
Jonkers Restaurant	46
Junction 28	193
Kimnel Arms	1
Lake Country House Hotel	91
Lake Vyrnwy Hotel	93
Llansantfraed Court	191
Left Bank Restaurant	138
Llanerchindda Farm	109
Llangoed Hall	73
Lloyds Hotel and Restaurant	92
Llwyndu Farmhouse	8
The Lobster Pot	28
The Lodge	58
Madhav	176
Manor House	111
Martin's Restaurant	36
Metropolis	177
The Mews Restaurant	154
Mill Farm	187
Miskin Manor Hotel	197
Morawelon	136
Morgan's Brasserie	144
Nant Ddu Lodge Hotel	76
Nantyffin Cider Mill	81
National Trust, Chirk Castle	13
National Trust, Erddig	61
National Trust, Penrhyn	5
National Trust, Plas Newydd	41
National Trust, Powis Castle	104
The Newbridge	199
New House Country Hotel	178
New Quay Honey Farm	101
Old Pharmacy Restaurant	142
The Old Rectory Country Hotel	15
The Olive Tree, Celtic Manor Hotel	194
Ye Olde Bull's Head	9
P.A's Wine Bar	129
Pale Hall	31
Pant-yr-Ochain	62
La Paysanne	17
Paxton's Restaurant	155
Penally Abbey	139
Penhelig Arms Hotel and Restaurant	66
Pentre Bach	22
Panteidal Organic Garden	65
Patrick's Restaurant	130
Penbontbren Farm Hotel	88
Penmaenuchaf Hall	21
Plantagenet House	156
Plas Bodegroes	53
Plas Café	26
Plas Dolmelynllyn	23
The Plough Inn	57
Y Polyn	132
Porth Tocyn Hotel	2
Portmeirion Hotel	52
Prince's Arms Country Hotel	59
The Priory Hotel	160
Quayside Brasserie	108
Queens Head	39
Razzi Restaurant, The Hilton Hotel	179
The Reef Café Bar	157
Richard's Bistro	37
Seeds Restaurant	90
Serendipity Restaurant	69
The Stable Door	120
Stables Restuarant and Paddock Bar	50
Stone Hall	116
St Tudno Hotel	38
Swallow Tree Gardens	141
Talk House	102
Tan-y-Foel Hotel	12
Tides Restaurant, St David's Hotel	180
La Trattoria	190
Three Cocks Hotel and Restaurant	75
Three Main Street	112
Tir-a-Môr	16
Treehouse Restaurant	70
Tregynon Farmhouse Restaurant	113
Tre-Ysgawen Hall Hotel	42
Trericket Mill Vegetarian Guest House	77
Tomlin's Restaurant	196
Tyddyn Llan Hotel	33
Ty'n Rhos Country House	11
Ty Croeso	82
The Walnut Tree	158
Warpool Court Hotel	145
The Waterfront Bistro	74
Welcome to Town Bistro	126
The West Arms	29
Whitehouse	140
The Wynnstay Arms	98
Windsor Lodge Hotel	152
Winnies Restaurant	133
The Wolfe Inn	117
Wolfscastle Country Hotel	118
Woods Bar and Brasserie	181
Woodland Restaurant and Bistro	195
Y Capel Bach @ The Angel	124
Ynyshir Hall	99
Yr Hen Fecws	51